THE INDIAN ARMY

THE INDIAN ARMY

by

BORIS MOLLO

New Orchard Editions
Poole · New York · Sydney

This edition published in the U.K. 1986 by
New Orchard Editions Ltd.
Robert Rogers House,
New Orchard,
Poole,
Dorset,
BH15 1LU

ISBN 1 85079 085 X

Distributed in the United States by
Sterling Publishing Co. Inc.,
2 Park Avenue, New York, N.Y. 10016, U.S.A.

Distributed in Australia by
Capricorn Link (Australia) Pty Ltd.,
P.O. Box 665, Lane Cove
N.S.W. 2066

Typeset in 11/12 pt Linotron Baskerville
by Polyglot Pte Ltd, Singapore

Printed in Portugal by Printer Portugesa

Contents

Introduction

While this book is primarily about the uniforms of the Indian Army, I give a general historical introduction to each section, with a resumé of the campaigns fought and notes on important changes in organisation. I then deal in turn with each arm; cavalry, infantry and artillery, and give changes of title, award of battle honours and details of uniform. I have chosen this arrangement because there is more in common, say, between the horse artillery of the three presidencies than between the native infantry and artillery of one particular presidency

The main emphasis is placed on the native cavalry and infantry, where the regimental organisation was complex and where there are many idiosyncrasies of dress to record. The artillery, engineers and European infantry, where the regulations of the corresponding arm of the British service were closely followed, are covered in less detail. Battle honours have been given up to 1914 only, as the earlier honours were often used on regimental appointments and the date of award of an honour is of assistance in dating an item of uniform on which that honour appears. Battle honours are given in small capital letters, i.e. ARCOT. Apart from appearing in the list of regimental titles in the Index, the Indian State Forces, Auxiliary Forces (India) and Frontier and Police units have not been included.

In acknowledging the help obtained from many sources in the preparation of this book I must give pride of place to the late Lieut-General Sir Reginald Savory, the last Adjutant-General (India), whose knowledge of, and love for, the Indian Army inspired my interest. My former colleague Bill Carman, whose books on the uniforms of the Indian Army are essential to those who wish to study the subject in greater depth, has always been generous in his help and advice. Among those former officers of the Indian Army who have helped, I must mention particularly Colonel Tony Mains. I am also grateful for the help received from Colonel Pip Newton of the Army Museums Ogilby Trust, Dr Joe Darracott of the Imperial War Museum, Tony Farrington and Pauline Rohatgi of the India Office Library and Giles Smith of the Parker Gallery. Colonel E. C. Pickard and the Hon David Mc Alpine kindly lent items to be photographed for use as illustrations. Among my colleagues at the National Army Museum I must acknowledge in particular the help received in preparing the illustrations from Marion Harding, Robin Sharp and the photographers Bob Goodall and Simon Dunstan.

Finally I dedicate this book to my wife Carolyn for all her love and devotion . . . and for Eugenie.

Acknowledgements

The publishers gratefully acknowledge the following, for permission to reproduce illustrations.
India Office Library 25, 56, 59, 60, 72, 73, 85, 111.
Imperial War Museum 144.
Scottish National Portrait Gallery 40.
Army Museums Ogilby Trust 9.
Sotheby & Co 8.
Christies Ltd 20, 21, 89.
Parker Gallery 36, 64.
Wallis and Wallis Ltd 51.
Private collections 6, 16, 17, 18, 30, 31, 152.
National Army Museum, Chelsea all other illustrations

1
The Early Years 1660–1824

EARLY YEARS IN INDIA

Britain's first foothold in India came in the form of trading stations or 'factories' set up with the permission of the local rulers. The East India Company was formed in 1600 to co-ordinate their activities and in 1611 the first factory was established at Surat, near Bombay. In 1662, King Charles II received Bombay itself from the Portuguese as part of the dowry of Catherine of Braganza. At first it was garrisoned by royal troops but in 1668, it was handed over to the Company and the garrison became company troops, later the Bombay European Regiment.

In Southern India, a factory was founded at Madras, and in 1639 Fort St George was built and garrisoned as the headquarters of the Southern Presidency. In the north-east the Presidency of Bengal was the last to be established, and its base became Fort William, Calcutta, begun in 1696.

In the 17th century, India was still under the nominal rule of the Mughal emperors, but their power had waned and after the death, in 1707, of the last emperor, Aurangzeb, the provincial governors became virtually independent princes. They vied with one another and there were frequent internal disputes. Into this growing anarchy came the European trading nations, Britain, France, the Netherlands and Portugal, all intent on establishing supremacy at the expense of the local rulers and each other. A power struggle developed which was to last nearly 100 years and which left the British as masters of India.

The British and French were the main rivals, and their troops in India found themselves at odds, not only through local affairs but also through wars waged in Europe and elsewhere. Thus the War of the Austrian Succession, 1742–1748 had its effect in India. Britain made several unsuccessful attempts to seize Pondicherry, the main French base in Southern India while the French, with more success, seized Madras in 1746. This was returned two years later at the Peace of Aix-la-Chapelle. The British noted the way in which the French used Indian troops, and the Madras Presidency began to form independent companies.

Although peace had been made in Europe, rivalry in India continued, as Britain and France became increasingly involved in India politics, particularly in the south where they supported rival claimants to the nawabdom of the Carnatic. In 1750 most of the available British troops were involved in helping their claimant in the defence of Trichinopoly. Robert Clive, a former clerk from one of the company factories, suggested that the war might be carried into the enemy's camp and was allowed to lead an expedition of some 500 troops to Arcot, the capital of the rival claimant. Clive duly captured Arcot and then successfully defended it, as the French and their allies came hot-foot from Trichinopoly. ARCOT, the oldest battle honour for operations in India, was awarded to the Madras European Regiment. Belated support from the British Government came in 1754 with the arrival of the first British regiment to serve in India, the 39th.

In Bengal, the French had formed an alliance with the local nawab, Siraj-ud-Daula, who, in 1756 captured Fort William, Calcutta, incarcerating his European prisoners in the notorious 'Black Hole'. There was a swift response from the British and a force under the joint command of Admiral Watson and Clive retook Calcutta and, as war had just broken out, went on to capture the French fort of Chandernagore. Clive then turned on the Nawab himself, and at Plassey on 23 June 1757, Clive's army of 3,000 defeated the local army of 55,000 in the most famous of Indian battles. The honour PLASSEY was awarded to the Bengal, Madras and Bombay European Regiments and to the 1st Bn Bengal NI. In 1759, the Dutch, who also had settlements near Calcutta, opened hostilities by threatening ships using Calcutta. Their troops were defeated at the battle of BADARA, an honour awarded to the Bengal European Regiment.

Meanwhile fighting broke out again in Madras, when the French landed a force under de Lally and captured the fort at Cuddalore and St Davids and once again threatened Madras itself. A small British force under Major Forde, sent to make a diversion, went much further, defeating the French twice, at CONDORE on 9 December 1758 and at MASULIPATAM on 8 April 1759 and persuading the local ruler to dismiss his French advisers and side with the British. Both honours were awarded to the Bengal European Regiment.

The scene was now set for the climax, in Southern India. Early in 1760, Colonel Eyre Coote landed in Madras with HM 84th Regiment and reinforcements for the Company's battalion. He defeated the main French force at WANDIWASH, an honour awarded only to the Madras European Regiment and went on to reduce the remaining French ports including PONDICHERRY. This honour was awarded to the Madras European Regiment for their service on this occasion and in two subsequent sieges in 1788 and 1793. By the Treaty of Paris in 1763, the French regained their factories; but their military power in India never recovered.

In 1764, the Nawab of Bengal suffered his final defeat at the hands of Colonel Sir Hector Munro at the battle of BUXAR, an honour awarded to the Bengal and Bombay European Regiments and to six Bengal NI battalions.

The British position in Bengal was further helped by the defeat of the Marathas by the Afghan armies of Ahmad Shah Durani at the battle of Panipat in 1761, which checked the growing strength of the Maratha Confederacy.

MYSORE WARS

In Madras the main French threat had been removed, but there were still powerful local rulers to contend with. Between 1767 and 1799, the British were involved in a series of four wars in southern India, with the Maharajahs of Mysore, Haidar Ali and his son Tipu Sultan.

1st Mysore War 1767–1769
At the beginning of the period, the British, with their base at Madras and some nineteen battalions of coast sepoys were not strong enough to face Haidar Ali alone and so an alliance was formed with the Nizam of Hyderabad.

In 1767 their combined armies invaded Mysore but they had only reached Bangalore when the Nizam and his army changed sides. The British infantry and Madras sepoys won a few minor skirmishes but their lack of cavalry meant that they could do little to prevent Haidar's men from ravaging the Carnatic. Within two years, Haidar's cavalry were at the gates of Madras and the British, too weak to drive them away, made peace.

2nd Mysore War 1780–1784
The next stage came in 1780 when, following British defeats in America, France declared war on Britain and found a ready ally in India in Haidar Ali. Haidar invaded the Carnatic, massacring the garrison at Pollibur and forcing the British once again back into Madras. Colonel Eyre Coote was sent with reinforcements from Bengal and on 1 July 1780 he took Porto Novo, a fortified position on the coast some 100 miles south of Madras, and on 27 September he defeated Haidar Ali at Sholinghur. The battle honour SHOLINGHUR was awarded in 1841 to the 3rd Regiment the Nawab of Arcot's Cavalry, later the 3rd Madras NC, to fourteen Carnatic battalions and to the Madras Pioneers. However, despite the victory there was still no answer to Haidar Ali's cavalry, and after their capture of the port of Trincomalee in 1782 the French were able to give Haidar Ali more active support.

In 1783, troops from Bombay took Mangalore and Bednore, but Tipu Sultan recaptured Bednore, and then laid siege to Mangalore, which was defended by the 42nd (later the Black Watch) and the 8th Bn Bombay Sepoys (later the 1st Bombay Grenadiers). This small garrison held out for six months before surrendering with the honours of war and the two regiments were awarded MANGALORE as a battle honour.

Meanwhile the war between Britain and France had ended and after the death of Haidar Ali in 1784, his son Tipu Sultan made peace. The Madras regiments involved in the war, the 3rd Cavalry, seventeen battalions and the Pioneers received the honour CARNATIC.

3rd Mysore War 1790–1792
In 1790, Tipu renewed the conflict by attack-

ing Travancore whose ruler was an ally of the British. The British reacted firmly by capturing the fortress of Bangalore (plate I) and laying siege to Tipu's capital, Seringapatam. It was during this campaign that the 1st Madras European Regiment gained the honour NUNDY DROOG for their part in the capture of the fortress, which lay some 30 miles north of Bangalore. In the autumn of 1791 bad weather forced the British to withdraw, but in Feb 1792 they attacked again and took the city by storm. Tipu sued for peace and half of his land in Mysore was divided between Britain and her allies and two of his sons were surrendered as hostages.

The regiments which took part in this campaign received the honour MYSORE.

4th Mysore War 1799

The final episode came in 1799 when Britain was once more at war with France and Tipu was accused of secret communication with the French. Tipu refused to acknowledge British control and Wellesley, the Governor-General, ordered two armies, one from Bombay in the west and the other from Madras in the south, to converge on Seringapatam. The Bombay column met Tipu near Seedaseer, on the frontiers of Coorg, but one brigade held off his attack, much enhancing the reputation of the

Plate 1. Death of Colonel Moorhouse at the siege of Bangalore 1791. On the right are British and native officers of the Governor's Bodyguard, Madras. Oil painting by Robert Home (detail).

9

Bombay sepoy. Three battalions were awarded the honour SEEDASEER. In May 1799 the columns met near Seringapatam and once again the city was taken by storm (plate 2). Tipu was killed in the fighting and British control of South India was complete. The honour SERINGAPATAM was awarded to three Madras Cavalry, ten Madras Infantry and five Bombay Infantry regiments.

MARATHA WARS

In western and central India the British were faced by the Maratha Confederacy made up of several powerful states named after their rulers. They included the Peshwa, Holkar, Sindia, Bhonsla and the Gaekwar, all hereditary ministers of the Rajah of Satara

1st Maratha War 1778–1782

The Bombay Presidency supported Ragunath Rao, a Maratha minister, against the Peshwa. 4,000 troops marched on Poona but were cut off and were only allowed to go free when their commander signed a treaty, which was later repudiated by his superior. To retrieve the situation, the Governor-General, Warren Hastings, sent six battalions of Bengal Infantry with supporting cavalry and artillery from Bengal to Surat, the first British force to cross India from coast to coast.

They linked up with a column sent from Bombay, comprising the Bombay European Regiment and some regiments of Bombay Native Infantry. Seventy years later the Bombay European Regiment was awarded the honour GUZERAT for this operation.

The Bengal Regiments received no battle honours, but all ranks who were involved in the columns which crossed and recrossed the sub-continent were awarded the Deccan Medal, the first issued by the East India Company.

In 1780 the British, by then reinforced, took Gwalior, Ahmadabad and Bassein. A peace was signed in 1782 with the Sindia, by which Britain retained the island of Salsette but restored other conquests.

2nd Maratha War 1803–1805

Under the Governor-Generalship of the Marquess Wellesley, the British continued the policy of 'divide and rule' in their bid to establish supremacy over the Confederacy. In 1802, their ally the Peshwa was defeated and overthrown, and when demands for his restoration were refused, Wellesley launched simultaneous offensives into the Deccan, led by his brother Sir Arthur Wellesley (later Duke of Wellington), and into Hindustan, led by General Gerald Lake. Sir Arthur Wellesley recaptured Poona and restored the Peshwa but found himself threatened by the Sindia. In August 1803 he captured Ahmednagar and in September defeated the armies of the Sindia and the Rajah of Berar, at Assaye in September and Argaum in November.

Wellesley's column included Madras native cavalry and infantry of which three cavalry and five infantry regiments were awarded the honour ASSAYE. No honours were awarded for Argaum although a clasp was issued with the India Medal.

Meanwhile Lake had similar success in his victories over the Marathas, by now under French command, at Delhi and Laswari where his infantry came into action after marching 65 miles in 48 hours. Lake's column comprised Bengal cavalry and infantry regiments and they received three battle honours, ALLY GHUR, a fortress taken on the way to Delhi, DELHI 1803 and LESWARREE.

In 1804 the British turned against the Holkar, who had ambushed and destroyed a small British force under Colonel Monson. Lake defeated the Maratha cavalry at Farrakhbad and then continued to Bhurtpore but failed after four attempts to capture it. Eventually the local rajah made peace. Lake pursued the Holkar into the Punjab and finally accepted his surrender at Amritsar in December 1805. An uneasy peace was made, but there was continuing unrest in Central India.

The 1804 campaign produced only one battle honour DEIG, commemorating the battle with the Holkar on 13 November and the capture of the city by assault on 23 December. Two Bengal Cavalry and six infantry regiments received the honour.

3rd Maratha War 1817–1818

The decline in the Maratha Confederacy and the resultant anarchy in the territories concerned, allowed robber bands, known as Pindaris and largely comprised of former

Maratha soldiers to flourish with the tacit support of Maratha chieftains. To deal with them, two British forces took the field, the Army of the Deccan under Sir T Hyslop from Madras and the Grand Army under the Commander-in-Chief, Lieutenant-General Sir F Rawdon Hastings, comprising troops from all the presidencies. The Marathas took the opportunity to attack reduced British garrisons, which for the most part held out. A number of battle honours were awarded for these actions. At KIRKEE on 5 November 1817, a force under Sir Lionel Smith, including four regiments of Bombay native infantry, all of which later received the honour, defeated the army of the Peshwa. A second battle between the same forces at Poona two weeks later was commemorated by the award of a clasp to the India medal. Also in November, the Nagpore garrison was attacked by the local Maratha Army of some 18,000 and withdrew to the fortified hill of SEETABULDEE where, on 26 November, they were attacked. The 6th Bengal Cavalry showed great spirit and on their own routed the attacking Nagpore infantry. They were awarded the honour together with two Madras NI battalions (1st/24th, later 1st and 1st/20th). Following

Seetabuldee, Major-General Doveton moved quickly to reinforce the Nagpore garrison. At NAGPORE on 16 December (plate 3), the Marathas were again repulsed and the fortress itself was recaptured. The honour was awarded to the 1st/22nd Bengal NI (later 6th Jat LI), the 6th Madras Cavalry, 8th Madras NI and 2nd Bn Berar Infantry of the Hyderabad Contingent.

The main battle of the war was fought at MAHEIDPOOR on 23 December 1817 between the Madras division of Sir Thomas Hyslop and the army of the Holkar, ending in the total defeat of the Holkar's forces. The honour was awarded to three Madras cavalry and five infantry regiments and to two battalions of Russell's Brigade, Hyderabad Contingent.

One minor episode which resulted in the award of a battle honour as well as entering the annals of the Bombay Army was the defence of CORYGAUM, 1 January 1818. While moving to reinforce the Poona garrison, a small force under Captain Staunton which included the 2nd/1st Bombay Grenadiers and the Poona Auxiliary Horse ran into the main body of the Peshwa's Army at Corygaum and held out against heavy odds until relieved on the following day.

Plate 2. The storming of Seringapatam, 4 May 1799. Engraving after Robert Ker Porter.

During the first six months of 1818, Hastings hunted down the Marathas and Pindaris, and the surrender of the Peshwa in June 1818 marked the end of Maratha power, British supremacy in Central India was assured.

OTHER OPERATIONS INVOLVING HEIC FORCES, 1774—1821

During the period of British expansion in India, both British and Company troops were engaged in many minor campaigns, subduing new enemies, maintaining control in territories already subdued and establishing control over the sea lanes around the sub-continent. There were too many of these to be covered in detail here, but some, in an apparently arbitrary way, were commemorated by the award of battle honours.

In 1774 a Bengal contingent under Colonel Champion operated in support of the King of Oudh against the incursion of the Marathas. The main battle was fought at Kutra near Bareilly on 23 April 1774. The honour ROHIL-CUND 1774 was awarded to the 2nd Bengal European Regiment and to six native battalions. A second honour for ROHILCUND was awarded for operations in 1794 to quell a rising in the state of Rampur which ended in a fierce battle at Betourah/Bitaura, near Bareilly. As for the earlier honour, the only surviving regiment to receive the honour was the 2nd Bengal European Regiment.

The most important campaign outside India in which Company troops were involved was the expedition to Egypt in 1801. The campaign's aim was to drive the French out of Egypt, removing their threat to the Mediterranean and preventing them from taking the opportunity to enter into alliances with local rulers in India. The main force of 17,000 was collected from Britain but the Governor-General was called upon to provide a force of 5,000 from India. By the time they had been gathered and set sail from Bombay at the end of March 1801, the main fighting in Egypt was over. Nevertheless the force, under Sir David Baird, comprising five British, one Bengal and two Bombay battalions made an epic march from the Red Sea across the desert to the Nile and arrived in time to take part in the final stages. In 1804, the honour EGYPT 1801 was awarded to the Bombay battalions, the 2nd/1st and the 1st/7th.

Plate 3. The last charge of the 6th Bengal Light Cavalry and the 6th Madras Light Cavalry at the battle of Nagpore, 16 December 1817. Engraving by Denis Dighton after Captain Robert Woolf, 6th Madras Light Cavalry (see also plate 17).

12

The battle honour COCHIN was conferred upon the 17th Madras NI for their defence, with HM 12th Regiment, of the residency of Cochin during the rebellion in Travancore on the south-west tip of India in 1809. A relief expedition defeated the local forces at Palamcottah where the 3rd Madras NI earned their title of Palamcottah Light Infantry.

Other honours were awarded for overseas expeditions to the East Indies, the Persian Gulf and the Indian Ocean. From the early days there had been rivalry between the British and Dutch in the East Indies, and after 1793, when Holland allied with France at the outbreak of the Wars of the French Revolution, the HEIC was called upon on several occasions to provide troops for maritime expeditions. The Madras European Regiment was awarded three honours for various operations against islands in the Molucca Seas; AMBOYNA 1796, BANDA 1796 and TERNATE 1801. These honours also covered operations during a further expedition to the area in 1810.

A more powerful expedition was mounted in 1811, when a force of 10,000 troops, half British and half native from Madras and Bengal, were landed in Java. After a week of fighting, Fort Cornelis and the French garrison surrendered. The honour JAVA was awarded to the Bengal Governor-General's bodyguard and the Bengal Marine Battalion.

Another haven for French privateers was the island of Bourbon (now Reunion) in the Indian Ocean, east of Mauritius. In September 1809 an expedition, which included HM 56th Regiment and the 2/2nd Bombay NI, landed and destroyed the forts at the principal port. The following July, reinforcements, which included the 6th and 12th Madras NI, captured the island and the island was held by the British until peace in 1814. All the native regiments involved received the honour BOURBON.

Operations in Persian Gulf were the responsibility of the Bombay Army, and several expeditions were mounted to combat pirates operating along the Arabian coast. The first expedition in 1809, comprising HM 47th and 65th regiments and the 1/2nd Bombay NI, took the pirate stronghold of Rus El Khima. Further expeditions were sent to the same area in 1819 and 1821. Honours awarded were ARABIA for the British regiments in 1809 and BENI BOO ALI for the 1/2nd NI, PERSIAN GULF for 1819, including the Bombay Marine Bn, and BENI BOO ALI for the 1821 expedition for the Bombay European Regiment and six native infantry battalions.

Mention must also be made of one campaign for which no battle honours were awarded, the Gurkha War of 1814-1816. The British had consolidated their position in Bengal up to Nepal, but suffered from frequent raids by Gurkhas across the border. In 1814, the Gurkhas occupied territory claimed by the East India Company. At first British attempts to dislodge them were unsuccessful, but General Sir David Ochterlony succeeded in cutting the main Gurkha army off from its base and eventually, on the Malaun Ridge, the Gurkhas surrendered. Peace talks were unsuccessful until Ochterlony renewed the offensive towards Katmandu, defeating the Gurkhas again at Makwanpur. The chiefs accepted British terms by which Kumaon and Garhwal were ceded to the British while Nepal itself remained independent. More important for the long term interests of the Indian Army, the first Gurkha regiments were accepted into British service as regiments of Bengal Local Infantry.

BENGAL ARMY 1757—1824

The first locally raised unit to be armed, clothed and drilled in the European fashion by the British was the Lal Paltan battalion raised by Clive in Calcutta in January 1757. They performed well at the battle of Plassey six months later, and in August the 2nd Battalion was raised. The 3rd was raised at Patna in 1761. Following the completion of Fort William, Calcutta, the British detachments from Madras and Bombay who volunteered to remain in Bengal were formed into the Bengal European Regiment.

Eighteen more native battalions were raised between 1758 and 1764, but the loss of three at Patna in 1761 brought the total down to eighteen. These were renumbered in 1764 according to the seniority of their captain.

In 1775, the battalions were renumbered, those in the 1st Brigade becoming 1st to 7th, those in the 2nd becoming 8th to 14th and those in the 3rd becoming 15th to 21st. The Nawab of Oudh agreed to maintain a force under British officers comprising two regiments of cavalry (later the 1st Bengal Native Cavalry), three regiments of artillery and nine battalions of infantry. Between 1778 and 1780, nine more battalions were raised. By 1781 there were 42 battalions, of which one was disbanded and a further six, serving in Bombay, were removed from the Bengal roll. The remainder were formed into 35 regiments each of two battalions. The return of the battalions from Bombay in 1784 led to the disbandment of the three junior regiments and a further three were disbanded for poor behaviour.

In 1796 the establishment of the Bengal Army was set at

European artillery, three battalions
European infantry, three regiments
Native cavalry, ten regiments
Native infantry, twelve regiments each of two battalions.

In 1803 James Skinner brought a regiment of irregular horse from Sindia's army into Company service, which later become the well-known Skinner's Horse.

After the fall of Malaun, in 1815, the first three battalions of Gurkhas were raised as Bengal local battalions, only one of which, the Nasiri Battalion, survived into modern times to become the 1st Gurkha Rifles. In 1816, the Kumaon Battalion, later the 2nd Gurkha Rifles, was raised.

MADRAS ARMY 1748–1824

In 1758 the Madras Government had in its service some 3,000 peons or native foot soldiers under native officers, who proved undisciplined and unreliable. It was decided therefore to form the foot soldiers into four native infantry battalions under European officers. Two were formed immediately, but the imminent approach of the French delayed the formation of the other two until 1759. The total size of the native infantry was fixed in 1761 at 6,300, but the number of battalions was increased to ten. By 1767 there were nineteen battalions, ten of which were paid for by the Nawab of the Carnatic.

In 1770, the native infantry was renumbered, those based in the south assuming the title Carnatic Battalions and taking the numbers 1 to 13, those in the north, Circar Battalions, 1st to 5th. Further increases took place in 1776–1777. In 1784 the distinction between Carnatic and Circar battalions was ended and all became known as Madras Battalions, with the former Carnatic battalions taking precedence. At the same time the four cavalry regiments paid for by the Nawab were taken into company service but promptly mutinied because of arrears of pay. Only the 3rd Regiment was retained and three new regiments were raised. Until 1788 the regimental precedence was based on the seniority of its commander. The numbering was then fixed on a permanent basis, although it meant that the oldest took the junior position.

In 1796 the establishment was set at

European infantry   two regiments
Native cavalry   four regiments
Artillery   two battalions each of five artillery companies and fifteen lascar companies
Native infantry   eleven regiments each of two battalions.

Because this meant a considerable reduction in the size of the native infantry, four extra battalions were retained and eventually brought on to establishment. Between 1796 and 1824 there was a steady increase to a total of 25 two-battalion regiments.

The mutiny at Vellore in 1806 over the introduction of European-style head-dress for the native infantry led to the disbandment of the 1st and 23rd regiments.

BOMBAY ARMY 1668–1824

Royal troops first arrived off Bombay in 1665, although it was another three years before the Portuguese were persuaded to hand over the city itself. In 1668 the King handed over Bombay to the Company and the garrison agreed to enter Company service. They later became the Bombay European Regiment. In the early days this contingent included both cavalry and artillery elements, but in 1748 a separate company of artillery was formed.

Local troops were raised as and when required and disbanded when not, but they fought under their own officers and with their own clothing and equipment. Clive's raising of native infantry in Bengal in 1758 had its effect,

Plate 4. A golandar of the Bengal Artillery, a sepoy of the Bengal Native Infantry and a subedar of the Governor-General's Bodyguard, c 1785. Watercolour by a company artist.

Plate 5. A sowar of the Bengal Native Cavalry, c 1780. Watercolour by a company artist.

and in 1759 the Bombay sepoy companies were reorganised along more disciplined lines, although still under their own officers.

In 1768, the British were emerging as the main power on the Indian continent and Bombay was the most important Western port. It was time for more attention to be paid to its army and in 1768 the first two regular sepoy battalions were formed, followed by a third in 1760 and a fourth in 1770. A marine battalion was also formed to take over military duties on board the Company's armed ships. In 1780 seven more battalions of native infantry (9th to 15th) were formed, largely with drafts from the older irregular corps. Following the end of the 1st Maratha and 2nd Mysore Wars, in both of which the Bombay Army was heavily involved, the Army was reduced to six battalions of native infantry, the Marine Battalion and the 8th NI which became the Grenadier Battalion.

In 1788, the seven battalions were increased to twelve and formed into two brigades of six battalions each. The new battalions were formed by expanding existing battalions and giving them a new order of precedence which took no regard of previous seniority.

In 1796, in common with the other presidencies, the Bombay Native Infantry battalions were formed into regiments of two battalions each. Again the renumbering had little to do with seniority or tradition. The reorganisation led to a drop from twelve to eight battalions, although extra battalions were gradually raised.

The presidency had no cavalry of its own and on campaign tended to rely on mounted contingents provided by its Indian allies. These were not always reliable and so, in 1803, sanction was given for the raising of two troops of regular cavalry. The first was raised in 1804, however, the second was not raised until 1816. During the 3rd Maratha War, the Peshwa agreed to maintain an auxiliary force of 5,000 cavalry and 3,000 infantry, to be trained and officered by British officers. The cavalry of this force became the Poona Horse and the infantry eventually became the basis of several regular Bombay Native Infantry battalions.

In 1817, the Gaekwar agreed to subsidise two cavalry regiments which were raised as regular light cavalry on the nucleus of the two existing troops. In 1820, a third regiment was added. During this period there were further increases in the regular infantry which eventually composed twelve regiments, each of two battalions.

BENGAL NATIVE CAVALRY 1773–1824

The Governor-General's Bodyguard at first wore a uniform similar to that of the native cavalry but retained their scarlet coats when the native cavalry changed to French grey (plate 7). Plate 4 shows a native officer who wears a blue cap with gold lace around the dial, scarlet coat with dark blue facings and gold lace (not silver as was worn later), crimson cummerbund, white shirt and breeches, and black boots.

British officers of Bengal Cavalry wore a crested helmet of similar pattern to that worn by the Madras Native Cavalry (plate 18) with a black body and red turban and crest. In 1802 regulations specified a helmet similar to the Tarleton pattern worn by British light

Plate 6. Captain Robert Frith, Bengal Cavalry, 1793.
Oil painting by Arthur William Devis, Madras, 1793.

Raised	Title	Uniform details coat/facings/lace	
		Pre 1810	Post 1810
1773	Governor's Troop of Moguls		
	1781 Governor-General's Bodyguard	red/blue/silver	red/blue/silver
1776	Oudh Cavalry		
	1787 1st Bengal Native Cavalry	red/blue/silver	French grey/orange/silver
1778	Kandahar Horse		
	1787 2nd Bengal Native Cavalry	red/yellow/silver	French grey/orange/silver
1796	3rd Bengal Native Cavalry	red/white/silver	French grey/orange/silver
1797	4th Bengal Native Cavalry	red/green/silver	French grey/orange/silver
1800	5th Bengal Native Cavalry	red/buff/silver	French grey/orange/silver
			1819 French grey/black/silver
1800	6th Bengal Native Cavalry	red/orange/silver	
		1808 red/grey/silver	French grey/orange/silver
1805	7th Bengal Native Cavalry	red/yellow/silver	French grey/orange/silver
1805	8th Bengal Native Cavalry	red/yellow/silver	French grey/orange/silver

In 1819 the Bengal Native Cavalry changed their title to Bengal Light Cavalry

Battle honours	Date of action	Date of award	Regiments granted award
DELHI	1803	1829	2nd, 3rd
LESWAREE	1803	1829	1st, 2nd, 3rd, 4th, 6th
DEIG	1804	1829	2nd, 3rd
JAVA	1811	1829	GGBG
SEETABULDEE	1817	1819	6th

dragoons with a bearskin crest, leopardskin turban, silver tassels and red and white feather. Before 1810 British officers (plate 6) wore a red jacket with collar and cuffs of facing colour and three rows of silver buttons connected by loops of silver cord, shoulder chains, a black waistbelt with large silver plate, and a sabretache of a style often seen in late 18th-century pictures of officers in India, of leopardskin, worn high on the left hip. These were officially abolished in 1802 but reappeared soon after in the more familiar shape worn by British cavalry, carried on longer slings. White breeches and black boots were also worn. By the early 1800s (plates 7 and 8) the number of silver lace loops had increased and scale wings were worn.

In 1809 orders were issued for the withdrawal of the red jacket, although the French grey replacement was not fully issued until 1811. Lace and buttons were silver and facings were orange for all regiments, except for the

5th which had black facings from 1818. The general style of uniform (plate 9) did not change although the helmet was replaced some time after 1815 by a bell-top shako with a star-shaped plate, a black cockade and a red and white plume. The lacing of the jacket was more solid and elaborate while shoulder scales were replaced by a single cord attached by a regimental button. A shoulder belt of light dragoon pattern with silver pickers was worn in review order, and a plain buff leather belt was worn in undress. The undress uniform (plate 10) included a dark blue jacket of silk or similar light material with orange facings and silver lace and brass shoulder scales. The uniform of the native ranks generally followed that of the officers. Plate 5 shows a sowar of the 1st Native Cavalry with a head-dress like a tarboosh, probably in black felt with silver trimmings, and a pale red jacket with blue facings and white lace (an order of 1793 stated that a sowar's coat should be 'aurora', a

Plate 7. Jacket of Major W H Rainey, Governor-General's Bodyguard, 1817–1820. Scarlet with dark blue facings and silver lace.

Plate 8. Colonel Walker Dawson Fawcett, 2nd Bengal Native Cavalry, c 1806. Miniature, artist unknown.

reddish brown colour, with 'cotton twisted cord and a loop on each shoulder of the same cord, metal or tin button'). More elaborate coats were specified for native officers and havildars.

During 1809–1811 the red jackets were altered to French grey with orange facings (plate 11). By then the head-dress was a dark blue bulbous turban with a dark blue knob on the top and white tape diagonally across the front and back.

BENGAL LOCAL HORSE 1803–1825

Many irregular cavalry regiments were raised for particular campaigns and subsequently disbanded. The first to be formally accepted into the Bengal Army was the regiment brought from the Sindia's service by James Skinner in 1803. Other regiments followed, known at first by the names of their colonel or the area in which they were raised. Most irregular cavalry operated on the traditional Indian 'sillidar' system whereby in return for a higher rate of pay, the recruit provided his own horse and equipment and was expected to provide for himself in the field. Only firearms and ammunition were found by the government. The sowars were permitted to wear their own loose flowing garments. The head-dress was either a turban or armoured helmet with sliding nose-piece. The main garment was the alkaluk, a long robe with a bib front, generally in regimental colour, with cummerbund.

British officers, at first, wore more formal uniforms, based on British cavalry, but often with unusual or invented features. Because there was no standardisation, it is necessary to deal with each regiment separately.

Skinner's Horse (plates 12, 13)
Officers: Tarleton helmet with leopardskin turban, dark blue jacket with red facings, heavy silver braiding and shoulder scales.

Raised	Title	1823 number	Uniform details coat/lace
1803	Skinner's Horse	1st	yellow/silver
1809	Gardner's Horse	2nd	green/silver
1815	1st Rohilla Cavalry	3rd	red/gold
1815	2nd Rohilla Cavalry	disbanded 1819	red/silver
1815	3rd Rohilla Cavalry	disbanded 1819	
1814	2nd Skinner's Horse or Baddeley's Frontier Horse	4th	yellow/silver
1815	3rd Skinner's Horse	disbanded 1819	
1823	Gough's Horse	5th	red/gold

No battle honours were awarded.

Native ranks: red turban or armoured helmet or peaked watering cap of brown fur with gilt crescent on front and red cords, yellow alkaluk, red cummerbund or red and yellow girdle.

Gardner's Horse
Native ranks: red cap or pugri, emerald green alkaluk with silver lace.

Rohilla Cavalry (plates 14, 15)
British officers: crested helmet with red horsehair mane, scarlet jacket with black facings and silver lace. The jacket was of an unusual pattern with three rows of buttons, broad lace down the front and around the edge but no cross lacing.
Native ranks: cap of tarboosh style, dark blue with yellow fittings, red alkaluk with yellow braid and blue piping, blue cummerbund, blue shabraque with yellow border.

MADRAS NATIVE CAVALRY 1778–1824
The first uniform of the Madras Native Cavalry (plate 16) was similar to that of the British light cavalry of the period, a crested helmet with gilt fittings, red crest and dark blue turban, a full length cutaway coat with blue lapels and gold lace chevrons on the sleeve, white waistcoat and breeches, and black boots. The painting of the death of Colonel Moorehouse (plate 1) shows Captain Alexander Grant of the Governor's Bodyguard with a Tarleton helmet, a red coat with silver lace loops set far apart in the style of the British

1784–96 light dragoon coat, and sabretache worn high on the left hip. Alongside is a native officer in similar uniform with a pink turban in place of the helmet.

The uniform of the sowars followed the same general lines as the uniform of the officers, apart from the head-dress. Water-

Plate 9. An officer of the 6th Bengal Native Cavalry, c 1815. Miniature, artist unknown.

Raised	Title	1788 number	1801 coat: scarlet facings/lace	1814 coat: blue lace: silver facings	1817–1820 coat: French grey lace: silver
1778	Governor's Bodyguard, Madras		scarlet/scarlet/silver		
1784	1st Native Cavalry	mutinied 1784			
1784	2nd Native Cavalry	mutinied 1784			
1784	3rd Native Cavalry	2nd	green/gold	orange	orange
1784	4th Native Cavalry	mutinied 1784			
1784	2nd Native Cavalry	3rd	buff/silver	buff	buff
1785	3rd Native Cavalry	4th disbanded 1796	yellow/silver	yellow	yellow
1785	4th Native Cavalry	5th			
1787	5th Native Cavalry	1st 1790 white/gold 1811 blue/gold		yellow	yellow
1799	5th Native Cavalry		black/silver	yellow	yellow
1799	6th Native Cavalry		French grey/silver	orange	orange
1800	7th Native Cavalry		yellow/silver	buff	buff
1804	8th Native Cavalry		yellow/silver	yellow	yellow

In 1819 the Madras Native Cavalry changed their title to Madras Light Cavalry

Battle honours	Date of action	Date of award	Regiments granted award
SHOLINGHUR	1781	1841	2nd
CARNATIC	1788–1791	1889	2nd
MYSORE	1788–1791	1889	1st, 2nd, 3rd, 4th
SERINGAPATAM	1799	1820	1st, 2nd, 3rd, 4th
ASSAYE	1803	1803	4th, 5th, 7th
SEETABULDEE	1817	1819	GBM
NAGPORE	1817	1826	6th
MAHEIDPOOR	1817	1819	3rd, 4th, 8th

colours in the Royal Collection show a native officer and a sowar of the Carnatic Cavalry, c 1785, with the long cutaway coat shown in plate 16. The native officers wore dark blue bulbous turbans with white cord running diagonally across them.

By 1800 (plate 17) the crested helmet had been replaced, for a while, by the Tarleton helmet, but after 1800 the cavalry reverted to a black metal, crested helmet with tigerskin turban, red mane and silver fittings (plate 18). Contemporary pattern-books also show an undress cap in the form of a shako wound round with red and yellow cord. The jacket was red with facings and lace of regimental colour. A scarlet sash and sword belt were worn either over or under the jacket according to the formality of the occasion. Also worn were white breeches and black boots. A portrait of an officer by Copley shows a leopard-skin shabraque on his horse. Behind are two sowars who both wear a small bulbous turban with a white knob. This head-gear remained in use for some time and may be seen more clearly in plate 49.

By a general order dated 17 February 1813 the cavalry were ordered to be clothed in dark blue with silver lace, and a new list of facings was laid down. The portrait of Major Morgan Chase (plate 19) indicates that the style of helmet did not change, although the lacing on the jacket became more elaborate and a light dragoon pouch-belt with silver pickers was introduced. The corresponding stable dress (plate 20) included a dark blue jacket, plain except for a broad band of silver lace around the collar and down the front.

An order of 5 March 1817 laid down that the dress of the native cavalry (known as light cavalry from 1819) should be changed to French grey, although a reminder issued in 1820 indicated that this change took some time to take effect (details are given in chapter 2).

Plate 10. *Major Francis Smalpage, 8th Bengal Native Cavalry, in undress, c 1820. Lithograph after W Whittaker.*

BOMBAY LIGHT CAVALRY 1804—1824

Raised	Title	Uniform details coat/facings/lace
1804	1st Troop (absorbed into 1st Light Cavalry)	
1816	2nd Troop (absorbed into 2nd Light Cavalry)	
1817	1st Light Cavalry	scarlet/white/gold
1817	2nd Light Cavalry	scarlet/white/silver
1820	3rd Light Cavalry	scarlet/white/silver

The 1st troop, raised in 1804, appear to have been clothed in red with helmets similar to those worn by the Madras Light Cavalry (plate 18). An 1817 order referred to a helmet cap with red horsehair mane. An order of 18 September 1819 laid down that the uniform should be French grey with orange facings and silver lace in line with the cavalry of the other presidencies. The portrait of Lieut John Owen (plate 21) illustrates this uniform and shows what is probably an undress pouch-belt of buff leather with silver pickers.

The Presidency of Bombay followed the example of Bengal in raising regiments of irregular cavalry, the earliest permanent regiment being the Poona Auxiliary Horse raised in 1817. At first no regular dress was enforced, but the sowars were encouraged to wear turbans, coats and cummerbunds of a uniform colour. The portrait of Charles Swanston (plate 24) shows him in a poshteen worn over a yellow alkaluk with black facings and gold lace. He also wears a yellow and black baldric, a crimson sash, and red overalls. At his feet is what appears to be a red turban with dark blue band edged in gold.

BOMBAY IRREGULAR CAVALRY 1817—1824

Raised	Title		Uniform details coat/facings/lace
1817	Poona Auxiliary Horse		yellow/black/gold
Battle honour	Date of action	Date of award	Regiment granted award
CORYGAUM	1818	1819	Poona Auxiliary Horse

Date	Organisation	Uniform details red coat/silver lace facings
1756	Bengal (European) Regiment	
1779	6 battalions	blue/black/yellow/green/buff/white
1796	3 regiments	buff/white/yellow
1798	2 regiments	buff/white
1803	1 regiment	buff
		c 1803 yellow
		c 1820 pompadour (purple)
		1822 sky blue

BENGAL NATIVE INFANTRY 1757—1824

The uniform of the officers of the Bengal NI (plate 22) followed fairly closely that worn by British line infantry, except that the style of head-dress did not change as often. Prior to 1800 tricornes or bicornes were usually worn, although officers were permitted white hats or white linen covers for their normal hats in hot weather. The round hat or shaped top hat appears from the 1790s, but did not necessarily replace the bicorne which is still depicted in the early 1800s. The stovepipe (1800–1812) and Waterloo (1812–1816) shakos do not seem to have been adopted in India, except by other ranks of the European infantry. After 1816, the

Plate 11. Native Troops, East India Company's Service.
1 Troops of the Bodyguard of the Governor-General.
2 Private of the Bengal Regular Cavalry.
3 Private of the Java Volunteers.
Aquatint after C Hamilton Smith,
published 1st March 1815.

bell-top shako came into use and thereafter British patterns were closely followed.

Coats were red with collar and cuffs of facing colour. They were worn open until the turn of the century, by the officers, and beyond that date by the sepoys. Buttons were usually in pairs and loops were plain. Epaulettes were worn in pairs until c 1800 when junior officers wore a single epaulette on the right shoulder. The shoulder-belt plates were either gilt or silver according to the regimental lace colour, and were oval or rectangular, with regimental number. The sword was suspended from a black or buff leather shoulder belt. Waistcoat and trousers were made of white linen for hot weather and of white cloth for other times. Black boots were generally worn.

The appearance of the sepoys (plates 4 and 25) was different, although their coats followed the same general rules as for officers. The difference was largely because of the distinctive appearance of their head-dress, known familiarly as 'sundial hats'. These were black or dark blue with embellishments signifying rank and regiment. They continued in use until c 1810, when they were replaced by a turban of more compact shape like a peakless shako (plate 23).

The coat had collar, cuffs and lapels of regimental facing colour and loops in pairs. Although as time went by the coats became shorter, they were worn open longer than in British service, probably until after 1810. Sepoys of battalion companies wore simple plaited shoulder cords, while those of grenadier and, from 1808, light companies, wore wings. Equipment was carried on black belts, later altered to buff, with a crossbelt plate.

Plate 12. Skinner's Horse returning from a review, c 1820 (detail). Watercolour by a company artist.

Plate 13. Skinner's Horse, 1824. 'Method of attack with the musket when meeting the enemy head on'. Watercolour by a company artist.

Raised	Title (Bn)	1764 (Bn)	1775 (Bn)	1781 Regt	1784 Regt
1757	1st	9th	16th	10th	17th
1757	2nd	destroyed 1763			
1758	3rd	destroyed 1763			
1758	4th	3rd	2nd	2nd Bombay	2nd Bengal
1761	5th	destroyed 1763			
1761	6th	1st	8th	2nd	8th
1761	7th	15th	10th	4th	mutinied 1784
1762	8th	2nd	1st	1st Bombay	1st Bengal
1763	9th	8th	9th	3rd	9th
1763	10th	13th	6th	6th Bombay	6th Bengal
1763	11th	7th	became Chittagong Local Corps, disbanded 1786		
1763	12th	6th	15th	9th	16th
1763	13th	4th	3rd	1st	3rd
1763	14th	10th	5th	5th Bombay	5th Bengal
1763	15th	12th	18th	12th	12th
1763	16th	14th	19th	13th	13th
1763	17th	5th	4th	4th Bombay	4th Bengal
1764	18th	17th	7th	7th Bombay	7th Bengal
1764	19th	18th	12th	6th	11th
1764	20th	16th	11th	5th	10th
1764	21st	11th	17th	11th	18th
1764		19th	20th	mutinied 1780	
1765		20th	13th	7th	14th
1765		21st	21st	14th	19th
1766		22nd	disbanded 1773		
1766		23rd	disbanded 1773		
1766		24th	14th	8th	15th
1766		25th	disbanded 1773		
1766		26th	disbanded 1773		
1766		27th	disbanded 1773		
1770			22nd	15th	mutinied 1784
1770			23rd	16th	20th
1770			24th	17th	disbanded 1784
1770			25th	18th	21st
1770			26th	19th	22nd
1770			27th	20th	23rd
1770			28th	21st	27th
1770			29th	22nd	28th
1776			30th	23rd	29th

Uniform details—all coats red

1796 Regt	1824 Regt	1796 facings/lace	1809 facings/lace	1819 facings/lace	1823 facings/lace
2/12th	1st	buff/silver	yellow/silver	white/gold	white/gold
1/2nd	5th	white/silver	yellow/silver	white/gold	white/gold
1/8th	9th	white/silver	yellow/silver	white/gold	white/gold
1/1st	2nd	yellow/silver	yellow/silver	yellow/silver	yellow/silver
1/9th	8th	white/silver	yellow/silver	yellow/silver	yellow/silver
1/6th	3rd	yellow/silver	yellow/silver	yellow/silver	yellow/silver
2/7th	10th	white/silver	yellow/silver	dark green/silver	dark green/gold
1/3rd	6th	yellow/silver	yellow/silver	yellow/silver	dark green/gold
1/5th	11th	yellow/silver	buff/gold	white/gold	white/gold
1/12th	12th	buff/silver	yellow/silver	white/gold	white/gold
2/1st	4th	yellow/silver	yellow/silver	yellow/silver	yellow/silver
1/4th	7th	buff/silver	yellow/silver	yellow/silver	dark green/gold
1/7th	13th	white/silver	yellow/silver	yellow/silver	dark green/gold
1/11th	15th	buff/silver	yellow/silver	buff/gold	buff/gold
1/10th	14th	yellow/silver			
drafted to 10th					
2/10th	16th	buff/silver	yellow/silver	buff/gold	buff/gold
2/11th	17th	buff/silver	yellow/silver	French grey/silver	French grey/silver
disbanded 1795					
2/6th	18th	yellow/silver	yellow/silver	yellow/silver	yellow/silver
drafted to 12th					
2/3rd	19th	yellow/silver	yellow/silver	dark green/gold	dark green/gold
2/5th	20th	yellow/silver	yellow/silver	white/gold	white/gold
drafted to 3rd					
drafted to 2nd					
2/9th	21st	white/silver	yellow/silver	yellow/silver	yellow/silver

Raised		1775 (Bn)	1781 Regt	1784 Regt	1796 Regt
1778		31st	24th	24th	drafted to 7th
1778		32nd	25th	25th	2/2nd
1778		33rd	26th	26th	drafted to 11th
1778	Ramgarh Light Infantry			31st	2/4th
1779		34th	27th	30th	2/8th
1779		35th	28th	31st	disbanded 1785
1779		36th	29th	32nd	disbanded 1785
1779		37th	30th	33rd	disbanded 1785
1779		38th	31st	34th	disbanded 1785
1779		39th	32nd	35th	disbanded 1785
1780		40th	33rd	disbanded 1784	
1780		41st	34th	disbanded 1784	
1780		42nd	35th	disbanded 1781	
1781			36th	disbanded 1784	
1786				32nd	drafted to 1st
1786				33rd	drafted to 8th
1786				34th	drafted to 9th
1786				35th	drafted to 5th
1786				36th	drafted to 6th
1795	Marine Battalion			1803	1/20th
1797					1/13th
1797					2/13th
1797					1/14th
1797					2/14th
1798					1/15th
1798					2/15th
1798					1/16th
1798					2/16th
1798					1/17th
1798					2/17th
1799					1/18th
1799					2/18th
1799					1/19th
1799					2/19th
1803					2/20th
1803					1/21st
1803					2/21st
1803					1/22nd
1803					2/22nd
1803					1/23rd
1803					2/23rd
1804					1/24th

1824 Regt	1796 facings/lace	1809 facings/lace	1819 facings/lace	1823 facings/lace
22nd	white/silver	yellow/silver	yellow/silver	white/silver
23rd	buff/silver	yellow/silver	dark green/gold	dark green/gold
24th	white/silver	buff/gold	white/gold	white/gold
25th	blue/gold	blue/gold	blue/gold	blue/gold
26th	white/silver	yellow/silver	red/gold	red/gold
27th	white/silver	yellow/silver	red/gold	red/gold
28th	yellow/silver	yellow/silver	dark green/gold	dark green/gold
29th	yellow/silver	yellow/silver	dark green/gold	dark green/gold
30th	buff/silver	yellow/silver	buff/gold	buff/gold
31st	buff/silver	yellow/silver	buff/gold	buff/gold
32nd	white/silver	yellow/silver	black/gold	black/gold
33rd	white/silver	yellow/silver	black/gold	black/gold
34th	yellow/silver	yellow/silver	scarlet/silver	scarlet/silver
35th	yellow/silver	yellow/silver	scarlet/silver	scarlet/silver
36th	yellow/silver	yellow/silver	lemon yellow/silver	lemon yellow/silver
37th	yellow/silver	yellow/silver	lemon yellow/silver	lemon yellow/silver
38th	yellow/silver	yellow/silver	dark green/gold	dark green/gold
39th	yellow/silver	yellow/silver	dark green/gold	dark green/gold
40th		blue/gold	blue/gold	blue/gold
41st		black/silver	yellow/silver	yellow/silver
42nd		black/silver	yellow/silver	yellow/silver
43rd		yellow/silver	pea green/gold	pea green/gold
44th		yellow/silver	pea green/gold	pea green/gold
45th		yellow/silver	dark green/gold	dark green/gold
46th		yellow/silver	dark green/gold	dark green/gold
47th		yellow/silver	yellow/silver	yellow/silver

Raised		1796	1824	1809	1819	1823
1804		2/24th	48th	yellow/silver	yellow/silver	yellow/silver
1804		1/25th	49th	yellow/silver	buff/gold	buff/gold
1804		2/25th	50th	yellow/silver	buff/gold	buff/gold
1804		1/26th	51st	yellow/silver	dark green/gold	dark green/gold
1804		2/26th	52nd	yellow/silver	dark green/gold	dark green/gold
1804		1/27th	53rd	yellow/silver	yellow/silver	yellow/silver
1804		2/27th	54th	yellow/silver	yellow/silver	yellow/silver
1815		1/28th	55th	white/silver	white/gold	white/gold
1815		2/28th	56th	white/silver	white/gold	white/gold
1815		1/29th	57th		buff/gold	buff/gold
1815		2/29th	58th		buff/gold	buff/gold
1815		1/30th	59th		Saxon green/gold	Saxon green/gold
1815		2/30th	60th		Saxon green/gold	Saxon green/gold
1817	Fatagarh Levy					
1823	Mainpura Levy	1/32nd	63rd			yellow/silver
1818	Benares Levy	1/31st	61st			yellow/silver
1818	Cawnpore Levy	2/31st	62nd			yellow/silver
1818	Mutra Levy	2/32nd	64th			yellow/silver
1823		1/33rd	65th			yellow/silver
1823		2/33rd	66th			yellow/silver
1823		1/34th	67th			yellow/silver
1823		2/34th	68th			yellow/silver

Note: facing colours varied so much with alteration in regimental numbers that it is impractical to provide any table of facings until the double battalion system was fixed in 1796. In 1765, when the regiments were formed into three brigades, those in the first wore blue facings, the second, black and the third, green, altered in 1799 to yellow. The six brigades formed in 1786 took the following facing colours:

1st blue	4th green
2nd black	5th buff
3rd yellow	6th white

In 1809, the whole of the Bengal NI except the Marine Battalion were ordered to wear yellow facings with white buttons and lace striped red, white and blue.

Battle honours	Date of action	Date of award	Regiments granted award (1824 titles)
PLASSEY	1757	1829	1st
BUXAR	1764	1829	2nd, 3rd, 5th, 8th, 9th, 10th
GUZERAT	1776–1782	1829	2nd, 3rd, 5th, 7th, 11th, 13th
CARNATIC	1788–1791	1889	4th, 5th, 12th, 22nd
MYSORE	1789–1791	1889	4th, 6th, 13th, 16th
SERINGAPATAM	1799	1820	14th, 16th, 36th, 37th, 38th, 39th
ALLYGHUR	1803	1829	7th, 23rd, 35th
LESWARREE	1803	1829	1st, 12th, 21st, 24th, 30th, 31st, 33rd
DEIG	1804	1829	5th, 7th, 9th, 30th, 31st, 33rd
DELHI	1803	1829	1st, 5th, 22nd, 23rd, 28th, 29th, 30th, 31st, 35th
JAVA	1811	1829	25th, 40th
NAGPORE	1817	1882	43rd

Beneath the coat was a white shirt with a cummerbund over the lower part allowing only an inch or two of the shirt to show below. The cummerbund was of dark blue linen and was fastened in place by white linen strips, giving the appearance of a saltire cross. Below were worn janghirs or shorts, white with a pattern of blue triangles and lines around the lower edge. White pantaloons were worn by native officers at all times, and by sepoys in cold weather, until after 1813 when they gradually replaced janghirs. Attention must also be drawn to the propensity of the native ranks for wearing necklaces and other jewellery which appear so often in illustrations (plate 4) that it must have been officially approved.

In addition to the regular native infantry, there were a succession of local corps, many of which had only a short existence. Uniform details are vague and sparse, and those known are summarised in chapter 2. Under this category came the Gurkha battalions, four of which, the 1st and 2nd Nasiri, Sirmoor and Kumaon battalions were taken into British service after the Gurkha War of 1814–1816. Except for periods spent as ordinary line regiments, from the start the Gurkhas adopted features of rifle uniform, and continue to do so to this day. Their head-dress was a black or dark green bonnet, possibly a tightly tied turban. Jackets were dark green, without lapels and with, at first, red collar and cuffs, although these were soon altered to black. Equipment was black with brass crossbelt plates and other fittings. The trousers were blue-grey and were worn with shoes. British officers wore bell-top shakos, silver epaulettes, and in hot weather, white linen trousers.

Plate 14. *Major George Cunningham, Rohilla Horse, c 1815. Oil painting by J Howe.*

MADRAS EUROPEAN INFANTRY

Date	Organisation	Uniform details red coat/silver lace facings
1748	Madras (European) Regiment	
1766	3 regiments	
1774	2 regiments each of 2 battalions	buff/black
1777	6 battalions	
1796	2 battalions	blue/white
1799	1 battalion	light blue 1810 French grey

Plate 15. *A sowar of the Rohilla Cavalry, in the full dress of the Corps. Watercolour, artist unknown.*

Raised	Coast Sepoys (Bn)	1769 Carnatic (Bn)	1784 Madras (Bn)	1796 Madras NI	1796–1824
1758	1st	1st	1st	1st/1st	1806 disbanded 1807 1st/24th 1818 1st/1st
1758	2nd	1st Circar	22nd	1785 disbanded	
1759	3rd	2nd	2nd	1st/2nd	
1759	4th	4th			
		1770 3rd	3rd	1st/3rd	1811 Palamcottah LI
1759	5th	5th			
		1770 4th	4th	1st/4th	
1759	6th	6th			
		1770 5th	5th	1st/5th	
1761	7th	7th			
		1770 6th	6th	1st/6th	
1761	8th	8th			
		1770 7th	7th	1st/7th	
1761	9th	9th			
		1770 8th	8th	1st/8th	
1762–1765	10th	10th			
		1770 9th	9th	1st/9th	
1765	11th	1769 disbanded			
1765	12th	2nd Circar	23rd	1785 disbanded	
1765	13th	3rd Circar	24th	1785 disbanded	
1766	14th	11th			
		1770 10th	10th	1st/10th	
1767	15th	12th			
		1770 11th	11th	2nd/9th	
1767	16th	13th			
		1770 12th	12th	2nd/8th	
1767	17th	3rd	1770 disbanded		
1767	18th	4th Circar	25th	1785 disbanded	
1767	19th	5th Circar	26th	1785 disbanded	
1770		6th Circar	27th	1785 disbanded	
1776		13th	13th	2nd/3rd	
1776		14th	14th	2nd/6th	
1776		15th	15th	2nd/4th	
1776		16th	16th	2nd/5th	
1776		7th Circar	28th	1785 disbanded	
1776		8th Circar	29th	1785 disbanded	
1777		17th	17th	2nd/1st	1806 disbanded 1807 2nd/24th 1818 2nd/1st
1777		18th	18th	1796 drafted into 8th	

1824 Madras NI	1758–1767 coat/facings	1769–1785 facings	1785 facings	1801 facings	1805 lace
	Uniform details—all coats red unless otherwise noted				
1st	red/blue	blue	green	white	gold
	red/yellow	blue	green		
2nd	red/green	blue	green	green	gold
3rd	red/black	blue	green	red	silver
				1812 green	gold
4th	red/red	blue	green	orange	silver
5th	yellow/red	blue	green	black	gold
6th	green lace	blue	green	buff	silver
7th		blue	green	French grey	silver
8th		blue	buff	yellow	silver
9th		blue	buff	green	silver
		blue			
		blue			
10th		blue	green	red	gold
11th		blue	green	green	silver
12th		blue	green	yellow	silver
		blue			
		blue			
		blue			
		blue			
13th		blue	buff	buff	silver
				1817 red	
14th		blue	green	buff	silver
15th		blue	green	orange	silver
16th		blue	buff	black	silver
17th		blue	yellow	white	gold
		blue	yellow		

Raised	Carnatic (Bn)	1784 Madras (Bn)	1796 Madras NI	1796–1824
1777	19th	19th	2nd/10th	
1777	20th	20th	2nd/7th	
1777	21st	21st	2nd/2nd	
1781	22nd	30th	1785 disbanded	
1781	23rd	31st	1785 disbanded	
1782	24th	32nd	1785 disbanded	
1782	25th	33rd	1785 disbanded	
1782	26th	34th	1785 disbanded	
1782	27th	35th	1785 disbanded	
1784	Grenadier Bn		1788 disbanded	
1786		22nd	1796 drafted to 3rd	
1786		23rd	1796 drafted to 1st	
1786		24th	1796 drafted to 2nd	
1786		25th	1796 drafted to 4th	
1786		26th	1796 drafted to 7th	
1786		27th	1796 drafted to 9th	
1786		28th	1st/11th	
1787		1st to 8th Revenue Bns		1792 disbanded
1788		29th	2nd/11th	
1788		30th	1796 drafted to 5th	
1790		9th to 14th Revenue Bns		1792 disbanded
1793		31st	drafted to 6th	
1793		32nd	drafted to 10th	
1794		33rd	1st/12th	1811 Wallajahabad LI
1794		34th	2/12th	
1794		35th	1st/13th	
1794		36th	2nd/13th	
1798		1st Extra	1st/14th	
1798		2nd Extra	2nd/14th	
1798		3rd Extra	1st/15th	
1799		Masulipatam Bn	2nd/15th	
1800			1st/16th	1811 Trichinopoly LI
1800			2nd/16th	
1800			1st/17th	
1800			2nd/17th	1811 Chicacole LI
1800			1st/18th	
1800			2/18th	
1800			1st/19th	
1800			2nd/19th	
1801			Madras Volunteer Bn	1804 2/20th

1824 Madras NI	1769–1785 facings	1785 facings	1801 facings	1805 lace
18th	blue	yellow	red	gold
19th	blue	yellow	French grey	silver
20th	blue	yellow	green	gold
		buff		
		yellow		
		buff		
		yellow		
		buff		
		buff		
21st		buff	buff	gold
22nd		buff	buff	gold
		yellow		
		yellow		
		yellow		
23rd		yellow	green 1819 dark green/gold	silver
24th		yellow	green	silver
25th		yellow	yellow	silver
26th		yellow	yellow	silver
27th			black	silver
28th			black	silver
29th			white 1819 white/gold	silver
30th			white 1819 white/gold	silver
31st			yellow	silver
32nd			yellow	silver
33rd			yellow	gold
34th			yellow 1819 dark green/gold	gold
35th			blue 1817 buff 1819 gold	silver
36th			blue 1817 buff 1819 gold	silver
37th			buff 1819 buff/gold	silver
38th			buff 1819 buff/gold	silver
40th			green	gold

Raised	1796 Madras NI	1796–1824	1824 Madras NI	1801	1805
1803	1st Extra	1804 1st/20th	39th	green	gold
1803	2nd Extra	1804 1st/21st	41st	yellow	gold
1803	3rd Extra	1804 1st/22nd	43rd	yellow	gold
1803	4th Extra	1804 2nd/21st	42nd	yellow	gold
1803	5th Extra	1804 1st/23rd 1806 disbanded 1807 25th 1819 1st/23rd	45th	white	gold
1803	6th Extra	1804 2nd/22nd	44th		
1803	7th Extra	1804 2nd/23rd 1806 disbanded 1807 2nd/25th 1819 2nd/23rd	46th	yellow	gold
1804	Madras Fencible Regt	1806 disbanded			
1804	1st–6th Extra Bns	1805 disbanded			
1807	1st/24th	1818 1st/1st	1st		
1807	2nd/24th	1818 2nd/1st	1st		
1807	1st/25th	1818 1st/23rd	45th		
1807	2nd/25th	1818 2nd/23rd	46th		
1810	Madras Volunteer Bn	1814 Madras Rifle Corps		green/black/gold	
1818	1st–4th Bns Hill Rangers	1819 disbanded			
1819	1st–6th Extra Bns	1821 disbanded			
1819	1st/24th		47th	buff	gold
1819	2nd/24th		48th	buff	gold
1819	1st/25th		49th	yellow	gold
1819	2nd/25th		50th	yellow	gold
1819	Madras Native Militia	1821 disbanded			

Battle honours	Date of action	Date of award	Regiments granted award (1824 titles)
CARNATIC	1788–1791	1889	1st, 2nd, 3rd, 4th, 5th, 6th, 7th, 8th, 9th, 12th, 13th, 14th, 15th, 16th, 17th, 19th, 20th
SHOLINGHUR	1781	1841	3rd, 4th, 5th, 6th, 8th, 9th, 12th, 13th, 14th 15th, 16th, 17th, 19th, 20th
MYSORE	1788–1791	1889	1st, 2nd, 3rd, 4th, 5th, 6th, 7th, 8th, 9th, 12th, 13th 14th, 15th, 16th, 19th, 20th, 21st, 22nd
SERINGAPATAM	1799	1820	1st, 6th, 8th, 11th, 13th, 19th, 20th, 21st, 22nd, 23rd, 24th
BOURBON	1810	1838	6th, 24th
ASSAYE	1803	1803	2nd, 4th, 8th, 10th, 24th
COCHIN	1809	1840	33rd
SEETABULDEE	1817	1819	1st, 39th
NAGPORE	1817	1826	1st, 2nd, 17th, 21st, 23rd, 26th, 28th, 39th
MAHEIDPOOR	1817	1819	3rd, 14th, 27th, 28th, 31st

The uniform of the British officers of the Madras NI followed closely that of the British infantry and the other presidencies. Head-dress followed the usual development from tricorne to bicorne to hat. A contemporary painting shows the latter as a black top hat with black fur or feather crest and a white plume on the left side. British infantry patterns of shako between 1800 and 1816 are illustrated in regulations, but there are no other indications that they were actually worn. The British pattern of bell-top shako was adopted after 1816.

The uniform coat was generally red with lapels, collar and cuffs of facing colour. The uniform worn by Captain George Jolland of the 7th Madras NI (plate 26) was an exception being dark green with red facings. This was because when facings were allocated in 1759, all the available colours had been used by the time the 7th were reached. It was decided to reverse one of the existing arrangements, that of the 3rd who wore red with green facings. Regulations issued in 1785 distinguish between 'full regimental cut' jackets, and coats, apparently of a simpler nature. In both cases only one epaulette was worn, except for officers of grenadier companies who wore wings. The 1801 regulations specified epaulettes in place of wings for flank companies with grenades or bugle horns. In 1801 a combined wing/epaulette was introduced for flank companies. Loops on the coat fronts were generally in two although the 1801 regulations specified that the 3rd, 6th, 13th and 17th regiments should have equal loops. According to regulations shoulder-belt plates were oblong with the regimental number embossed.

Native officers followed the general style of British officers, except for the head-dress, while the main difference in the sepoys' uniform was to be found in head-dress and netherwear. The earliest head-dress shown (plate 26) was a blue turban of a loose flat pancake shape. This varied both in size and in the angle at which it was worn. They were replaced at the turn of the century by a stiff bell-topped head-dress (plate 28) probably consisting of an iron or leather framework around which a cloth was wound and on which regimental devices were mounted. The

Plate 16. Captain Thomas Dallas, Madras Cavalry, 1786. Oil painting by Alexander Nasmyth.

weight and similarity to European head-dress proved unpopular, so the heavy framework was replaced with a framework made of bamboo. The early coats were long with narrow lapels and loops in pairs, but by the turn of the century they were shorter with standing collars. Hamilton Smith's print of 1815 shows a short, single-breasted jacket similar to that worn by British infantry. Flank company wings began as simple strips sewn at right angles, but became more elaborate as time went on. Equipment was generally of buff leather although examples of black are found. A white shirt and blue cummerbund ornamented with white stripes of varying pattern was worn under the coat. Native officers and NCOs wore white trousers while sepoys wore white janghirs, longer than those of the Bengal Army, reaching almost to the knee. These were edged in blue of varying pattern. Pantaloons were permitted for foreign service in 1810, and for general use in 1812. In the early

Raised	Title Bombay Sepoys	1788 Bombay Sepoys	1796 Bombay Native Infantry
1768	1st	7th	2nd/4th
1768	2nd	2nd–6th	1st/2nd
1769	3rd	drafted to 10th and 11th	
1770	4th	12th	drafted to 2nd/3rd and 2nd/4th
1775	5th	7th–9th	2nd/2nd
1775	6th	2nd–6th	2nd/3rd
1777	1st Marine Bn		1818 1st/11th
1778	7th	1785 disbanded	
1778	8th	1st	1st/1st Grenadier Battalion
1780	9th	1784 absorbed into 5th	
1780	10th	1785 disbanded	
1780	11th	1784 disbanded	
1780	12th	1784 drafted to 1st	
1780	13th	1784 drafted to 1st	
1780	14th	1784 drafted to 1st	
1780	15th	1784 drafted to 1st	
1788		3rd	1st/3rd
1788		4th	1st/4th
1788		5th	2nd/1st 1798 1st/5th
1788		8th	drafted to 1st/3rd and 1st/4th
1788		10th	drafted to 2nd/1st and 2nd/2nd
1788		11th	drafted to 1st/2nd and 2nd/2nd
1796		13th	1st/5th 1798 2nd/1st 1818 Grenadiers
1797			2nd/5th
1796			1st/6th
1798			2nd/6th
1800			1st/7th
1800			2nd/7th
1800			1st/8th
1800			2nd/8th
1803 Bombay Fencible Regt			1st/9th
1803			2nd/9th
1817			1st/10th
1817			2nd/10th
1818			2nd/11th
1820			1st/12th
1820			2nd/12th Marine Battalion
1820			1st Extra
1820			2nd Extra

Prior to 1791 all regiments had red coats and blue facings except for the Marine Battalion which had green facings. In 1791 all regiments had yellow facings. *See page 191 for table of battle honours.

1824 Bombay NI	1812 facings/lace	1812–1824 changes
8th	white/silver	
3rd	sky blue/silver	
4th	sky blue/silver	
6th	black/silver	
21st	green/silver	1822 green/gold
1st	orange/silver	1822 white/gold
5th	black/silver	
7th	white/silver	
9th	green/silver	1822 black/gold
2nd	orange/silver	1822 white/gold
10th	green/silver	1822 black/gold
11th	buff/silver	
12th	buff/silver	
13th	green/silver	1822 buff/gold
14th	green/silver	1822 buff/gold
15th	pompadour/silver	1822 buff/silver
16th	pompadour/silver	1822 buff/silver
17th	yellow/silver	
18th	yellow/silver	
19th	yellow/gold	
20th	yellow/gold	
22nd	green/gold	
23rd	green/silver	
24th	green/silver	
25th	yellow/silver	
26th	yellow/silver	

Plate 17. *Lieutenant Robert Woolf, 6th Madras Cavalry, c 1810. Watercolour by himself (see also plate 3).*

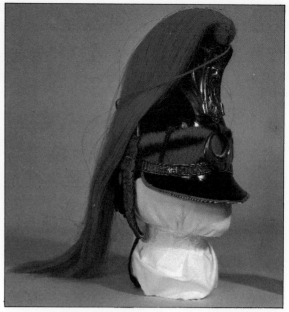

Plate 18. *Officer's helmet of the 3rd Madras Native Cavalry, worn by Colonel James Russell, c 1800.*

days sepoys went barefoot, but sandals or chapplis were later provided, although they are not shown in contemporary illustrations until after 1810.

While the Madras Army did not have local or irregular corps, they did introduce rifles and light infantry. The Madras Rifle Corps was raised as the Madras Volunteer Corps in 1810 and became rifles in 1814. They wore green with black facings and gold lace, with green trousers.

In 1811, four battalions, the 1/3rd, 1/12th, 1/16th and 2/17th were converted to light infantry. An order of 12 November 1812 laid down that they should have dark green facings and gold lace. Trousers were white for hot weather and black for other times.

BOMBAY EUROPEAN REGIMENTS

		Uniform details red coat facings/lace
1662	Raised as independent companies	
1668	Bombay Regiment	
1688	Bombay (European) Regiment	
1788	2 regiments	
	1st	blue/gold
	2nd	blue/silver

BOMBAY INFANTRY 1768—1824

British officers of the Bombay NI followed much the same development as their counter-parts in Britain and in the other presidencies although, as the table of facings show, there was probably more uniformity in Bombay than elsewhere. Once again, there is little evidence that the early pattern shakos were worn by officers, and the first to be specified was the 1816 pattern. Illustrations from the early 1800s show the top hat in use, often with a white cover. The coat and jacket followed developments similar to those in Bengal and Madras. The 1816 regulations laid down the distinctions of rank by means of epaulettes. Field officers wore two epaulettes, a colonel wore a crown over a star, a lieutenant colonel a crown, and a major a star; Captains and subalterns wore a single epaulette, except those of flank companies who wore wings on each shoulder. An order of 14 September 1808 laid down that gorgets should be worn by officers on duty. The shoulder belt plate was oval with the regimental number, and after 1796, the battalion number engraved thereon. In July 1806 a shell jacket was authorised. It was single breasted with buttons in pairs, gold or silver cord loops on the shoulder and plain collar and cuffs of facing colour.

The main difference in uniform between

Plate 19. Lieutenant Morgan Charles Chase, 1st Madras Native Cavalry, c 1810. Oil painting, artist unknown.

officers and native ranks lay in the native ranks' head-dress and netherwear. During the earlier period, the head-dress was a turban, but its form and colour are uncertain. The 1773 print of 'seapoys' (plate 29) shows a loosely bound turban of light-coloured material. By 1788 the turbans were dark blue. Gradually they developed fronts of metal or leather mounted with regimental devices, and eventually the confection shown in plate 30 evolved with a high body and fur-trimmed front plate bearing the regimental number.

After 1814 this was replaced by a peakless shako (plate 63).

The uniform coat followed standard patterns of the day, although the method of wearing it buttoned down the front (plate 29) was unusual. Cummerbunds do not feature in illustrations of Bombay NI, and it appears that there was less emphasis on them than in the other presidencies. The sepoy in plate 30 wears a British-style soldier's jacket with buff crossbelts but without any form of waistband. Janghirs were midway between the Bengal

Plate 20. An officer of the Madras Light Cavalry, in undress, c 1820. Miniature by George Patten.

Plate 21. Lieutenant Conrad John Owen, 1st Bombay Light Cavalry, c 1820. Oil painting, artist unknown.

and Madras patterns in length, and were similarly decorated with a variety of patterns of blue triangles and stripes. Janghirs were not replaced by trousers until 1824, rather later than in the other presidencies.

BENGAL HORSE ARTILLERY

The first experimental troop of horse artillery was formed in 1806. By 1809 there were three troops and by 1818 seven troops including a rocket troop. For a short while, the first troop included native drivers, but they were replaced by Europeans and the regiment remained all-European until 1818 when three native troops were added.

There is little information about the early uniform of the Corps but it closely followed that of the Royal Horse Artillery. The first regulations issued in 1809 still followed the general style with some important differences, notably in the head-dress. Apparently the Corps began with the Tarleton helmet, but by 1809 regulations specified the Roman helmet with black skull, red horse-hair mane, gilt scales and leopardskin turban. The jacket was dark blue with red facings and gold lace. The lace of the jacket was flat and in wavylines. A crimson and gold girdle, and white pantaloons completed the uniform.

Native ranks wore a bulbous head-dress similar to that of the cavalry, also in dark blue. They also wore plain blue jackets with red collar and cuffs and white overalls.

The first company of foot artillery was formed in 1748 and was manned by Europeans and natives. An all native company or Golundauz was formed in 1777, and the number of both European and native companies was gradually built up.

BENGAL FOOT ARTILLERY

European officers and other ranks followed the pattern of Royal Artillery uniforms (plate 31). Head-dress developed through tricorne and bicorne to hats in white material, or swathed in white, and, eventually, the 1816 bell-top shako. The coat was dark blue with red facings and gold lace, becoming shorter with closed front and loops down the front at the turn of the century.

The native ranks, or lascars, wore a simpler version of this combination. The natives in the background of plate 31 wear a dark blue turban with red piping in a flat pancake style, similar to that of the Madras NI rather than to the sundial cap of the Bengal NI. However, the 'golandar' in plate 4 wears a blue sundial cap with red piping and white star. The coat was dark blue with red cuffs and narrow lapels. The cummerbund was red with blue or purple tapes. White janghirs with blue decoration were worn.

By the early 19th century the lascars wore the same bulbous head-dress as the native cavalry, in dark blue with yellow decoration. The dark blue jacket had red facings and yellow lace, and janghirs were abolished in favour of white trousers sooner than in the native infantry.

MADRAS ARTILLERY

The first troop of Madras Horse Artillery was raised in 1805 and by 1819 this had been built up to two European troops, a rocket troop and three native troops. The foot artillery was formed in 1748 and the first native company in 1784.

The uniform of both the horse and foot artillery followed that of the Royal Regiment and the Bengal regiments already described, although certain variations and details should be noted. The horse artillery appear to have used the Tarleton helmet, at least up to 1816 and possibly later, until it was replaced by a bell-top shako. 1806 regulations specify that the clothing should be dark blue with red collar and cuffs and yellow trimmings and 'of the fashion of cloathing of Cavalry Regiments'.

Plate 22. LEFT: Lieutenant William Vincent, 6th Bengal Native Infantry, c 1800. Oil painting, artist unknown.

Plate 23. Subedar and sepoy of the 21st Bengal Native Infantry, c 1815. Watercolours by Captain J Williams of the regiment, published as illustrations to his Historical Account of the Rise and Progress of the Bengal Native Infantry.

There is more pictorial evidence than usual for the European gunners of the foot artillery, notably plate 27 which shows in good detail the white hat which replaced the tricorne in hot weather, the blue jacket with yellow loops on the sleeves and the brass crossbelt plate stamped with the battalion number (the 2nd Battalion was formed in 1786).

The uniforms of the native lascars are shown in plate 32. All wear the same stiff turban as the Madras NI, in red for officers and dark blue for NCOs and lascars, both ornamented with white cord. The officer and NCO wear crimson sashes and white breeches; the lascars wear blue cummerbunds with white braid and white janghirs almost down to the knee, with blue ornamentation on the lower edge.

BOMBAY ARTILLERY

The first troop of horse artillery was formed in 1811. The first artillery company was formed in 1748, but there was no native artillery until 1824.

Uniform followed closely the pattern of the other presidencies. The Roman helmet of the horse artillery is not described until 1829, so the Tarleton helmet was probably worn before then. The shoulder-belt plate of the foot artillery is shown in plate 33, worn with an undress jacket.

ENGINEERS, SAPPERS AND MINERS, PIONEERS

In Bengal, companies of engineers and pioneers were formed in 1764, although the pioneers were disbanded shortly after. In 1803 an engineer lascar company and a corps of pioneers were formed.

43

Plate 30. ABOVE LEFT: 'Se-Poy' (sic) of the 1st Bombay Native Infantry, Grenadier Battalion, c 1805. Watercolour by a company artist.

Plate 31. ABOVE RIGHT: Lieutenant James Mayaffre, Bengal Artillery, 1773. Oil painting by Tilly Kettle.

Plate 32. Subedars and lascars of the Madras Artillery, 1796. Watercolour by Charles Gold 'sketched from life at Trichinopoly 1796'.

They wore black shakos, dark green jackets with black facings, black buttons, yellow lace and green trousers. The Corps of Sappers and Miners was formed in 1819, and they were clothed in traditional engineer uniform of red coats, dark blue facings and yellow lace. A jacket of an officer of the Bengal Engineers preserved in the National Army Museum is red with black velvet facings and gold lace.

In Madras, companies of pioneers were formed in 1780. In the 1790s they wore blue coats, black velvet facings and gold lace. By 1819 they had changed to red coats with dark blue velvet facings and gold lace. A corps of Madras sappers and miners were formed in 1818 but disbanded in 1821. They wore dark blue coats, black facings and yellow lace.

In Bombay, a company of pioneer lascars were formed in 1777 and in 1781 they became a corps of pioneers, dressed in blue turbans, dark green coats, black facings and gold lace. Sappers and miners were formed in 1820, with British officers from the Bombay Engineers who wore red coats, black velvet facings and gold lace.

Plate 33. Lieutenant Christopher Hodgson, Bombay Artillery, 1814. Oil painting by William Newton.

2
The Sepoy Army
1824–1857

The defeat of the Marathas in 1818 had confirmed the East India Company as the supreme power in southern and central India, but the Company still had some way to go to establish its supremacy over the warrior states to the north-west. The British also faced hostility from Burma to the east.

1st Burma War 1824–1826

There had been long-standing disputes between India and Burma over border territories, including Assam and Manipur. In 1819 Burma had conquered Assam, and in 1822 its attempts to take Manipur had been resisted by British troops sent to help the native rulers. In March 1824 Britain declared war and attacked the Burmese at three points, in Assam and in Arakan with columns from Bengal, and with a seaborne expedition comprising mainly Madras troops against Rangoon.

In Assam and Arakan the small British columns made little progress, but Rangoon was taken unopposed. When the Burmese found that the British showed no sign of advancing further into the country, they gathered their forces together and launched a furious counter-attack in December which was decisively repulsed. For their defence of a key point in the Rangoon defences, the 26th Madras NI received an immediate award of the battle honour KEMMENDINE.

In the early months of 1825, the British advanced up the Irrawaddy, and in April they took the main Burmese base of Danabyu. After settling into Prome for the monsoon season, the British resumed their advance in November, defeating the Burmese again at Pagahm. Their way was now clear to Ava, the capital, but as they approached, the Burmese sued for peace. Under the terms, the Burmese surrendered Assam, Arakan and the Tenasserim coast, giving the British virtually the whole of Burma's western coastline.

The main battle honour for the war, AVA, was awarded to the Madras regiments which took part, including the European Regiment, the Governor-General's Bodyguard, the 1st Light Cavalry and seventeen native infantry regiments together with one Bengal regiment, the 40th Native Infantry. The Bengal regiments received separate honours for ARRACAN (Gardner's Horse and five native infantry regiments) and ASSAM (46th and 57th NI).

2nd Burma War 1852–1853

Friction between the British traders in Rangoon and the Burmese Government led to a further outbreak of hostilities in 1852. In April, an expedition which included native troops from Bengal, Madras and the Punjab, occupied Rangoon. After a halt for the monsoon season, the campaign was resumed in the autumn with an attack on the Swe Dagon, the Great Pagoda. The British went on to occupy the other main towns of Southern Burma, including Bassein, Prome and Pegu, and annexed the province.

The battle honour PEGU was awarded for this campaign to four Bengal and seven Madras native infantry regiments and to the recently raised 4th Sikh Local Infantry.

In the West and North-West, Britain still had to face the remnants of Maratha independent power, and the powerful and warlike Sikh nation of the Punjab.

BHURTPORE 1826

In 1803–1804 Bhurtpore had held out against Lord Lake's forces, which made four attempts to storm it, and it had become the last independent stronghold of the Marathas. When, in 1826, it became the subject of a disputed succession, Lord Combermere, the Commander-in-Chief, decided to use the opportunity to reduce it. He assembled in Bengal a force of one cavalry and two infantry divisions. The siege began on 28 December 1825, and the breaches were successfully stormed, at some cost, on 17 January 1826. The honour BHURTPORE was awarded to the Bengal European Regiment, six regiments of light cavalry, two of local horse, sixteen native infantry and three local infantry regiments.

Plate 34. 'A Coffee Party' with officers of the Bengal irregular cavalry, native infantry, light cavalry and horse artillery. Lithograph after Philip Trench, c 1850.

Plate 35. Skinner's Horse at exercise, c 1840. Oil painting by Joshua Reynolds Gwatkin.

A further ripple of Maratha power came in Gwalior, in 1843, when the death of the Sindia led to disputes over succession. The British felt that this was a threat to their communications with the north-west, a sensitive area after the disasters in Afghanistan. The Governor-General decided that the Gwalior army must be disbanded, and for this purpose two forces were assembled. They crossed the Chambal River into Gwalior, hoping that their presence would discourage the local forces from fighting. However, at Maharajpur on 29 December 1843, Gough found the Rani of Gwalior and her forces firmly entrenched and after a determined battle, defeated them. On the same day, Gray defeated the remainder of the Gwalior forces at Paniar

The honour MAHARAJPORE was awarded to the Governor-General's Bodyguard, five light cavalry, and one irregular cavalry, seven native infantry and one local infantry regiment, while PUNNIAR was awarded to three light cavalry, one irregular cavalry and four native infantry regiments.

1ST AFGHAN WAR 1838–1842

Britain's main preoccupation now was with the north-west frontier of India. The underlying factor affecting British policy was a fear of Russian expansion into Central Asia, intensified by Russian support for the Persian invasion of Afghanistan in 1836–1838. In December 1838, the British used this as a pretext to invade Afghanistan with the object of replacing the Amir, Dust Mohammed, by the former ruler, Shah Shujah. The ruler of the Punjab, Ranjit Singh refused to allow the British force passage through his territory, and the British force was compelled to detour south, across the Sind desert and through the Bolam Pass to Kandahar, which they occupied in April 1839. They took the fortress of Ghazni by storm and in August 1839 reached Kabul where Shah Shujah was restored. A garrison of some 4,500 troops was left, and the main army returned to India.

This stage of the campaign was signified by the award of the honours AFGHANISTAN 1839 and GHUZNEE 1839 to the regiments of the Bengal and Bombay armies which took part. Battles against Baluchi forces threatening the British lines of communications led to the award of three other honours, KHELAT (4th Local Horse, Bombay Sappers and Miners and 31st Bengal NI), KAHUN (5th Bombay NI) and CUTCHEE (1st and 2nd Scinde Horse).

Everything remained comparatively quiet, until November 1841 when the Afghans in Kabul rose in revolt, killed the British envoy and surrounded the garrison. In January terms were agreed by which the British force was allowed to return to India, but on their way through the Khyber Pass they were surrounded and massacred. Only Dr Brydon escaped to bring the news to Jalalabad. Other garrisons were attacked, Ghazni was taken but Jalalabad, Kandahar and Kelat-i-Ghilzai held out.

These actions were commemorated by the honours JELLALABAD awarded to the 5th Bengal LC and 35th NI, and KELAT-I-GHILZAI awarded to a regiment of Bengal local infantry recruited from Shah Shujah's forces which adopted the honour as their title.

A punitive expedition was hastily raised, and in April a force set out from Bombay, relieving Kelat and Jalalabad and recapturing Ghazni. The force joined up with a column from Kandahar under General Nott, and the combined army entered Kabul in September. Three battle honours, CANDAHAR 1842, GHUZNEE 1842 and CABOOL 1842 were awarded to the Bengal and Bombay regiments which took part in this final phase.

The war in Afghanistan had two effects. Those Indian nations still independent of the British, particularly the Baluchis and the Sikhs, had been shown that British troops were not invulnerable, and they felt more confident about facing British troops on the battlefield. At the same time, the British realised that if their north-west frontier was to be secure, these nations had to be under their control.

SIND WAR 1843

The first clash came in Sind, which the British had occupied during the Afghan War, and

Plate 36. The 26th Bengal Native Infantry at Mahomde Ushah Fort, 1st Afghan War, 12 September 1842. Watercolour, artist unknown.

where they wished to retain their bases and control over the rivers. The ruling amirs were replaced, but in February 1843 the Baluchis responded by attacking the British residency at Hyderabad.

The British reacted swiftly, and a force of 2,500 troops under Sir Charles Napier defeated ten times their number of Baluchis at the battle of Miani on 17 February. After a forced march, Napier met the enemy again on 24 March outside the gates of Hyderabad and dispersed the force which had been besieging the residency. Over the following six months, the British marched the length and breadth of Sind and in a number of minor actions finally defeated the Baluchis.

Napier's native regiments, mainly from Bombay (apart from the 9th Bengal Light Cavalry) were awarded the battle honours MEEANEE and HYDERABAD. The western frontier of India had been stabilised and the River Indus, vital to communications had been secured.

SIKH WARS

Relations with the Punjab had depended on the powerful ruler, Ranjit Singh, who had remained on reasonably friendly terms with the British. However, after his death in 1839, the new rulers were more hostile. The Sikh Army was superior to others which the British had met in India, being trained on European lines, and the British reverses in Afghanistan had given the Sikhs greater confidence.

1st Sikh War: The Sutlej Campaign
1845–1846
Matters came to a head in December 1845 when a Sikh army crossed the Sutlej into British territory. On 18 December they attacked Sir Hugh Gough's troops at Mudki but were repulsed with heavy losses. With his army reinforced, Gough pressed on to attack the Sikhs' entrenched position around Ferozeshah and after a fierce battle spread over two days, the Sikhs withdrew across the Sutlej. A further Sikh foray across the Sutlej was defeated at Aliwal on 28 January 1846. The climax of the campaign came on 10 February when the British carried the war back across the Sutlej and defeated the Sikhs at Sobraon. The British went on to occupy Lahore, and Punjab became a British protectorate.

49

The battle honours for the 1st Sikh War, MOODKEE, FEROZESHAH, ALIWAL and SOBRAON were awarded to regiments of the Bengal Army, including the 1st Bengal European Regiment and the Governor-General's Bodyguard.

2nd Sikh War: The Punjab Campaign
1818–1849

The Council of Regency appointed by the British had problems maintaining control, and the Sikh Army still felt that it could defeat the British.

In April 1848 two British officers were killed at Multan. A British force under General Whish was sent to retake Multan and after a siege which lasted from July until the following January, the Sikh garrison surrendered.

Meanwhile, on 9 November, an army of 15,000 under General Sir Hugh Gough had crossed the Sutlej and had met the Sikhs in an inconclusive battle at Ramnagar. The armies met again on 13 January 1849, in the bitterly fought battle of Chillianwallh, where the Sikhs were driven out of their positions at heavy loss to the British and without being decisively beaten. With the addition of General Whish's troops from Multan, Gough attacked again on 21 February at Gujerat and at last gained the decisive victory. British rule over the Punjab was established and the British, recognising the quality of their late enemies, began forming regiments in the territory.

Gough's force, which included both Bengal and Bombay regiments was awarded the battle honours MOOLTAN, CHILLIANWALLAH and GOOJERAT and the campaign honour PUNJAUB. Regiments of the newly raised Punjab Frontier Force were awarded the honours MOOLTAN, GOOJERAT (Lumsden's Guides) and PUNJAUB (Lumsden's Guides and the 1st and 2nd Sikh Local Infantry).

Again during this period, Company troops were also involved in operations away from the Indian mainland.

1ST CHINA WAR 1840–1842

The 1st China War is notable because it marks the first use of Indian troops in an operation which was not directly concerned with India, but was intended to further the aims of British expansion in the Far East. China had been reluctant to allow foreign traders into its territory, and in 1839 stocks of opium imported by British traders were impounded. In July 1840, an expedition under Sir Hugh Gough seized the island of Chusan and attempts were made to arrange peace terms with China.

Little progress was made, so in January 1841 reinforcements were sent, including a number of Madras regiments, enabling Gough to seize the forts guarding Canton, and in May Canton itself was taken. Despite appalling administration, which led to more British casualties than did the fighting, another year's campaigning brought the British force up the Yangtse to threaten Nanking. The Chinese finally agreed on peace terms, by which Hong Kong was ceded to Britain and five Chinese ports were opened to foreign trade.

The honour CHINA and the emblem of the China dragon were awarded to the Madras Sappers and Miners, and to the 2nd, 6th, 14th, 37th and 41st Madras NI.

ADEN 1839

The Bombay Army continued to take responsibility for operations around the Arabian Sea.

In 1835 an agreement had been reached with the local Arab ruler, by which, in return for a cash subsidy, Britain could use Aden as a coaling station. Other Arab rulers objected, and it became necessary for the British to install a garrison, which had to be done in the face of some resistance. The 1st Bombay European Regiment, the Marine Bn and the 24th NI were awarded the honour ADEN.

PERSIAN WAR 1856–1857

The Persian campaign arose from causes similar to those which led to the 1st Afghan War. Despite British warnings, the Persians invaded Afghanistan and captured Herat, regarded as the key to any invasion of India from the North-West. A strong force was assembled under Lieutenant-General Sir James Outram, the native contingent being found by the Bombay Army. The first landings were made on 5 December 1856 and after three short sharp engagements, the Persians sued for peace and withdrew from Afghanistan.

Thanks to Outram, a generous allocation of

Plate 37. Uniform of Captain J Caulfield, 4th Bengal Light Cavalry, c 1832.

Plate 38. Lieutenant James Irving, 1st Bengal Light Cavalry, in undress, 1839. Oil painting by Rajah Sansome.

battle honours, PERSIA, RESHIRE, BUSHIRE and KOOSH AB, were awarded to the Bombay regiments involved.

BENGAL ARMY 1824–1857

In 1824, the native infantry battalions were separated into regiments and renumbered according to their date of formation, to form 68 regiments.

During the 1st Burma War, the 47th were disbanded for refusing to take part in the expedition to Arakan, and were replaced by a new regiment originally given the number 69, but renumbered 47th in 1828. Also in 1824, the Sylhet Local Battalion (later 8th Gurkha Rifles) was raised. Six extra regiments raised in 1825 were given the numbers 69 to 74.

In 1840, three light infantry regiments were formed, from light companies of various battalions. The 34th were disbanded in 1843, as a result of problems during the campaign in Sind when many soldiers opted for discharge rather than go on campaign.

There was a further increase in size, as a

51

result of the demands on the Bengal Army during the 1st Sikh War and eight new irregular cavalry regiments, numbered 10th to 17th, were formed. In 1847, The Bundelkhund Legion were brought in as the 10th and all the others moved down one number. Ten infantry levies of 1,000 men each, and eighteen depot battalions were formed, but these were mostly reduced after the war.

The fighting qualities of the Sikhs impressed the British so much that, in 1846, the first two regiments of Sikh infantry were raised, the regiments of Ferozepore (later 14th Sikhs) and of Ludhiana (later 15th Sikhs). In the same year a frontier brigade was raised for police and general duties comprising a Corps of Guides, four regiments of Sikh infantry and a light battery.

The conquest of the Punjab in 1849 brought the British into contact with the Pathan tribes of the North-West Frontier, and this led to the formation of what later became the Punjab Frontier Force, comprising the Frontier Brigade raised in 1846, five regiments of Punjab irregular cavalry and five regiments of Punjab irregular infantry. In addition the Sind Camel Corps was transferred from the Bombay Presidency to become the 6th Punjab Infantry. In 1850, foreign service allowance was withdrawn from regiments serving in the Punjab, causing several mutinies, the worst being in the 66th NI which was disbanded. Its place in the line was taken by the Nasiri Gurkha Battalion.

MADRAS ARMY 1824–1857

In 1824 the 25 regiments of native infantry were reorganised into 50 single battalion regiments. Two more regiments were raised in 1826 and in 1830, and the Madras Rifle Corps was abolished and its companies dispersed as rifle companies to other regiments. With the emphasis on conquest and pacification to north-west, Madras became something of a backwater, and there were no further changes of any significance in the organisation of the army until 1861.

BOMBAY ARMY 1824–1857

In 1839 the availability of indigenous horse-

Plate 39. Colonel J S G Ryley, 5th Bengal Light Cavalry, c 1850. Pastel by Isidore-Jean-Baptiste Magues.

men led to an increase in the irregular cavalry, with the formation of the Gujerat Irregular Horse and the Scinde Irregular Horse (raised from the Cutch Levy, formerly part of the Poona Horse). In 1850 the South Mahratta Horse was raised.

The aquisition of Sind and Baluchistan, in 1844, brought a valuable new element into the Bombay Army, with the raising of the 1st Belooch Battalion in 1844, and the 2nd in 1846. Also in 1846, John Jacob was authorised to raised a 2nd regiment of Scinde irregular horse. Earlier, in 1843, Napier had created the Scinde Camel Corps which, in 1852, became the 6th Regiment Punjab Irregular Force.

The need for extra troops to garrison Sind led to the formation of three more regular infantry regiments, the 27th, 28th and 29th.

BENGAL LIGHT CAVALRY 1825–1857

Although there were several changes of headdress between 1824 and 1857, the uniform of the Bengal light cavalry remained fairly constant in other respects. The shako introduced in 1818 continued in use until 1830 when it was replaced by a shako with a Maltese cross badge, with the regimental number in the

BENGAL LIGHT CAVALRY 1825–1857

Raised	Title	Uniform details all coats French grey/all lace silver facings	
1773	Governor-Generals Bodyguard	scarlet/blue/silver	
1776	1st	Orange	
1778	2nd	Orange	disbanded in 1841 for misconduct in Afghanistan
1796	3rd	Orange	
1797	4th	Orange	
1800	5th	Black	
1800	6th	Orange	
1805	7th	Orange	
1805	8th	Orange	
1825	9th	Orange	raised as 1st Extra Regiment, became 9th in 1826
1826	10th	Orange	raised as 2nd Extra Regiment, became 10th in 1826
1842	11th	Orange	became 2nd Light Cavalry in 1850

All regiments were disbanded during the Indian Mutiny.

Battle honours	Campaign	Date of action	Date of award	Regiments granted award
DELHI (1803)	2nd Maratha War	11 Sept 1803	23 Feb 1829	2nd, 3rd
LESWAREE	2nd Maratha War	1 Nov 1803	23 Feb 1829	1st, 2nd, 3rd, 4th, 6th
DEIG	2nd Maratha War	Nov–Dec 1804	23 Feb 1829	2nd, 3rd
SEETABULDEE	3rd Maratha War	26–27 Nov 1817	27 Feb 1819	6th
AVA	1st Burma War	1824–1826	22 Aug 1826	GGB
BHURTPORE	Bhurtpore	18 Jan 1826	30 May 1826	3rd, 4th, 6th, 8th, 9th, 10th
GHUZNEE	1st Afghan War	23 Jul 1839	4 Oct 1842	2nd, 3rd
JELLALABAD(*)	1st Afghan War	Jan–Apr 1842	4 Oct 1842	5th
CABOOL	1st Afghan War	1839–1842	4 Oct 1842	1st, 5th, 10th
AFGHANISTAN 1839	1st Afghan War	1839	19 Nov 1842	2nd, 3rd
MAHARAJPORE	Gwalior	29 Dec 1843	4 Jan 1844	GGB, 1st, 4th, 5th, 8th, 10th
PUNNIAR	Gwalior	29 Dec 1843	4 Jan 1844	2nd, 5th, 8th
MEEANEE	Sind	17 Feb 1843	1843	9th
HYDERABAD	Sind	24 March 1843	1843	9th
MOODKEE	1st Sikh War	18 Dec 1845	12 Dec 1846	GGB, 4th, 5th
FEROZESHUHUR	1st Sikh War	21–22 Dec 1845	12 Dec 1846	GGB, 4th, 5th, 8th
ALIWAL	1st Sikh War	28 Jan 1846	12 Aug 1846	GGB, 1st, 3rd, 5th
SOBRAON	1st Sikh War	10 Feb 1846	12 Aug 1846	GGB, 3rd, 4th, 5th
PUNJAUB	2nd Sikh War	1848–1849	7 Oct 1853	1st, 2nd, 5th, 6th, 7th, 8th
MOOLTAN	2nd Sikh War	Sep 1848–Jan 1849	7 Oct 1853	2nd
CHILLIANWALLAH	2nd Sikh War	13 Jan 1849	7 Oct 1853	1st, 5th, 6th, 8th
GOOJERAT	2nd Sikh War	21 Feb 1849	7 Oct 1853	1st, 5th, 6th, 8th

(*) With mural crown.

BENGAL LOCAL HORSE/IRREGULAR
CAVALRY 1825—1857

Raised		Title	Uniform details coat/lace	Outcome
1803	1st	Skinner's Horse	yellow/silver	1st Bengal Cavalry
1809	2nd	Gardner's Horse	green/silver	2nd Bengal Cavalry
1815	3rd	1st Rohilla Cavalry	red/gold	mutinied 1857
1814	4th	Skinner's Horse	yellow/silver	3rd Bengal Cavalry
1823	5th	Gough's	red/gold	mutinied 1857
1824	6th	Fitzgerald's Horse		disbanded 1829
1824	7th	Hawke's Horse		disbanded 1829
1824	8th	Skinner's Horse		disbanded 1829
1838	6th	Oudh Auxiliary Cavalry	red/gold	4th Bengal Cavalry
1841	7th		red/gold	5th Bengal Cavalry
1842	8th		red/gold	6th Bengal Cavalry
1844	9th	formed from Christie's Horse in service of Shah Shujah		part mutinied 1857 remainder disbanded 1861
1838	10th	Cavalry of Bundelkund Legion became 10th B I C 1847	blue/gold	disbanded 1857
1846	11th	originally 10th	scarlet/gold	mutinied 1857
1846	12th	originally 11th	green/silver	part mutinied 1857 remainder disbanded 1861
1846	13th	originally 12th	blue/gold	mutinied 1857
1846	14th	originally 13th		mutinied 1857
1846	15th	originally 14th	red/gold	mutinied 1857
1846	16th	originally 15th	red/gold	disarmed 1857
1846	17th	originally 16th	scarlet/gold	7th Bengal Cavalry
1846	18th	originally 17th	blue/gold	8th Bengal Cavalry

All regiments of Bengal Local Horse were renamed Bengal Irregular Cavalry in 1840.

Battle honours	Campaign	Date of action	Date of award	Regiments granted award
ARRACAN	1st Burma War	1825	22 Apr 1826	2nd
BHURTPORE	Bhurtpore	18 Jan 1826	30 May 1826	1st, 8th
AFGHANISTAN 1839	1st Afghan War	1839	19 Nov 1842	4th
CANDAHAR	1st Afghan War	10 Mar 1842	4 Oct 1842	1st
GHUZNEE	1st Afghan War	6 Sept 1842	4 Oct 1842	4th
KHELAT	1st Afghan War	1839	15 Feb 1840	4th
MAHARAJPORE	Gwalior	29 Dec 1843	4 Jan 1844	4th
PUNNIAR	Gwalior	29 Dec 1843	4 Jan 1844	8th
MOODKEE	1st Sikh War	18 Dec 1845	12 Dec 1846	4th, 8th, 9th
FEROZESHUHUR	1st Sikh War	21–22 Dec 1845	12 Dec 1846	4th, 8th, 9th
ALIWAL	1st Sikh War	28 Jan 1846	12 Aug 1846	4th
SOBRAON	1st Sikh War	10 Feb 1846	12 Aug 1846	2nd, 8th, 9th
MOOLTAN	2nd Sikh War	Sep 1848–Jan 1849	7 Oct 1853	7th, 11th
CHILLIANWALLAH	2nd Sikh War	13 Jan 1849	7 Oct 1853	9th
GOOJERAT	2nd Sikh War	21 Feb 1849	7 Oct 1853	9th, 11th, 12th, 13th, 14th
PUNJAUB	2nd Sikh War	1848–1849	7 Oct 1853	2nd, 7th, 9th, 11th, 12th 13th, 14th, 15th, 16th, 17th

centre (plates 37 and 38). This was replaced in 1847 by a dark-coloured fur busby with red bag, red and white plume and silver cords (plate 39). The undress cap had a dark blue crown with silver lace and welts (plate 34).

The full dress jacket was French grey with elaborate silver braiding and orange collar and cuffs (except for the 5th LC who had black). Plate 39 shows the rank badge on the collar and a more elaborate shoulder cord than was used earlier. The undress jacket (plate 38) was dark blue, with broad silver lace down the front and orange (or black) facings. Brass shoulder scales were worn with this jacket, and plate 38 shows the full dress shako, pouch-belt, red and gold girdle and sabretache. In 1835 the colour of the undress jacket was ordered to be French grey, but this was cancelled a few months later. This alteration was introduced on a permanent basis in 1847.

The scarlet and gold barrel sash shown in plate 37 was replaced by a scarlet and gold girdle. The full dress pouch-belt was of silver lace with orange train, silver fittings and a silver pouch with the device BLC in gilt. The sabretache and shabraque were of dark blue cloth with silver lace and embroidery, overalls were dark blue with a double silver stripe until 1847 when they were changed to French grey.

The native ranks' uniform followed the same general lines. At the beginning of the period, the bulbous turban was replaced by a peakless shako which continued up to the mutiny worn on occasions with a white cover. The jacket and overalls were of French grey, and some illustrations show brass shoulder scales, while others show a simple shoulder cord. Breeches were dark blue to 1847 and French grey thereafter.

BENGAL IRREGULAR HORSE 1825—1857

While the number of regular light cavalry regiments remained relatively static during this period, there was a steady increase in the number of irregular cavalry regiments. This was partly because of the success of the sillidar system, and partly because the concept appealed to the more romantically minded British officers of the time. It was a reflection of the two opposing forces of European civilisation which were meeting head-on all over Europe. On the one hand there was the traditional formality of the absolute monarchs who expected the soldier to be a stiff, immaculately dressed automaton, and on the other hand there was the liberalism of the romantic revival as personified by Byron. The loosely clothed, independent sillidar cavalryman fitted beautifully into the latter mould. In chapter 1 we saw that the British officers of irregular cavalry still wore regular cavalry-style uniform. Now (plate 34) we find them adopting the clothing of their sowars, an example which eventually spread to most regular Indian cavalry regiments.

Regulations covered no more than the basic uniform details of the irregular cavalry, and for further details we must rely on contemporary illustrations or descriptions. Available evidence is summarised below:

1st (plate 35) polished steel helmet with blue pugri, yellow alkaluk, black sword belt with yellow decoration, red and yellow girdle, red pyjamas.

2nd (From a portrait of Sir John Hearsey) green alkaluk heavily laced with silver, red cummerbund, red pyjamas.

3rd (From a watercolour in National Army Museum) black fez with blue turban, red alkaluk with blue decoration, red and gold cummerbund, yellow pyjamas, sabretache with black velvet face.

4th (From a watercolour in National Army Museum) helmet with blue and gold pugri, yellow alkaluk with heavy silver embroidery and dark blue facings, blue and gold girdle, black cummerbund with white decoration, red pyjamas.

5th (From a portrait of Colonel Hill) white turban, red alkaluk with dark blue facings and silver lace, crimson cummerbund.

6th (From a watercolour in National Army Museum and a print published by Ackermann) black helmet with white plume and gilt fittings or yellow turban, red alkaluk with blue facings and gold lace, blue sabretache with gold lace, shabraque of red and yellow squares with blue border.

7th (From a watercolour in National Army Museum) hussar busby with green cloth bag and yellow lace or fez with blue turban and red crown, red alkaluk with blue facings and gold lace, blue cummerbund.

8th (Plate 40) red turban, red alkaluk with blue facings and gold lace, scarlet and gold girdle, white breeches.

9th (From a watercolour in National Army Museum) yellow turban with blue stripes, red alkaluk with yellow lace, blue cummerbund, black equipment, yellow pyjamas, red and yellow shabraque.

10th (From a portrait of Sir John Lauder and a print published by Ackermann) black fur busby with red bag and gold cords (or white turban, blue alkaluk with heavy gold embroidery, and scarlet facings; red cummerbund, red pyjamas, blue shabraque.

11th As table

12th (From a watercolour in National Army Museum) crimson turban, dark blue alkaluk with yellow piping, crimson sash, yellow pyjamas, black equipment, red and yellow shabraque.

13th As table.

14th As table.

15th (From a portrait of Surgeon Gee in National Army Museum) dark blue turban, red alkaluk with black facings and gold lace, dark blue cummerbund, gold lace pouchbelt with black silk train.

16th As table.

17th As table.

18th (Plate 41) red turban, blue alkaluk with scarlet facings and yellow lace, red cummerbund, brown equipment, red pyjamas, dark blue shabraque with red braid.

PUNJAB CAVALRY 1846–1857

The Corps of Guides, limited at first to one troop of cavalry and two companies of infantry, were raised on 12 December 1846 by Harry Lumsden who wrote to his father that 'the arming and dressing is to be according to my own fancy'. Lumsden had conceived the highly unorthodox notion that tight scarlet tunic with high stock was not the most suitable garment in which to wage war on the plains of the Punjab in hot weather. He therefore bought all the white cotton he could find locally, and sent it down to the local river where it was soaked and impregnated with mud. Shortly after the increase in the establishment in 1849, Lumsden wrote to his second-in-command, Major W S R Hodson to the effect that he had '. . . made up my mind to have all the cavalry and infantry in mud colour and want cloth enough to make a man each a coat, pantaloons and greatcoat'. The Guides went into action in their new uniforms later that year, which must rate as the first official use of khaki in action.

The five Punjab cavalry regiments raised in 1849 adopted more conventional attire. British officers wore a dragoon pattern helmet in felt with metal binding and plume, and either an alkaluk similar to that worn by a native officer,

Plate 40. Jemedar of the 8th Bengal Irregular Cavalry, 1855. Watercolour by Charles Grant.

Plate 41. Sowars of the 18th Bengal Irregular Cavalry, c 1850. Watercolour, artist unknown.

or a European style coat. A tailor's book of the period described the jacket of the 1st Punjab Cavalry as dark blue with buff collar and cuffs, edged all round in silver lace with silver shoulder cords.

The uniform of the native ranks (plate 42) followed a similar pattern for each regiment. The alkaluk followed the traditional pattern, with officers having elaborate embroidery in regimental lace colour, the sowars having piping in facing colour. The pouch-belt was black with silver pickers and a black leather pouch. A crimson cummerbund and a black leather sword belt were worn, pyjamas were light-coloured, yellow or white, and were worn with high boots.

PUNJAB CAVALRY 1846–1857

		Uniform details			
Raised	Title	turban	alkaluk	facings	lace
1846	Guides	drab	drab	drab	drab
1849	1st Punjab Cavalry	scarlet	dark blue		silver
1849	2nd Punjab Cavalry	dark blue	scarlet	black	silver
1849	3rd Punjab Cavalry	dark blue	dark blue		silver
1849	4th Punjab Cavalry	scarlet	dark green	scarlet	gold
1849	5th Punjab Cavalry		dark green	scarlet	gold

All regiments remained loyal during the Indian Mutiny and retained their titles after 1861.

Battle honours	Campaign	Date of action	Date of award	Regiments granted award
MOOLTAN	2nd Sikh War	Sep 1848-Jan 1849	7 Oct 1853	Guides
GOOJERAT	2nd Sikh War	21 Feb 1849	7 Oct 1853	Guides
PUNJAUB	2nd Sikh War	1848-1849	7 Oct 1853	Guides

Plate 42. Native ranks of the 4th Punjab Cavalry. Watercolour by W Carpenter, Kohat, 1855.

MADRAS LIGHT CAVALRY 1824–1857

From 1808, the Governor's Bodyguard, Madras, had no official existence but was formed on an *ad hoc* from other cavalry regiments. The Bodyguard continued to wear a distinctive and elaborate uniform, which is well documented in the prints of Hunsley and Ackermann as well as in original pictures of the period. The British officer in plate 43 has a black helmet with silver fittings and red crest, like the light cavalry, although a scarlet shako with silver lace and black plume would be more usual. The jacket is scarlet with dark blue facings and silver lace. Also worn is a silver pouch-belt with dark blue train in lace, a scarlet and gold girdle, white breeches and boots, and shabraque and sabretache scarlet with silver decoration. Native ranks wore a turban, like the light cavalry, scarlet for native officers, dark blue for other ranks.

Uniforms of the Madras Light Cavalry from 1824 to 1857 followed a similar development to those of the Bengal Light Cavalry with little basic change, except in the style of head-dress for the Brtish officer. Regulations appeared frequently, and apart from those covering the Madras Army as a whole (1838 and 1851), the regimental standing orders issued in 1833 and 1848 had sections which specified four orders of dress:

Review order   for levees, parades, etc

Plate 43. Sowar of the 6th Madras Light Cavalry, c 1845. Watercolour, artist unknown.

Heavy marching order	on lines of march, service and inspections
Light marching order	exercise and guard duties
Stable dress	in barracks

By 1830, British officers wore a Roman-style helmet, japanned black, with silver fittings and a flowing red horsehair mane. By 1839 the mane had been replaced by a red horsehair crest (plate 45), and Ackermann's print of 1845 shows a crest and a mane. The matter was resolved by the 1846 regulations, which introduced a shako similar to the British light dragoon 1844 pattern, black with a gilt and silver plate, gold lines and white plume. An example, worn by a British NCO, with white braid in place of silver lace is shown in plate 46. The undress cap was blue, with silver lace band and black peak.

The dress jacket was French grey with three rows of buttons, silver lace and buff collar and cuffs. The 1846 regulations altered the style of jacket to five rows of buttons; with it was worn a crimson and gold barrel sash or girdle and a silver light-cavalry pattern pouch-belt and pouch. The undress jacket was described in the 1823 regulations as being plain shell pattern, with collar and cuffs of facing colour but no lace, except a loop on the shoulder. The stable jacket shown in an Ackermann print of 1846 is much more elaborate, with silver studs and two bands of lace down the front, lace around collar and cuffs, and silver shoulder scales. By this time the British officer was also authorised to wear a dark blue frock coat with

MADRAS LIGHT CAVALRY 1824–1857

Raised	Title	Uniform details French grey coat/silver lace facings	1861 title
1787	1st	pale yellow	1st Madras Light Cavalry
1784	2nd	orange	2nd Madras Light Cavalry
1784	3rd	buff	3rd Madras Light Cavalry
1785	4th	deep yellow	4th Madras Light Cavalry
1799	5th	pale yellow	disbanded 1860
1799	6th	orange	disbanded 1860
1800	7th	buff	disbanded 1860
1804	8th	deep yellow	disbanded 1857

All regiments adopted light buff facings in 1846.

Battle honours	Campaign	Date of action	Date of award	Regiments granted award
SHOLINGHUR	2nd Mysore War	27 Sept 1781	1841	2nd
CARNATIC	2nd Mysore War	1788–1791	1889	2nd
MYSORE	2nd Mysore War	1788–1791	1889	1st, 2nd, 3rd, 4th
SERINGAPATAM	4th Mysore War	8 Mar 1799	26 Dec 1820	1st, 2nd, 3rd, 4th
ASSAYE	2nd Maratha War	23 Sept 1803	30 Oct 1803	4th, 5th, 7th
NAGPORE	3rd Maratha War	Dec 1817	10 Mar 1826	6th
MAHEIDPOOR	3rd Maratha War	21 Dec 1817	29 Sept 1819	3rd, 4th, 8th
AVA	1st Burma War	1824–1826	22 Apr 1826	1st

roll collar and black loops down the front. Trousers were sky blue with two silver lace stripes, reduced to one by the 1846 regulations.

Native ranks (plates 43 and 49) followed the same outline, except that throughout the period they wore the bulbous turban, in red with silver trimmings for native officers and in black with white trimmings for sowars.

HYDERABAD CONTINGENT CAVALRY 1824–1857

British officers were dressed after the Madras light cavalry pattern, with similar helmets, but with dark green hussar jackets with white facings and gold lace, barrel sash, gold lace pouch-belt and green overalls with silver or white stripe. Native officers (plate 47) wore a small red and gold turban, green alkaluk, red

HYDERABAD CONTINGENT CAVALRY 1824–1857

Raised	Title		Became
1826	1st Regiment Nizam's Cavalry	1854	1st Cavalry Hyderabad Contingent
1826	2nd Regiment Nizam's Cavalry	1854	2nd Cavalry Hyderabad Contingent
1826	3rd Regiment Nizam's Cavalry	1854	3rd Cavalry Hyderabad Contingent
1826	4th Regiment Nizam's Cavalry	1854	4th Cavalry Hyderabad Contingent
1826	5th Regiment Ellichpur Horse (later Hyderabad Cavalry)	1853	disbanded

All regiments wore green uniforms, with white facings and gold lace.

After 1861   1st to 4th regiments were retained

BOMBAY CAVALRY 1824–1857

LIGHT CAVALRY

Raised	Title	Uniform details coat/facings/lace	1861
1817	1st Light Cavalry 1842 1st Bombay Lancers	French grey/white/silver	1st Light Cavalry
1817	2nd Light Cavalry	French grey/white/silver	2nd Light Cavalry
1820	3rd Light Cavalry	French grey/white/silver	3rd Light Cavalry

IRREGULAR CAVALRY

Raised	Title	Uniform details coat/facings/lace	1861
1817	Poona Auxiliary Horse 1847 Poona Irregular Horse	dark green/red/gold	4th Bombay Cavalry
1839	Gujerat Irregular Horse	dark green/red/gold	disbanded 1865
1839	Scinde Irregular Horse 1846 1st Scinde Irregular Horse	green/—/silver	5th Bombay Cavalry
1846	2nd Scinde Irregular Horse	green/—/silver	6th Bombay Cavalry
1850	South Mahratta Horse		disbanded 1865

Battle honours	Date of action	Date of award	Regiments granted award
CORYGAUM	1 Jan 1818	29 Sep 1819	Poona
GHUZNEE 1839	23 Jul 1839	4 Oct 1842	1st LC, Poona
CANDAHAR	10 Mar 1842	4 Oct 1842	Poona
CABOOL	1839–1842	4 Oct 1842	3rd LC
GHUZNEE 1842	6 Sep 1842	4 Oct 1842	3rd LC
AFGHANISTAN 1839	1839	19 Nov 1842	1st LC, Poona
CUTCHEE	1839–1842	1855	1st Scinde, 2nd Scinde
MEANEE	17 Feb 1843	1843	Poona, 1st Scinde, 2nd Scinde
HYDERABAD	24 Mar 1843	1843	Poona, 1st Scinde, 2nd Scinde
MOOLTAN	Sep 1848–Jan 1849	7 Oct 1853	1st LC, 1st Scinde, 2nd Scinde
GOOJERAT	21 Feb 1849	7 Oct 1853	1st Scinde, 2nd Scinde
PUNJAUB	1848–1849	7 Oct 1853	1st LC, 1st Scinde, 2nd Scinde
RESHIRE	9 Dec 1856	1858	3rd LC, Poona
BUSHIRE	10 Dec 1856	1861	3rd LC, Poona
KOOSH AB	8 Feb 1857	1858	3rd LC, Poona
PERSIA	1856–1857	1858	3rd LC, Poona, 1st Scinde

piping and cuff, gold lace, black pouch and sword belt, and white breeches. Native other ranks were similarly dressed but with a plain green alkaluk with white lining.

BOMBAY CAVALRY 1824–1857

The 1st (until 1841), 2nd and 3rd regiments of Bombay Light Cavalry followed the same uniform developments as the light cavalry of the other presidencies. By 1824 the helmet had been replaced by a bell-top shako with silver lace, gold lines and a white and red hackle. The 1850 regulations specified a fur cap, but there is no evidence that this was ever worn. On the other hand, there are examples of a dragoon helmet, silver with gilt plate and white horehair plume, which probably came into use after 1850.

The full dress jacket was French grey with silver lace and white facings. At first the jacket had three rows of buttons, but later it had five. The undress uniform (plate 48) comprised a

Plate 44. British officer of the Governor's Bodyguard, Madras, c 1830. Watercolour, artist unknown.

dark blue cap with silver lace and piping, French grey stable jacket with plain collar and cuffs, silver studs down the front, silver lace around the edges, and French grey overalls with single silver stripe.

In 1842, the 1st became lancers and adopted a lancer uniform (plate 50). This included a black lancer cap with red crown, gold lace and black plume. The jacket was described as 'cavalry grey', but portraits show a dark blue-grey colour with white facings and silver lace, silver epaulettes, cavalry grey pouch and sabretache, with silver lace on a white leather backing, and cavalry grey overalls with single silver stripe. The native ranks wore a similar uniform, including lance caps and brass shoulder scales in place of epaulettes.

The Bombay Irregular Cavalry were not included in the official regulations and by and large seem to have pleased themselves in matters of dress. While, for the most part, British officers wore native style uniforms, some very European elements still appeared. As with Bengal, it is best to deal with each regiment individually.

Poona Auxiliary Horse: red turban, dark green alkaluk with red facings and gold lace,

red cummerbund. A set of illustrated regulations, produced by the regiment in 1853, show the British officers with a dragoon helmet, plain double-breasted coatee with boxed epaulettes, light cavalry pouch-belt and silver pouch with regimental device. Undress included a pith helmet with spike, a shell jacket and a frock coat.

Scinde Irregular Horse: red turban, green alkaluk with red facings and silver lace, red cummerbund. An Ackermann print of 1849 shows a British officer in silver dragoon helmet with black plume, dark green hussar jacket with silver lace, green and silver barrel sash, and dark green overalls. The sowars wore a grey turban, green alkaluk with yellow cord, and a yellow and green girdle. Colonel Harry Green (plate 55), wears a helmet without plume, but with red pugri (an interesting precursor of the familiar Wolseley helmet and pugri of the late 19th century), a yellow poshteen over green alkaluk, green pyjamas with double red stripe, and black and silver lace equipment. A sowar in the background wears a red turban, yellow poshteen over green alkaluk, green pyjamas, and a green and red shabraque.

BENGAL INFANTRY 1824–1857

The uniform for both officers and other ranks followed the British pattern very closely. The pattern of officer's shako (plate 51) changed in 1830 to the bell-top shako with star plate, and 1844 saw the introduction of the Albert shako. The uniform cap was dark blue with gold lace and black peak.

The full dress jacket was laced down the front until 1830, and thereafter was plain with two rows of buttons in pairs, after 1831 all lace was gold. Epaulettes were boxed and varied in size according to rank (flank company officers wore wings). Collar and cuffs were of regimental facing colour and the long coat skirts had embroidered regimental tailornaments. The undress jacket had collar and cuffs of facing colour, and a row of buttons down the front, but was otherwise plain. The jacket was often worn open (plate 34), in a style predicting the mess jacket. British officers were also allowed to wear a single-breasted frock coat, with eight

Plate 45. British officer's helmet, 3rd Madras Light Cavalry, c 1832.

Plate 46. British NCO's shako, Madras Light Cavalry, c 1850.

BENGAL EUROPEAN REGIMENT 1824—1857

Date	Title	Uniform details all coats red facings/lace
1839	1st Bengal (European) Regiment	
		1824 sky blue/silver
		1831 sky blue/gold
1841	1st Bengal (European) Light Infantry	
1846	1st Bengal (European) Fusiliers	
		1847 dark blue/gold
1859	1st Bengal Fusiliers	
1862	tfd to British Army as 101st Regiment (Royal Bengal Fusiliers) later 1st Bn Royal Munster Fusiliers	
1839	2nd Bengal (European) Fusiliers	white/gold
1859	2nd Bengal Fusiliers	
1862	tfd to British Army as 104th Regiment (Bengal Fusiliers) later 2nd Bn Royal Munster Fusiliers	
1853	3rd Bengal (European) Light Infantry	white/gold
1859	3rd Bengal Light Infantry	
1862	tfd to British Army as 107th Regiment (Bengal Infantry) later 2nd Bn Royal Sussex Regiment	

BENGAL NATIVE INFANTRY 1824—1857

Raised	Title	Pre 1824	Uniform details all coats red facings/lace	Outcome
1757	1st	2/12th	white/gold	mutinied 1857
1762	2nd	1/1st	yellow/silver*	disarmed 1857
1763	3rd	1/6th	yellow/silver*	mutinied 1857
1763	4th	2/1st	yellow/silver*	disbanded 1861
1758	5th	1/2nd	white/gold	mutinied 1857
1763	6th	1/3rd	dark green/gold	mutinied 1857
1763	7th	1/4th	dark green/gold	mutinied 1857
1763	8th	1/9th	yellow/silver*	mutinied 1857
1761	9th	1/8th	white/gold	mutinied 1857
1763	10th	2/7th	dark green/gold	mutinied 1857
1763	11th	1/5th	white/gold	mutinied 1857
1763	12th	1/12th	white/gold	mutinied 1857
1764	13th	1/7th	dark green/gold	mutinied 1857
1764	14th	1/10th	buff/gold	mutinied 1857
1764	15th	1/11th	French grey/silver*	mutinied 1857
1765	16th	2/10th	buff/gold	became grenadier regiment 1845 disarmed 1857
1765	17th	2/11th	French grey/silver* 1853 black/gold	mutinied 1857
1770	18th	2/6th	yellow/silver*	mutinied 1857
1770	19th	2/3rd	dark green/gold	disarmed 1857
1770	20th	2/5th	white/gold	mutinied 1857
1776	21st	2/9th	yellow/silver*	1861 1st Bengal NI
1778	22nd	2/2nd	white/silver*	mutinied 1857
1778	23rd	2/4th	dark green/gold	mutinied 1857
1779	24th	2/8th	white/gold	disarmed 1857
1795	25th	1/20th	dark blue/gold	disbanded 1857
1797	26th	1/13th	red/gold	became light infantry in 1843 mutinied 1857
1797	27th	2/13th	red/gold	disbanded 1857
1797	28th	1/14th	dark green/gold	mutinied 1857
1797	29th	2/14th	dark green/gold	mutinied 1857
1798	30th	1/15th	buff/gold	mutinied 1857
1798	31st	2/15th	buff/gold	1861 2nd Bengal NI
1798	32nd	1/16th	black/gold	1861 3rd Bengal NI
1798	33rd	2/16th	black/gold	1861 4th Bengal NI
1798	34th 1846 Infantry of Bundelkund Legion	1/17th	scarlet/silver* blue/gold	disbanded 1844 mutinied 1857
1798	35th	2/17th	scarlet/silver*	became light infantry 1843 disbanded 1857
1799	36th	1/18th	yellow/silver*	Bengal Volunteers mutinied 1857
1799	37th	2/18th	yellow/silver*	Bengal Volunteers mutinied 1857
1799	38th	1/19th	dark green/gold	Bengal Volunteers mutinied 1857

1799	39th	2/11th	dark green/gold	Bengal Volunteers disbanded 1857
1803	40th	2/20th	dark blue/gold	mutinied 1857
1803	41st	1/21st	yellow/silver*	mutinied 1857
1803	42nd	2/21st	yellow/silver*	became light infantry 1842 1861 5th Bengal Light Infantry
1803	43rd	1/22nd	pea green/gold	became light infantry 1842 1861 6th Bengal Light Infantry
1803	44th	2/22nd	pea green/gold	disbanded 1857
1803	45th	1/23rd	dark green/gold	mutinied 1857
1803	46th	2/23rd	dark green/gold	mutinied 1857
1804 1824	47th raised as 69th, 1828 renumbered 47th	1/24th	yellow/silver*	disbanded 1824 1861 7th Bengal NI
1804	48th	2/24th	yellow/silver*	mutinied 1857
1804	49th	1/25th	buff/silver*	disbanded 1857
1804	50th	2/25th	buff/silver*	mutinied 1857
1804	51st	1/26th	dark green/gold	disarmed 1857
1804	52nd	2/26th	dark green/gold	mutinied 1857
1804	53rd	1/27th	yellow/silver*	mutinied 1857
1804	54th	2/27th	yellow/silver*	mutinied 1857
1815	55th	1/28th	white/gold	mutinied 1857
1815	56th	2/28th	white/gold	mutinied 1857
1815	57th	1/29th	buff/gold	mutinied 1857
1815	58th	2/29th	buff/gold	disarmed 1857
1814	59th	1/30th	Saxon green/silver*	1861 8th Bengal NI
1814	60th	2/30th	Saxon green/silver*	mutinied 1857
1818	61st	1/31st	yellow/silver*	mutinied 1857
1818	62nd	2/31st	yellow/silver*	disarmed 1857
1817	63rd	1/32nd	yellow/silver*	1861 9th Bengal NI 1901 9th Gurkha Rifles
1818	64th	2/32nd	yellow/silver*	disarmed 1857
1823	65th	1/33rd	yellow/silver*	1861 10th Bengal NI
1823 1815	66th became 66th Bengal NI (1850)	2/33rd 1st Nasiri	yellow/silver* white/gold	mutinied 1850 1861 11th Bengal NI 1861 1st Gurkha Regiment LI
1823	67th	1/34th	yellow/silver*	disarmed 1857
1823	68th	2/34th	yellow/silver*	mutinied 1857
1824	69th	See 47th		
1825	69th	1st Extra	yellow/silver*	disarmed 1857
1825	70th	2nd Extra	yellow/silver*	1861 11th Bengal NI
1825	71st	3rd Extra	yellow/silver* 1831 black/gold	mutinied 1857
1825	72nd	4th Extra	yellow/silver*	mutinied 1857
1825	73rd	5th Extra	yellow/silver*	disbanded 1857
1825	74th	6th Extra	yellow/silver*	mutinied 1857

*All regiments with silver lace adopted gold lace in 1831.

Battle honours	Campaign	Date of action	Date of award	Regiments granted awards
PLASSEY	7 Years War	23 Jun 1757	23 Feb 1829	1st
BUXAR	7 Years War	23 Oct 1764	23 Feb 1829	2nd, 3rd, 5th, 8th, 9th, 10th
GUZERAT	1st Maratha War	1776–1782	23 Feb 1829	2nd, 3rd, 5th, 7th, 11th, 13th
CARNATIC	2nd Mysore War	1788–1791	1889	4th, 5th, 12th, 22nd
MYSORE	2nd Mysore War	1789–1791	1889	4th, 6th, 13th, 16th
SERINGAPATAM	4th Mysore War	8 Mar 1799	1820	14th, 16th, 36th, 37th, 38th, 39th
ALLYGHUR	2nd Maratha War	4 Sept 1803	23 Feb 1829	7th, 23rd, 35th
DELHI	2nd Maratha War	11 Sept 1803	23 Feb 1829	1st, 5th, 22nd, 23rd, 28th 29th, 30th, 31st, 35th
LESWARRIE	2nd Maratha War	1 Nov 1803	23 Feb 1829	1st, 12th, 21st, 24th 30th, 31st, 33rd
DEIG	2nd Maratha War	Nov–Dec 1804	23 Feb 1829	5th, 7th, 9th, 30th, 31st, 33rd
JAVA	East Indies	Aug 1811	23 Feb 1829	25th, 40th
NAGPORE	3rd Maratha War	Dec 1817	1882	40th
AVA	1st Burma War	1824–1826	22 Apr 1826	40th
ASSAM	1st Burma War		22 Apr 1826	46th, 57th
ARRACAN	1st Burma War	1825	22 Apr 1826	26th, 28th, 40th, 42nd, 62nd
BHURTPORE	Bhurtpore	18 Jan 1826	30 May 1826	6th, 11th, 15th, 18th, 21st, 23rd, 31st, 32nd 33rd, 35th, 36th, 37th, 41st, 58th, 60th, 63rd
GHUZNEE	1st Afghan War	23 Jul 1839	19 Nov 1839	2nd, 16th, 35th, 38th, 48th
KHELAT	1st Afghan War	13 Nov 1839	15 Feb 1840	31st
JELLALABAD	1st Afghan War	Jan–Apr 1842	4 Oct 1842	35th
CANDAHAR	1st Afghan War	10 Mar 1842	4 Oct 1842	2nd, 16th, 38th, 42nd, 43rd
GHUZNEE	1st Afghan War	6 Sept 1842	4 Oct 1842	

regimental buttons down the front. Trousers were normally dark blue with red stripe, but white trousers were permitted in hot weather.

The stiff turban of the native ranks, described in chapter 1, was replaced in 1827 by a shako of British style but without peak (plate 52). This could be worn with a black oilskin or white linen cover according to season. It was never popular with native troops and when the kilmarnock cap was introduced in 1847 as an undress item (replacing an earlier forage cap introduced in 1844), it took over from the shako for most occasions (plates 53, 54, 56). The kilmarnock cap was dark blue with the regimental number on the front, and was often worn with a white cover (plate 53). The uniform jacket was red with collar and cuffs of facing colour, single breasted with five pairs of white braid loops down the front. Sepoys of battalion companies had white-edged shoul-

Plate 47. Jemedar of the Hyderabad Contingent Cavalry, c 1837. Watercolour by Thomas James Ryves.

CABOOL	1st Afghan War	1839–1842	4 Oct 1842	2nd, 6th, 16th, 26th, 30th, 33rd, 35th, 38th, 42nd, 43rd, 53rd, 60th, 64th
AFGHANISTAN 1839	1st Afghan War	1839	4 Oct 1842	16th, 31st, 35th, 37th, 42nd, 43rd, 48th
MAHARAJPORE	Gwalior	29 Dec 1843	4 Jan 1844	2nd, 14th, 16th, 31st, 39th, 43rd, 56th
PUNNIAR	Gwalior	29 Dec 1843	4 Jan 1844	39th, 50th, 51st, 58th
MOODKEE	1st Sikh War	18 Dec 1845	12 Dec 1846	2nd, 16th, 24th, 26th 42nd, 45th, 47th, 48th, 73rd
FEROZESHUHUR	1st Sikh War	21/22 Dec 1845	12 Dec 1846	2nd, 12th, 14th, 16th 24th, 26th, 33rd, 42nd, 44th, 45th, 47th
ALIWAL	1st Sikh War	28 Jan 1846	12 Aug 1846	24th, 30th, 36th, 47th, 48th
SOBRAON	1st Sikh War	10 Feb 1846	12 Aug 1846	7th, 16th, 26th, 33rd, 41st, 42nd, 43rd, 47th, 59th, 68th
MOOLTAN	2nd Sikh War	Sept 1848–Jan 1849	7 Oct 1853	8th, 49th, 51st, 52nd, 72nd
CHILLIANWALLAH	2nd Sikh War	13 Jan 1849	7 Oct 1853	15th, 20th, 25th, 30th, 31st, 36th, 45th, 46th, 56th, 69th, 70th
GOOJERAT	2nd Sikh War	21 Feb 1849	7 Oct 1853	8th, 13th, 15th, 20th, 25th, 30th, 31st, 36th, 45th, 46th, 51st, 52nd, 56th, 69th, 70th, 72nd
PUNJAUB	2nd Sikh War	1848–1849	7 Oct 1853	1st, 3rd, 4th, 8th, 13th, 15th, 18th, 20th, 22nd, 25th, 29th, 30th, 36th, 37th, 45th, 46th, 49th, 50th, 51st, 52nd, 53rd, 56th, 69th, 70th, 71st, 72nd, 73rd
PEGU	2nd Burma War	1852–1853	18 May 1858	10th, 40th, 67th, 68th

der straps with a woollen fringe, while those in flank companies had white woollen wings. In drill order, the jacket was white with plain collar and cuffs and evenly spaced buttons down the front (plate 52). The trousers were like those of the officers, dark blue or white. However, as plate 36 indicates, on active service the sepoys reverted to loose pyjamas, which they found more comfortable. Equipment was white with a brass crossbelt plate. In 1844 the old square knapsack was replaced by a haversack. Sepoys of rifle companies (plate 53) wore dark green double-breasted jackets and trousers, with black lace and black equipment.

BENGAL LOCAL INFANTRY 1824–1857
At this time the local battalions raised in Nepal, who eventually became Gurkha Rifles, were referred to as 'Local Hill Corps.' Their

Plate 48. Undress uniform of an officer of the 1st Bombay Light Cavalry, c 1840.

Raised	Title	1823	1826
1792	Bhagalpur Hill Rangers	3rd	3rd
1792	Dinajpore	4th	disbanded
1795	Ramgarh LI	2nd	2nd
1795	Calcutta Native Militia	1st	1st
1815	Champarau LI	5th	disbanded
1815	1st Nasiri	6th	4th
1815	2nd Nasiri	7th	5th
1815	Sirmoor	8th	6th
1815	Kumaon	9th	7th
1817	Cuttack Legion	10th Rangpur LI	8th Assam
1817	Fatagarh Levy	1/32 NI	63rd NI
1818	Gorakhpur LI	11th	disbanded
1818	1st Rampura	12th	disbanded
1818	2nd Rampura	13th	disbanded
1822	Mharwara	14th	9th
1822	Bencoolen	15th	10th
1824	Sylhet LI	16th	11th
1825	Mundlaiser	15th	disbanded
1830	Arracan		
1830	New Nussaree Bn		
1835	Assam Sebundy		
1835	Shekhawati		
1836	1st Oudh		
1836	2nd Oudh		
1836	Harriana LI		
1838	Shah Shuja's Force		
1840	Mulwa Bhil Corps		
1840	Meywar Bhil Corps		
1846	Ferozepore		
1846	Ludhiana		
1853	Pegu LI		
1856	Bengal Military Police Bn		

	Date of action	Date of award	Regiments granted award
BHURTPORE	28 Jan 1826	30 May 1826	1st Nasiri, Sirmoor, Fatagarh
KELAT I GHILZIE	Nov 1841–May 1842	4 Oct 1842	Regiment of Kelat-i-Ghilzie
CANDAHAR	10 Mar 1842	4 Oct 1842	Regiment of Kelat-i-Ghilzie
GHUZNEE	6 Sep 1842	4 Oct 1842	Regiment of Kelat-i-Ghilzie

	Uniform details *coat/facings/lace*	*Post-1861*
		Police Corps
1835 Ramgarh LI	green/black/—	1857 mutinied
1859 Alipore Rgt		18th Bengal NI
	green/black/silver	
1850 66th Bengal NI	green/black/black	1st Gurkha Rifles
1829 disbanded		
	green/black/black	2nd Gurkha Rifles
	green/black/black	3rd Gurkha Rifles
1844 1st Assam LI	green/black/black	42nd Bengal NI later 6th Gurkha Rifles
		9th Bengal NI later 9th Gurkha Rifles
	green/black/gold	
	red/dark green/silver	
	red/dark green/silver	
		Police Corps later 44th Infantry
1829 disbanded	red/green/silver	
		48th Bengal NI
	green/black/black	later 1/8th Gurkha Rifles
	green/black/black	Police Corps
		disbanded
1844 2nd Assam LI	green/black/black	43rd Bengal NI later 2/8th Gurkha Rifles
	red/white/gold	13th Bengal NI
1856 Oudh Irregular Force		1857 mutinied
1856 Oudh Irregular Force		1857 mutinied
	green/black/black	1857 mutinied
1842 Regiment of Kelat-i-Ghilzie		12th Bengal NI
	green/black/black	Police Corps
	green/black/black	Police Corps
	red/yellow/green	14th Bengal NI
	red/yellow/green	15th Bengal NI
		Police Corps
	drab/blue/silver	45th Bengal NI

CABOOL	1839–1842	4 Oct 1842	Regiment of Kelat-i-Ghilzie
MAHARAJPORE	29 Dec 1843	4 Jan 1844	Regiment of Kelat-i-Ghilzie
ALIWAL	28 Jan 1846	12 Aug 1846	1st Nasiri, Sirmoor, Shekhawati
SOBRAON	10 Feb 1846	12 Aug 1846	1st Nasiri, Sirmoor, 63rd NI (formerly Fatagarh)

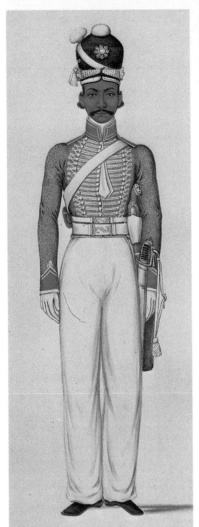

Plate 49. *Native ranks of the Madras Army, c 1835. Light cavalry, infantry, rifle corps, horse artillery, foot artillery, pioneers. Watercolours by a native artist.*

BENGAL ARMY, IRREGULAR CONTINGENTS 1824—1857

Raised	Title	Cav	Inf	Arty	Uniform details coat/facings/lace	Outcome
1835	Judpur Legion	C	I	A*	green/black/black	mutinied 1857
1838	Bundelkund Legion	C	2	A	red/blue/silver	disbanded 1844 infantry to 34th NI
1838	Gwalior Contingent	2	7	4		mutinied 1857 IBN → 45th/41st NI
1843	Kotah Contingent					mutinied 1857
1845	Mulwa Contingent	C	I	A		mutinied 1857
(1845)	Bhopal Contingent	C	I	A		mutinied 1857
(1845)	Nimour Police Corps	C	I	—		?
1854	Nagpore Irregular Force	1	3	1		disbanded 1859 (?)
1856	Oudh Irregular Force	3	10	3		mutinied 1857
1856	Oudh Military Police	C	I			disbanded 1859 (?)

PUNJAB INFANTRY 1846—1857

Raised	Title	1856	Uniform details coat/facings/lace	1859
1846	Guides		drab/drab/drab red/yellow	
SIKH INFANTRY				
1846	1st	red/yellow/gold		drab/yellow/drab
1846–1847	2nd or Hill Regt	green/black/black		drab/black/drab
1846–1847	3rd	red/yellow		drab/yellow/drab
1846–1847	4th	drab/dark green/drab		

1846—Infantry of the Frontier Brigade
1847—Sikh Local Infantry
1857—Sikh Infantry
1857—Sikh Infantry, Punjab Irregular Force

PUNJAB INFANTRY

1849	1st	green/green/black
1849	2nd	drab/black/drab
1849	3rd	drab/green/green
1849	4th	drab/French grey/drab
1849	5th	drab/green/drab
1843	Scinde Camel Corps*	
	1853 6th	red/green/drab

1851—Infantry, Punjab Irregular Force

*Motto: Ready Aye Ready.

Battle honours	Date of action	Date of award	Regiments granted award
MOOLTAN	Sept 1848–Jan 1849	7 Oct 1853	Guides
GOOJERAT	21 Feb 1849	7 Oct 1853	Guides
PUNJAUB	1848–1849	7 Oct 1853	Guides, 1st Sikh, 2nd Sikh
PEGU	1852–1853	18 May 1855	4th Sikh

uniform was laid down in an Adjutant General's circular of 9 Jan 1829.

British officers wore a black bell-top shako with black lace, bronzed ornaments and black tuft. The jacket was dark green, rifle pattern,

Plate 50. An officer of the 1st Bombay Lancers, 1848. Oil painting by T Bone.

Plate 51. Officer of the 2nd Bengal Native Infantry, c 1828. Miniature, artist unknown.

72

with black collar and cuffs, three rows of black buttons down the front and black braid. Pouch-belt and pouch were of black leather with bronze ornaments, trousers were dark green with double black stripe. An undress jacket, without trimmings, was also specified.

Native ranks (plate 57) also wore peaked shakos (unlike the regular Bengal NI who wore peakless shakos). The jackets had five bastion loops down the front, and they wore black equipment with brass crossbelt plates. Trousers were green. In 1847 the Kilmarnock cap was introduced, and a stiffened version is still worn by Gurkhas in the ceremonial dress of today. The cap was generally dark blue with a dark green band, but the Sirmoor Battalion adopted a diced red and green band. In 1850 the Nasiri Battalion became the 66th Bengal NI and adopted standard native infantry uniform with red coats.

PUNJAB INFANTRY 1846—1857

Little firm evidence of the early uniform of the Punjab Infantry survives, apart from two illustrations (plates 58 and 59) which both show Lumsden's influence, in the drab colour, loose appearance and, for that period, modern cut. The 1st Punjab Infantry are shown in multi-coloured turbans, dark blue tunics with concealed buttons and red piping, and dark blue trousers with yellow stripe. One of the native officers wears a fur-lined poshteen. The 4th are shown with drab turbans, drab loose-fitting jackets and pyjamas, with brown equipment. The subedar wears a green scarf, and the havildar wears a crimson sash. The 5th, according to their regimental history, were originally dressed in red with black equipment, but changed in 1853, to a drab tunic with green facings.

The four Sikh regiments raised in 1846–1847 were dressed more conventionally, in red with yellow facings and dark blue trousers, apart from the 2nd who wore green with black facings. After a request to change to drab had been granted in 1852, the white summer clothing was dyed khaki but drab cloth tunics and trousers were not issued until 1859. At first the head-dress was a turban, but this was altered in 1847 to a dark blue kilmarnock cap with a yellow band. It was changed again to a drab pattern cap in 1853, and to a drab turban with yellow in 1857.

Plate 52. A sepoy of the 66th Bengal Native Infantry, in undress, 1842. Oil painting by Alex Hunter, Barrackpore, 1842.

Plate 53. Sepoys of the rifle and battalion companies of the 41st Bengal Native Infantry, c 1850. Lithograph after C Wyndham.

Plate 54. Subedar of the 12th Bengal Native Infantry, Mooltan, 1852. Watercolour, artist unknown.

73

MADRAS EUROPEAN REGIMENT 1824-1857

Raised	Title	Uniform details all coats red facings/lace
1839	1st Madras (European) Regiment	white/gold
1843	1st Madras (European) Fusiliers	dark blue/gold
1859	1st Madras Fusiliers	
1862	tfd to British Army as 102nd Regiment (Royal Madras Fusiliers) later 1st Bn Royal Dublin Fusiliers	
1839	2nd Madras (European) Light Infantry	pale buff/gold
1859	2nd Madras Light Infantry	
1862	tfd to British Army as 105th Regiment (Madras Light Infantry) later 2nd Bn King's Own Yorkshire Light Infantry	
1854	3rd Madras (European) Infantry	pale yellow/gold
1859	3rd Madras Infantry	
1862	tfd to British Army as 108th Regiment (Madras Infantry) later 2nd Bn Royal Inniskilling Fusiliers	

MADRAS NATIVE INFANTRY 1824—1857

Raised	Title	1796	Uniform details all coats red facings/lace	Changes 1824–1857
1758	1st	1/1st	white/gold	
1759	2nd	1/2nd	green/gold	
1759	3rd	1/3rd	green/gold	Palamcottah Light Infantry
1759	4th	1/4th	orange/silver*	
1759	5th	1/5th	black/gold	
1761	6th	1/6th	buff/silver*	
1761	7th	1/7th	French grey/silver*	
1761	8th	1/8th	yellow/silver*	
1762	9th	1/9th	gosling green/silver*	
1766	10th	1/10th	red/gold	
1767	11th	2/9th	gosling green/silver*	
1767	12th	2/8th	yellow/silver*	
1776	13th	2/3rd	red/silver*	1839 white facings
1776	14th	2/6th	buff/silver*	
1776	15th	2/4th	orange/silver*	
1776	16th	2/5th	black/silver*	
1777	17th	2/1st	white/gold	
1777	18th	2/10th	red/gold	disbanded 1864
1777	19th	2/7th	French grey/silver*	1853 sky blue facings
1777	20th	2/2nd	green/gold	
1786	21st	1/11th	buff/gold	
1788	22nd	2/11th	buff/gold	1853 buff facings
1794	23rd	1/12th	green/gold	Wallajahabad Light Infantry
1794	24th	2/12th	willow green/silver*	
1794	25th	1/13th	yellow/silver*	1853 dark green facings

Plate 55. Colonel Harry Green, Scinde Horse, 1848. Watercolour by W H Sitwell, 1848.

Plate 56. 'Blessing the Colours', 35th Bengal Light Infantry, 1843. Watercolour by a native artist.

Raised	Title	1796	Uniform details all coats red facings/lace	Changes 1824–1857
1794	26th	2/13th	yellow/silver*	1853 dark green facings
1798	27th	1/14th	black/silver*	
1798	28th	2/14th	black/silver*	
1798	29th	1/15th	white/silver*	Malay Native Infantry
1799	30th	2/15th	white/silver*	
1800	31st	1/16th	dark green/gold	Trichinopoly Light Infantry
1800	32nd	2/16th	yellow/silver*	
1800	33rd	1/17th	black/gold	
1800	34th	2/17th	dark green/gold	Chicacole Light Infantry
1800	35th	1/18th	pale buff/silver*	
1800	36th	2/18th	pale buff/silver*	Nundy Regiment
1800	37th	1/19th	buff/gold	1841 Grenadier Regiment 1853 blue facings
1800	38th	2/19th	buff/gold	
1803	39th	1/20th	green/gold	
1801	40th	2/20th	green/gold	
1803	41st	1/21st	yellow/gold	
1803	42nd	2/21st	yellow/gold	disbanded 1864
1803	43rd	1/22nd	yellow/gold	disbanded 1864
1802	44th	2/22nd	yellow/gold	disbanded 1864
1803	45th	1/23rd	white/gold	disbanded 1862
1803	46th	2/23rd	white/gold	disbanded 1862
1810	Madras Volunteer Battalion			
	1814 Madras Rifle Corps		green/black/green	disbanded 1830
1819	47th	1/24th	pale buff/gold	1852 white facings disbanded 1862
1819	48th	2/24th	pale buff/gold	disbanded 1862
1819	49th	1/25th	yellow/gold	disbanded 1862
1819	50th	2/25th	yellow/gold	disbanded 1862
1826	51st	1st Extra	white/gold	disbanded 1862
1826	52nd	2nd Extra	pale buff/gold	disbanded 1862
1826		3rd Extra		disbanded 1830
1826		4th Extra		disbanded 1830

*All regiments with silver lace adopted gold lace in 1832.

Battle honours	Date of action	Date of award	Regiments granted award
CARNATIC	1788–1791	1889	1st, 2nd, 3rd, 4th, 5th, 6th, 7th, 8th, 9th, 12th, 13th, 14th, 15th, 16th, 17th, 19th, 20th
SHOLINGHUR	1781	1841	3rd, 4th, 5th, 6th, 8th, 9th, 12th, 13th, 14th, 15th, 16th, 17th, 19th, 20th
MYSORE	1788–1791	1889	1st, 2nd, 3rd, 4th, 5th, 6th, 7th, 9th, 12th, 13th, 14th, 15th, 16th, 19th, 20th, 21st, 22nd
SERINGAPATAM	1799	1820	1st, 6th, 8th, 11th, 13th, 19th, 20th, 21st, 22nd, 23rd, 24th
BOURBON	1810	1838	6th, 24th
ASSAYE	1803	1803	2nd, 4th, 8th, 10th, 24th
COCHIN	1809	1840	33rd
SEETABULDEE	1817	1819	1st, 39th

NAGPORE	1817	1826	1st, 2nd, 17th, 21st, 23rd, 26th, 28th, 39th
MAHEIDPOOR	1817	1819	3rd, 14th, 27th, 28th, 31st
AVA	1824–1826	1826	1st, 3rd, 7th, 9th, 10th, 12th, 16th, 18th, 22nd, 26th, 28th, 30th, 32nd, 34th, 36th, 38th, 43rd
KEMMENDIE	Dec 1824	1825	26th
CHINA 1840*	1840	30 Oct 1843	2nd, 6th, 14th, 37th, 41st
PEGU	1852–1853	18 May 1855	1st, 5th, 9th, 19th, 26th, 35th, 49th

*With dragon.

Plate 57. 'Goorkhas of the Sabathu Battalion.' The Nasiri Battalion, later the 1st Gurkha Rifles, were based at Sabathu. Watercolour, artist unknown, dated 11 October 1834.

Plate 58. The 1st Punjab Infantry, c 1855. Lithograph after Walter Fane.

77

Plate 59. 4th Punjab Infantry, c 1855. Watercolour by Walter Fane.

MADRAS NATIVE INFANTRY 1824—1857

Uniform for the Madras NI followed the same general outline as for the Bengal NI, and the British officers' uniform was virtually identical. Native ranks wore the distinctive Madras head-dress, a stiff bamboo basketwork, covered with dark blue (or black) lacquered cloth polished like leather (plates 49,60,62). At the apex of the head-dress was a knob with a groove traditionally intended to act as a musket rest. In marching order, the head-dress was worn with a white cover (plate 60).

Native officers (plate 62) wore a plain single-breasted jacket with ten buttons in pairs, gold lace around the collar and gold spools on the cuff. They wore a white sword-belt with a gilt plate, and a crimson sash. NCOs also wore a crimson waist sash. Sepoys wore white loops, with a line of facing colour woven in. All native ranks wore sandals and loose trousers, dark blue or white according to the season.

The Madras Rifle Corps (plate 49) existed as a separate unit from 1810 until 1830, when it was split up, and its companies were sent to eight different regiments, the 1st, 5th,

16th, 24th, 26th, 36th, 38th and 49th. As rifle companies, they retained their dark green uniforms. According to the 1824 regulations, British officers wore single-breasted dark green jackets with black facings, gold wings and dark green overalls with a single black stripe. By 1838, this had been changed to a hussar-style jacket. The sepoys wore a black turban with a silver bugle-horn badge, dark green single-breasted jacket with black facings, black equipment and dark green trousers.

In 1811 four battalions were designated light infantry, and in the 1824 reorganisation, these became the 3rd, 23rd, 31st and 34th Light Infantry. They wore a uniform similar to line regiments, but with dark green facings, gold lace and short light infantry skirts to their jackets (plate 60). They wore a black shako with dark green plume, later changed to a tuft, and a bugle badge; officer also wore a black pouch-belt with gilt plate, whistle and chain and a black pouch with a bugle on the flap.

BOMBAY NATIVE INFANTRY 1824—1857

The Bombay NI followed a general development similar to the NI of other presidencies, with certain differences in head-dress. British officers' jackets had one unusual feature: a portrait of an officer of the 1st Grenadiers shows gold embroidered grenades on the collar of the jacket.

Native ranks (plate 63) adopted a peakless shako in about 1814, and this continued in use until the 1850s. Grenadier companies had a white plume, light companies had a green tuft, and battalion companies had a white on red plume. The shakos were also worn with foul-weather covers. Kilmarnock undress caps were introduced in the 1850s. Jackets had seven white loops down the front, and equipment included white crossbelts and waistbelt, with brass plates bearing the regimental number.

BENGAL HORSE ARTILLERY

Officers' uniform for this period is fully described in 'Standing Orders of the Bengal Artillery' for 1828 and 1845, and existing portraits and examples of uniform conform to

Date	Title		Uniform details all coats red facings/lace
1839	1st Bombay (European) Regiment		1833 white/gold
1844	1st Bombay (European) Fusiliers		1843 dark blue/gold
1859	1st Bombay Fusiliers		
1862	tfd to British Army as 103rd Regiment (Royal Bombay Fusiliers) later 2nd Bn Royal Dublin Fusiliers		
1839	2nd Bombay (European) Light Infantry		pale buff/gold
1859	2nd Bombay Light Infantry		1843 white/gold
1862	tfd to British Army as 106th Regiment (Bombay Light Infantry) later 2nd Bn Durham Light Infantry		
1853	3rd Bombay (European) Regiment		pale yellow/gold
1859	3rd Bombay Regiment		
1862	tfd to British Army as 109th Regiment (Bombay Infantry) later 2nd Bn Leinster Regiment		

BOMBAY NATIVE INFANTRY 1824—1857

Raised	Title	Pre 1824	Uniform details all coats red unless stated facings/lace	Changes 1824–1857
1778	1st	1/1st	white/gold	Grenadier Regiment since 1783
1796	2nd	2/1st	white/gold	Grenadier Regiment since 1818
1768	3rd	1/2nd	sky blue/silver*	
1775	4th	2/2nd	sky blue/silver*	1841 Rifle Corps
1788	5th	1/3rd	black/silver*	1841 Light Infantry
1775	6th	2/3rd	black/silver*	
1788	7th	1/4th	white/silver*	
1768	8th	2/4th	white/silver*	
1788	9th	1/5th	black/gold	
1797	10th	2/5th	black/gold	
1796	11th	1/6th	buff/silver*	
1798	12th	2/6th	buff/silver*	
1800	13th	1/7th	buff/gold	
1800	14th	2/7th	buff/gold	
1800	15th	1/8th	light buff/silver*	
1800	16th	2/8th	light buff/silver*	
1803	17th	1/9th	yellow/silver*	
1803	18th	2/9th	yellow/silver*	
1817	19th	1/10th	yellow/gold	
1817	20th	2/10th	yellow/gold	
1777	Marine	1/11th	green/silver*	1861 21st Bombay NI
1820	21st	2nd Extra	yellow/silver*	1857 mutinied
1818	22nd	2/11th	green/gold	
1820	23rd	1/12th	dark green/silver*	1841 Light Infantry

BOMBAY NATIVE INFANTRY 1824—1857 (continued)

Raised	Title	Pre 1824	Uniform details all coats red unless stated facings/lace	Changes 1824–1857
1820	24th	2/12th	dark green/silver*	
1820	25th	1st Extra	yellow/silver*	
1825	26th	2nd Extra	light buff/gold	
1825	3rd Extra	1826 1st Extra		1829 disbanded
1825	4th Extra	1826 2nd Extra		1829 disbanded
1844	1st Baluch		green/red/black	1861 27th Bombay NI
1846	27th		white/gold	1858 mutinied
1846	28th		yellow/gold	
1846	29th		yellow/gold	1861 disbanded
1846	2nd Baluch		green/red/black	1861 29th Bombay NI

*All regiments with silver lace adopted gold lace in 1832.

Battle honours	Date of action	Date of award	Regiments granted award
MANGALORE	1783	1841	1st
MYSORE	1789–1791	1889	1st, 3rd, 4th, 5th, 7th, 8th, 9th
SEEDASEER	1799	1823	3rd, 5th, 7th
SERINGAPATAM	1799	1823	3rd, 4th, 5th, 6th, 7th, 9th
EGYPT 1801	1801	1804	2nd, 13th
BOURBON	1810	1855	4th
KIRKEE	1817	1823	2nd, 12th, 13th, 23rd
CORYGAUM	1818	1818	2nd
PERSIAN GULF	1819	1854	Marine Bn
BENI BOO ALI	1821	1831	3rd, 4th, 5th, 7th, 13th, 18th, Marine Bn
ADEN	1839	1841	24th, Marine Bn
BURMAH	1825	1854	Marine Bn
GHUZNEE 1839	1839	13 Nov 1839	19th
KAHUN	1840	1841	5th
AFGHANISTAN 1839	1839	19 Nov 1842	19th
MEANEE	17 Feb 1843	1843	12th, 25th
HYDERABAD	24 Mar 1843	1843	1st, 12th, 21st, 25th, Marine Bn
MOOLTAN	Sept 1848–Jan 1849	7 Oct 1853	3rd, 4th, 9th, 19th
GOOJERAT	21 Feb 1849	7 Oct 1853	3rd, 19th
PUNJAUB	1848–1849	7 Oct 1853	3rd, 4th, 9th, 19th, Marine Bn
RESHIRE	9 Dec 1856	1858	4th, 20th, 2nd Baluch
BUSHIRE	10 Dec 1856	1861	4th, 20th, 2nd Baluch
KOOSH AB	8 Feb 1857	1858	4th, 20th, 26th
PERSIA	1856–1857	1858	4th, 11th, 15th, 20th, 23rd, 26th, 2nd Baluch

these regulations (plate 64). The dress helmet was of black metal, with gilt fittings, a broad leopardskin pugri and the long red horsehair mane always associated with this regiment. The jacket was dark blue with red facings, heavily laced in gold. The pouch-belt was of light cavalry pattern, with gold lace with red train, silver pickers and silver pouch. Around the waist was a red and gold barrel sash and waistbelt, and sword slings of gold lace with a

BOMBAY LOCAL CORPS 1824—1857

Raised	Title	Uniform details uniform/facings/lace	
1825	Khandish Bhil Corps	—/blue/gold	
1845(?)	Kolapore Local Infantry		
1845(?)	Guzerat Provincial Bn		
1845(?)	Sawunt Warree Local Corps		
1847(?)	Ghaut Light Infantry Corps		1857 Ghaut Police Corps
1852(?)	Rutnagherry Rangers		
1852(?)	Guzerat Police Corps	red/yellow/gold	
1857(?)	Settara Local Corps		

HYDERABAD CONTINGENT INFANTRY 1824—1857

Raised	Pre 1824 title	1826	1854
1813	1st Bn Russell Brigade	1st Infantry Nizam's Army	1st Infantry Hyderabad Contingent
1813	2nd Bn Russell Brigade	2nd Infantry Nizam's Army	2nd Infantry Hyderabad Contingent
1797	1st Bn Berar Infantry	3rd Infantry Nizam's Army	3rd Infantry Hyerabad Contingent
1794	2nd Bn Berar Infantry	4th Infantry Nizam's Army	4th Infantry Hyderabad Contingent
c 1795	3rd Bn Berar Infantry	5th Infantry Nizam's Army	1853 disbanded
c 1795	4th Bn Berar Infantry	6th Infantry Nizam's Army	1853 disbanded
1788	1st Bn Ellichpur Brigade	7th Infantry Nizam's Army	5th Infantry Hyderabad Contingent
1788	2nd Bn Ellichpur Brigade	8th Infantry Nizam's Army	6th Infantry Hyderabad Contingent

Battle honours	Regiments granted award
NAGPORE	4th
MAHEIDPOOR	1st, 2nd
NOWAR	1st, 2nd, 3rd

Plate 60. Sepoys of the 30th Madras Native Infantry, order c 1840. Watercolours by a company artist.

Plate 61. British officer of the 3rd Madras Light Infantry, c 1825. Watercolour by a company artist.

Plate 62. Subedar and sepoys of the 40th Madras Native Infantry, c 1835. Watercolour by a company artist.

Plate 63. Bombay Native Infantry, 1825. Grenadier sepoys of the 10th and 22nd, light company sepoy of the 21st. Watercolour by L W Hart, 1825.

Plate 64. Officer of the Bengal Horse Artillery, c 1850. Oil painting, artist unknown.

Plate 65. Native trooper, Abercrombie's troop, Bengal Horse Artillery, Mooltan, 1852. Watercolour, artist unknown.

red train. Overalls were dark blue (replacing white breeches in 1828) with a double gold stripe. Sabretache and shabraque were dark blue with gold embroidery. It should be noted that, unlike the Royal Artillery, the Bengal HA received particular battle honours, some of which were carried on their accoutrements.

The undress uniform included a peaked forage cap, with gold band and red piping, and a plain dark blue stable jacket, altered in 1841 to a more elaborate style; laced down the front, along the bottom and around the pockets, worn with gold shoulder cords.

European other ranks wore a similar helmet, and a jacket with yellow lacing in place of gold. They continued to wear white breeches after 1828, and did not change to dark blue until 1847. A photograph of a European gunner in undress 1855, shows him with a full-dress helmet similar to an officer's, a plain jacket with thirteen buttons down the front, shoulder cords, a white pouch-belt, and white sword slings, worn under his jacket.

The uniform of the native other ranks is shown in plate 65. It includes a kilmarnock cap, introduced in 1847, of dark blue with a red band, a dark blue jacket with red facings and yellow braid, a red and yellow girdle, and blue-grey overalls.

BENGAL FOOT ARTILLERY

The Foot Artillery (plate 66) had the same pattern shako as the infantry. The short jacket was replaced, in 1828, by a long-tailed plain-fronted coatee, which was dark blue, with red facings and elaborate gold oakleaf-pattern lace (later replaced by a simpler pattern of flat lace), boxed gold epaulettes, with a silver wire grenade on the strap. The shoulder-belt plate included the inscription 'Bengal Artillery'. A crimson sash, and dark blue trousers, with broad red stripe, were also worn.

MADRAS HORSE ARTILLERY

British officers probably wore a shako between 1828 and 1838, although this is not

Plate 66. British officer of the Bengal Foot Artillery, Light Field Battery, 1854. Watercolour, artist unknown.

Plate 67. An officer of the Madras Foot Artillery, 1843. Watercolour by Francois Theodore Rochard, 1843.

documented outside regulations. In 1838, the Roman-pattern helmet was introduced (plate 69), which was black with gilt fittings and red horsehair mane. The plate had an ordnance shield, with an East India Company lion above and the honours AVA and MAHIDPOOR below. A photograph shows this helmet with a dark cover and only the plate exposed. The dark blue jacket had red facings and heavy gold lace. The pouch-belt was buff leather, 3 in. wide (7·5 cm), with an ornamental gilt plate with pickers and honour scrolls. The pouch was black with gilt circular plate. A crimson and gold girdle and buff sword belt and slings were worn around the waist. Trousers were sky blue in 1832, altered, in 1846, to dark blue with a single gold stripe.

The undress uniform included a blue cloth cap, with gold lace band and black peak, a

dark blue jacket with red collar, cuffs and lining, gilt studs down the front and gold lace edging. In the 1840s a white jacket decorated with white cotton braid was introduced for hot weather. Undress trousers were sky blue with double red stripe.

European other ranks wore black helmets with brass fittings (shield, label and binding only) and red crest, plain dark blue jackets, red cummerbunds, white swordbelts, and sky blue overalls with double red stripe.

Native ranks (plate 49) wore the distinctive Madras turban, red for officers and dark blue for other ranks, with gilt chin scales and yellow braid. The jacket was dark blue with red collar and cuffs and yellow braiding. Equipment was white. Trousers were white at first, but later changed to dark blue with a double red stripe.

MADRAS FOOT ARTILLERY

The uniform for British officers (plate 67) followed the same outline as in Bengal. The bell-top shako, worn from 1829–1846, had a star plate with the Royal Arms within a garter bearing the words 'Madras Artillery'. A dark blue coatee was worn, with gold epaulettes, crimson waist sash and dark blue trousers with gold stripe.

The Golundauz or native artillery (plate 49) wore a dark blue turban, with yellow decoration and grooved knob similar to that worn by the infantry. The jacket was dark blue with red collar and cuffs, and yellow braid, including seven bastion-shaped loops down the front. Equipment was white with brass plates. The trousers were white, but were later altered to grey with a red stripe.

BOMBAY HORSE ARTILLERY

The uniform of the Bombay Horse Artillery (plate 68) was laid down in the standing orders of the Brigade of Horse Artillery (Bombay), which quotes a general order of 1 March 1829. The helmet was Roman pattern, japanned black, with cheetahskin turban, gilt fittings and black mane; on the front was a shield bearing the words 'Horse Artillery'. In place of the shield, the 1st (or Leslie's) Troop wore an eagle with a banner in each talon, bearing the words 'Afghanistan' and 'Hyderabad'. The jacket was dark blue, with red facings and gold lace. The pouch-belt was of gold lace with a red train, silver pickers and a pouch which was specified as gilt in 1829, silver in 1844 and black patent leather in 1850. A crimson and gold barrel sash and gold lace swordbelt and slings were worn around the waist. Dark blue overalls, with single gold stripe were also worn. The undress jacket was dark blue, with red collar and cuffs laced around with 1 in. lace. The jacket had gilt studs down the front, and gilt shoulder scales.

Other ranks' uniform, described in the 1844 orders, was distinguished from officers' uniform by the same features that distinguished it in the other presidencies.

Plate 68. Captain William Brett, Bombay Horse Artillery, c 1845. Watercolour, artist unknown.

BOMBAY FOOT ARTILLERY

The only distinguishing feature to note, was the title 'Bombay Artillery' worn on the shako, shoulder-belt and waist-belt plates.

ENGINEERS, SAPPERS AND MINERS, PIONEERS

The Bengal Sappers and Miners followed a pattern of uniform similar to the native infan-

Plate 69. Colonel George Bonner, Madras Horse Artillery, c 1840. Watercolour by Richard Buckner.

try, adopting the peakless shako, and then adopting the kilmarnock cap. Colour remained as before, red with dark blue facings and yellow lace.

Madras Pioneers, up to 1831, are shown in plate 49. The pioneers wore a black turban with white decoration, a dark green jacket with black facings and silver lace, black equipment and white trousers. After 1831, they were converted to sappers and miners, and wore engineer uniform. A native officer wore a black turban, red coat, black or dark blue patch on collar and cuff, gold lace, black swordbelt, and dark blue trousers with broad red stripe. Native ranks wore a similar arrangement, with dark blue shoulder scales with yellow cord edging.

In Bombay, the pioneers were also absorbed by the Sappers and Miners in 1830 and wore engineer uniform.

3
The Great Mutiny
1857–1861

There had been rapid British expansion in the previous fifteen years and, in many of the newly annexed provinces, positions of responsibility had been transferred into British hands. British laws and reforms were introduced, and local practices such as Sati (widow-burning) and thagi (strangling of travellers), both sanctified by Hindu custom, were abolished. Miles of railway lines and telegraph wires were further evidence of the spreading British presence.

By 1857 the army in India was composed as follows

Bengal	137,500
Madras	49,000
Bombay	48,000
Local forces	40,000
Military police	39,000
Total Indian	313,500
Total British	38,000
Total overall	351,500

Mutiny was not unknown in the armies of the East India Company, however, the Indian Mutiny of 1857–1858 was distinguished by its scale and by the support the mutineers received from the community in disaffected areas. The causes were, on the whole, deep-seated and long standing, and a situation had been created where a small and apparently trivial spark could set off a conflagration.

These changes caused unrest among Indians in general, and among the sepoys of the Bengal Army in particular. The sepoys were unhappy because their conditions of service had been affected. Although a regiment normally served within its own presidency, the sepoys were prepared to serve elsewhere during hostilities, particularly as they were paid compensation for field service. The sepoys were less happy about continuing to serve elsewhere after the end of hostilities on garrison duties, particularly where a new territory had been annexed and they no longer qualified for field service pay. Furthermore, in 1856, recruits had to accept a commitment for overseas service and many had religious objections to crossing the sea. The army was further weakened by the drain of British officers to the

Plate 70. The mess of the 3rd European Bengal Cavalry, at Allahabad, c 1860. Drawing by Lieutenant H C Kenible.

Plate 71. Hodson's Horse at Rhotuck, 1858. Lithograph after Captain George Francklin Atkinson.

political and civil services then expanding to administer new territories. More often than not, the younger and more active officers left, leaving regiments officered by the elderly and disinterested, and morale suffered accordingly. Against this tense background, a new muzzle-loading Enfield rifle was issued. Drill required the end of the cartridge to be bitten off before loading, and the story spread that the cartridges were greased with the fat of pigs (unclean to Muslims) and the fat of cows (holy to Hindus). This led to the rumours that the British planned to pollute and then Christianise the whole sepoy army.

The Mutiny, originally a military revolt, assumed a wider character, as many Indian princes sought to regain their former power. However, other princes supported the army, as did, for the most part, the sepoys of Bombay and Madras, the Sikhs of the Punjab, the Gurkhas and Garwhalis of the north, and the Rajputs of the west. The Mutiny was therefore largely confined to the Bengal Army and the northern plains, particularly the recently annexed province of Oudh where there was much residual loyalty to Bahadur Shah, the last symbol of Moghul power in Delhi.

In May 1857, sepoys at Meerut refused to touch the Enfield cartridges and were court-martialed and imprisoned. Their fellow sepoys mutinied, broke into the prison and released them. Together they killed their British officers and marched on Delhi.

The British were shaken and frightened by the outbreak. Many atrocities were committed by the mutineers, notably at Cawnpore, where the British, with their families, surrendered on promise of safe conduct but were subsequently massacred (plate 76). Accounts of this and other incidents, many of which were exaggerated, infuriated the British who responded with great ferocity, showing little mercy to mutineers who fell into their hands. The British even resorted to the old Moghul custom of blowing prisoners from guns; the disintegration of the body, according to local religious belief, affected the after-life of the victim. At first the Mutiny spread rapidly. In May 1857 the mutineers from Meerut occupied Delhi, although not before the ordnance staff had blown up the magazines to prevent their capture. The mutineers killed all the Europeans and Christians they could find, and proclaimed Bahadur Shah as Emperor. The British, under Sir John Lawrence, hastily gathered a force of 3,000 men and rushed them to Delhi where they laid siege to the city. Further reinforcements were sent from the Punjab and, in September, Delhi was successfully stormed.

At Lucknow, the capital of Oudh and the centre of the disaffected area, Lawrence's brother, Henry organised the defence of the

Plates 72 and 73. British and Indian officers of the 2nd Punjab Cavalry, 1859.

residency until he was killed in July and was replaced by Brigadier John Inglis. In September, Sir Henry Havelock fought his way through to Lucknow with a force of 3,000 to reinforce the garrison, but the rebels closed in again. Finally, in November, another force under Sir Colin Campbell relieved the garrison and evacuated the residency, which was not finally retaken until the following March.

In Central India, the Europeans in Jhansi had been massacred after surrendering the fort to the mutineers in early June 1857, and the Rani of Jhansi set up government. In March 1858, Sir Hugh Rose with two brigades from the Bombay Army laid siege to Jhansi and, in April, he both defeated the rebel army under Tantia Topi and captured the town. The Rani fled with Tantia Topi to Gwalior, where they subverted the local army and drove out its loyal ruler, the Sindia. In June, Sir Hugh Rose arrived with his army, recaptured Gwalior and again defeated Tantia Topi. The Rani was killed and Tantia Topi was eventually captured and executed. Although sporadic fighting went on for a further six months, the mutiny was defeated.

Plate 74. Lieutenant H Goschen, 2nd Punjab Cavalry, c 1860. Tinted photograph.

89

Plate 75. Defence of Arrah House against a large body of insurgents under Koer Singh, 1857. Lithograph after W Taylor.

Plate 76. Cawnpore, the scene of the massacre, with men of the Bengal European Regiment, 1857. Lithograph after Lieutenant W G Sankey.

In the confusion which followed the outbreak of the Mutiny, and with the breakdown in Government control and communications, many new regiments were raised from loyal natives and from recently annexed territories without any official order, often on the basis of verbal instructions only. In particular, the Sikhs of the Punjab proved to be loyal and excellent soldiers, and they provided a large number of the new regiments, including four regiments of Sikh irregular cavalry and eighteen regiments of Punjab infantry. In 1860 these were transferred from the control of the Government of the Punjab to the Commander-in-Chief of the Bengal Army.

Plate 77. 1st Bengal European Fusiliers, officers and soldiers in various orders of dress.

Cavalry

In 1858, four regiments of European cavalry were formed to replace the eight regiments of Bengal light cavalry, all of which had mutinied. After the mutiny, these were transferred to the British Army as the 19th, 20th and 21st Hussars.

In 1861 the native cavalry was reorganised. There had been twenty-nine irregular cavalry regiments under the C-in-C Bengal, and seventeen under the Government of India. Of the latter, the Guides Cavalry, five Punjab cavalry regiments, two regiments of Central India Horse, and four cavalry regiments of the Hyderabad Contingent, were retained. Of the twenty-nine under the C-in-C Bengal, ten were disbanded and nineteen were retained as regular regiments in the new Bengal Cavalry list.

Infantry

At the end of 1860 the number of infantry regiments was as follows

Under the C-in-C Bengal	15 Regular
	30 Irregular and Extra
	18 Punjab
Under the Government of India	7 Punjab
	5 Sikh and Guides
	6 Hyderabad Contingent
	3 Nagpur Irregular Force
	7 Local Corps

In 1861, twelve of the fifteen regular regiments were retained, the remaining three being disbanded. Twenty-five of the thirty irregular regiments, and fourteen of the eighteen Punjab regiments, were retained. The regiments under Government of India control remained unchanged.

Within six months, the five Gurkha Corps were withdrawn from the line and numbered separately, the 5th (or Hazara) Gurkhas being transferred from the Punjab Irregular Force, leaving a total of forty-eight Bengal infantry regiments.

The European cavalry and infantry had been transferred to the British Army. The artillery and engineers were transferred to the Royal Artillery and Royal Engineers, although the Bengal Sappers and Miners remained as a separate body under the C-in-C Bengal.

THE MADRAS ARMY 1857—1861

The Madras Army was not much affected by the Mutiny, but did not prove very effective in the provision of reinforcements for the Mutiny's suppression, and a few extra units were raised for local security purposes only.

In 1857 the 8th Light Cavalry refused to embark for service in Bengal and the regiment was disbanded.

In the post-mutiny reorganisation, the 5th, 6th and 7th Light Cavalry were disbanded with effect from 31 December 1860.

The following infantry regiments were raised during the Mutiny. All were disbanded in 1860

1st Extra Regiment
2nd Extra Regiment
3rd Extra Regiment
Madras Sappers Militia

Plate 78. Subedar Bussawah Singh, 8th Punjab Infantry, 21 December 1858. Watercolour, artist unknown.

Pegu Police Battalion
4th Extra Regiment

The extra regiments were raised to provide garrisons in place of regular battalions ordered for service outside Madras. The Madras Sappers Militia was to garrison Fort St George and the Pegu Police Battalion was for service in Pegu (Burma).

THE BOMBAY ARMY 1857—1861

The Indian Mutiny was largely confined to the Bengal Army, and although similar temptations faced its members, the Bombay Army did not, on the whole, succumb. This was because the Bombay Army was less bound by the caste system, and the sepoys had retained their traditional attachment to their Colours and their officers. Of thirty-two infantry battalions, only six gave grounds for anxiety and, of these, only two, the 21st and 27th actually mutinied. The Government of Bombay was able to send most of his British regiments to the centres of fighting and was also to keep

secure the southern end of the North-West Frontier.

As with the other presidencies, in 1861 the Bombay European infantry and artillery were transferred to the crown. Except for the 3rd Sinde Horse and the 30th Jacob's Rifles, most of the units raised during the mutiny were disbanded. The 29th were reduced, the Marine Battalion was brought into the line as the 21st, and the 1st and 2nd Belooch Battalions became the 27th and 29th regiments respectively. The native artillery disappeared, except for two companies, which were retained as mountain batteries.

THE BENGAL EUROPEAN CAVALRY 1857—1861

In November 1857 the Bengal Government found itself perilously short of cavalry, as seven of the ten regular light cavalry regiments had mutinied and two had been disbanded. It was therefore decided to form four regiments of European light cavalry, to be recruited in England. Recruiting was so brisk, that the numbers required were raised in three weeks and were immediately embarked for Calcutta. In June 1858 they arrived at Allahabad where, after an initial period of chaos, they were formed into regiments, principally officered by surviving officers of the regular light cavalry. The new recruits wore white helmets, with drab covers on service, or undress peaked forage caps (plate 70). They also wore blue serge tunics with white facings, white pouchbelts, and blue overalls with double white stripe. The planned full dress, which was probably never issued in any quantity, included a Roman helmet and a dark blue hussar tunic with five rows of white cord down the front.

Europeans were also recruited for the Bengal Yeomanry Cavalry, raised in Calcutta in July 1857. Their uniform of grey helmet with white pugri, blue flannel jumper, brown corduroy trousers and jack boots had a modern ring to it.

BENGAL LIGHT CAVALRY 1857—1861

The uniform of the light cavalry had not

Plate 79. The new Nussaree Battalion, a Gurkha battalion raised in 1830 and disbanded after the mutiny.

altered much between the 1847 regulations and the Mutiny, and the swift demise of all the regiments cut short further developments. Surviving officers continued to serve, attached to other corps, and one of them was described by a contemporary writer as wearing a drab braided frock coat and white overalls.

BENGAL IRREGULAR HORSE 1857–1861

The eight regiments which remained loyal, retained the uniforms described in chapter 2. Many additional regiments were raised during the Mutiny, partly to offset the shortage of cavalry caused by the defection of the light cavalry regiments, and partly because of the need for mobility on the part of loyal forces. Many of the new regiments were raised by enterprising and progressive officers like William Hodson and Dighton Probyn, and it was natural that their preference should have been for the drab-coloured loose fitting clothing worn by the Punjab Irregular Force (plates 71, 72 and 73).

Uniform
British officers wore wicker helmets in a drab colour, with pugris or turbans like their sowars. Tunics were usually single-breasted in drab or dark colours; alternatively, officers wore kurtas which were replacing the alkaluk. Equipment was of brown or black leather, with sword-belt worn over a cummerbund. Drab overalls, or white breeches, and boots were worn.

The native ranks wore turbans, alkaluks, kurtas or loose blouses with cummerbunds and loose pyjamas. Combined with long flowing beards, and riding untamed-looking horses, the effect must have been daunting to friend and foe alike.

BENGAL IRREGULAR CAVALRY: REGIMENTS RAISED DURING THE INDIAN MUTINY

Title	1861 outcome
1st Hodson's Horse	9th Bengal Cavalry
2nd Hodson's Horse	10th Bengal Cavalry
3rd Hodson's Horse	disbanded
Alexander's Horse	disbanded
1st Mahratta Horse	disbanded
2nd Mahratta Horse	18th Bengal Cavalry

93

Plate 82. *The 22nd Madras Native Infantry moving from Vellore, c 1857. Watercolour by Captain F Bannerman Philips.*

1st Sikh Irregular Cavalry, Wales' Horse	11th Bengal Cavalry
2nd Sikh Irregular Cavalry	12th Bengal Cavalry
3rd Sikh Irregular Cavalry	disbanded
4th Sikh Irregular Cavalry	13th Bengal Cavalry
Behar Irregular Cavalry	disbanded
Lahore Light Horse	disbanded
Benares Horse	disbanded
Lind's Pathans	disbanded
Ramghur Irregular Cavalry	disbanded
Meerut Horse	disbanded
Rohilkund Horse	16th Bengal Cavalry
Muttra Horse, Robart's Horse	17th Bengal Cavalry
Jat Horse Yeomanry, Murray's Jat Horse	14th Bengal Cavalry
Multani Regiment of Cavalry, Cureton's Multanis	15th Bengal Cavalry
Fane's Horse	19th Bengal Cavalry

Plate 80. OPPOSITE TOP: *Sepoys at rifle practice, 1857. Lithograph after Captain George Francklin Atkinson.*
Plate 81. OPPOSITE BOTTOM: *The Sirmoor Rifles at Delhi, 1858. Watercolour by E A Judge, 1893, from a contemporary original.*

Uniform

Details of uniforms are recorded for a few regiments only:

1st Hodson's: wicker helmet with red pugri, single-breasted drab tunic; red cummerbund, and black equipment. Sowars wore red turbans.

2nd Hodson's: dark blue alkaluk with red facings and piping, brown equipment.

1st Sikh Irregular Cavalry: blue turban, drab kurta, red cummerbund, red pyjamas.

4th Sikh Irregular Cavalry: British officers wore a dark coloured tunic with five small black loops, leather crossbelt and waistbelt over cummerbund, white breeches and boots. Native officers wore a mixture of dark and light-coloured alkaluks and blouses.

Robart's Horse: red turban, drab jackets with red cummerbunds, drab pyjamas.

Jat Horse: red turban, blue kurta, red cummerbund, black equipment, white pyjamas.

Fane's Horse: helmet with drab pugri, drab tunic, brown equipment, drab breeches. Sowars wore red turbans.

Plate 83. 'A Faithful Sepoy, Madras Army'. Pen and ink sketch by Henry Hope Crealock, 1858.

MADRAS LIGHT CAVALRY 1857—1861

The Madras Light Cavalry replaced the short hussar jacket with a hussar tunic of French grey with buff facings and five rows of silver hussar cord. They also wore sky blue overalls with single silver or white stripe. Native ranks wore the old black turban with white cords. The hussar tunic was worn for a short time only, as the native-style uniform described in chapter 4 was introduced in 1859.

BOMBAY LIGHT CAVALRY 1857—1861

The Bombay Light Cavalry also introduced a hussar tunic, some time after 1856. An example in the National Army Museum is powder blue with white facings and silver lace. During the Mutiny and the Persian War, the light cavalry generally wore undress, with peaked forage cap, with white cover and veil, undress jacket with shoulder scales and trousers with cloth stripes.

PUNJAB CAVALRY 1857—1861

Like the Bengal Irregular Cavalry, the Punjab Cavalry preferred to fight in loose-fitting native clothing. British officers still wore European-style dress, and plate 74 shows an officer of the 2nd Punjab Cavalry in black helmet, with elaborate turban and white plume, red tunic, with black facings and gold cord around collar and cuffs, dress pouch-belt and waist-belt worn over a multi-coloured cummerbund, white breeches and boots.

The Punjab Cavalry were fond of local variations. W H Russell described the Colonel of the 1st Punjab Cavalry as wearing a Persian-style helmet and armoured gauntlet, while Sir Dighton Probyn recalled an officer of the 2nd sewing the curb chains from his horse's bridle on to his shoulders, to protect against sword cuts, the origin of the shoulder chains worn by British cavalry to this day.

BOMBAY IRREGULAR CAVALRY REGIMENTS RAISED DURING THE INDIAN MUTINY

Title	1861 outcome
Macauley's Horse	3rd Scinde Horse
2nd Southern Mahratta Horse	2nd Southern Mahratta Horse
2nd Poona Horse	disbanded
4th Scinde Horse	disbanded
3rd Southern Mahratta Horse	disbanded
2nd Gujerat Horse	disbanded

CENTRAL INDIA HORSE

Raised	Title	1861 outcome
1858	Mayne's Horse	1st Central India Horse
1858	Beatson's Horse	2nd Central India Horse

A contemporary watercolour in the National Army Museum shows a British officer in drab helmet with purple pugri, drab kurta, purple cummerbund, and drab breeches. Native ranks wore the same, with purple turban and brown equipment.

BENGAL INFANTRY REGIMENTS RAISED DURING THE INDIAN MUTINY

Title	Raised as/from	1861 titles	
		1st	*2nd*
7th Punjab Infantry	Punjab Police Battalion	23rd	19th
8th Punjab Infantry	From 4th and 5th Punjab Infantry	24th	20th
9th Punjab Infantry	From 3rd and 6th Punjab Infantry	25th	21st
Extra Gurkha Regiment		19th	4th Gurkha Regt
10th Punjab Infantry		disbanded	
11th Punjab Infantry	From 1st Sikh Infantry and 3rd Punjab Police Battalions	26th	22nd
12th Punjab Infantry		disbanded	
13th Punjab Infantry		disbanded	
14th Punjab Infantry		disbanded	
15th (Pioneer) Regiment of Punjab Infantry		27th	23rd
16th Punjab Infantry		28th	24th
17th Punjab Infantry	Lahore Punjab Battalion	29th	25th
18th Punjab Infantry		30th	26th
19th Punjab Infantry	Regiment of Rawalpindi	31st	27th
20th Punjab Infantry	Ferozepore Punjab Battalion	32nd	28th
21st Punjab Infantry		33rd	29th
22nd Punjab Infantry		34th	30th
23rd Punjab Infantry	Cortlandt's Levy	35th	31st
24th (Pioneer) Regiment Punjab Infantry	Punjab Pioneers	36th	32nd
Regiment of Lucknow	13th, 48th and 71st Bengal NI	20th	16th
Allahabad Levy		37th	33rd
Mhair Regiment		Police Battalion	
Kamroop Regiment		discontinued	
Fatehgarh Levy		38th	34th
Mynpoorie Levy		39th	35th
Bareilly Levy		40th	36th
Meerut Levy		41st	37th
Agra Levy		42nd	38th
Aligarh Levy		43rd	39th
Loyal Purbeah Levy	3rd, 36th and 61st Bengal NI	21st	17th
25th Punjab Infantry	Hazara Gurkha Battalion	7th Inf Punj Irr Fce	5th Gurkha Regt
Shajehanpur Levy		44th	40th
Cawnpore Levy		discontinued	
Moradabad Levy		discontinued	
1st Gwalior Regiment		45th	41st
Sealkote Infantry Levy		discontinued	
Goojramwallah Levy		discontinued	
Kemaoon Levy		discontinued	
2nd Gwalior Regiment		discontinued	
Bhopal Levy	from Bhopal, Gwalior and Mulwa contingents	Bhopal Battalion	

Plate 84. Bengal Horse Artillery in Action, 1857. Lithograph after Captain George Francklin Atkinson.

EUROPEAN INFANTRY 1857–1861

The European Infantry regiments followed the 1855–1856 changes of British regiments, and adopted the French-style sloping shako and the new tunic (plates 76 and 77). An example of the tunic in the National Army Museum is red with dark blue facings and gold lace, crown on collar, slash cuff and white piping. These regiments played an important part in the suppression of the Mutiny, and a wide variety of uniforms appeared in contemporary illustrations. Officers wore the 1855 shako, possibly with white cover or wicker helmet in white or drab, or peaked forage cap, sometimes stiff, sometimes floppy, with covers or pugri. The Madras Fusiliers, unable to find white shako covers, adopted pale blue instead, and earned the nickname 'Neill's bluecaps'. Officers also wore the full dress red tunic, or white shell jacket, or drab frock, crimson shoulder sash, and dark blue or white trousers. A photograph of an officer of the Bombay Fusiliers shows him in hot weather dress with slate-coloured frock with flat shoulder straps, red sash over shoulder and slate-coloured trousers. Soldiers wore the same uniform as officers,

with the addition of white blouses (plate 76) or white shorts, and white equipment.

BENGAL NATIVE INFANTRY 1857–1861

The officers of the Bengal NI, and the sepoys who remained loyal, generally fought in undress. Plate 80 shows a typical group. The officers wear white peaked forage caps, plain undress jackets, sword belts and white trousers. The sepoys wear kilmarnocks with white covers, full dress jackets, with single white cartouche belt, waistbelt with pouch for percussion caps, and white trousers. Some wear the single-breasted white undress jacket.

To replace the mutinied regiments, many local corps were brought into the line or new regiments formed from loyal elements of the mutinied regiments. These, for the most part, wore the same uniform as the regular regiments, although the Sikh regiments reverted to their national dress of turban and loose blouse for fighting. Fifteen new Punjab regiments were also raised of which all but four eventually took their place in the line as regular regiments. Plate 78 shows a subedar of the 8th Punjab Infantry. He wears a drab turban, drab tunic with brown equipment and drab trousers. Most of the regiments wore

Plate 85. Officers of the Bombay Horse Artillery, Sind, 1860.

drab at first, and five retained this as their main uniform colour after the Mutiny, the remainder changing to scarlet. In action the regiments preferred their less formal native attire, of blouse shirts and tight pyjamas.

GURKHA REGIMENTS 1857–1861

The Gurkha regiments did not follow the popular trend towards loose drab uniform, presumably because they had pride in their rifle-green dress, which was in itself a practical colour. Plate 79 and 81 show gurkhas wearing kilmarnock caps (in one case with white covers), double-breasted dress coatees, black equipment and dark green trousers. A photograph taken during the Mutiny, of the 2nd Gurkha Rifles, shows one gurkha in a tunic, indicating that tunics were probably coming into use at about this time. The two Gurkha regiments raised during the Mutiny, the Extra Gurkha Regiment and the Hazara Gurkha battalions, wore loose drab clothing at first but adopted dark green clothing with black facings after the war.

PUNJAB IRREGULAR FORCE INFANTRY 1857–1861

The infantry of the Punjab Irregular Force are generally described as wearing turbans and drab clothing with black or brown leather equipment.

MADRAS NATIVE INFANTRY 1857–1861

In 1857 tunics were ordered for use by British officers, but they were not actually issued until 1859–1860. The British officers in plate 82 wear a white wicker helmet, with white cover and pugri (sanctioned for use in 1854), a red, (probably undress) tunic, with piping down the back seam and sword belt worn under, and dark blue trousers with red stripe. The sash, not worn here, was to be worn over the shoulder from 1856. By 1859 authorisation had been given for khaki to be worn as summer dress and at the same time, a khaki cover for the wicker helmet was authorised. In 1860 a red serge frock was introduced in place of the shell jacket.

The sowars (plate 83) retained the stiff turban until 1860, but generally preferred to wear the peakless forage cap. In plate 82, the bandsmen wear peaked forage caps with white covers, while the sepoys wear turbans with white covers (as in plate 60).

BOMBAY NATIVE INFANTRY 1857–1861

Title	1861 outcome
1st Regiment, Jacob's Rifles	30th Bombay Infantry
2nd Regiment, Jacob's Rifles	disbanded

Plate 86. Rebel artilleryman and rebel trooper. Pencil drawings by James Atkinson, c 1857.

3rd Belooch Battalion	disbanded
30th Bombay NI (from loyal elements of 21st NI)	disbanded
31st Bombay NI (from loyal elements of 27th NI)	disbanded
1st Extra Battalion	disbanded
2nd Extra Battalion	disbanded
3rd Extra Battalion	disbanded

Wicker helmets were authorised for wear in the Bombay Army in 1859, although they had been in unofficial use for some time. Tunics 'of the pattern prescribed for the Royal Army' were introduced in January 1857, with crimson shoulder sash and badges of rank on the collar. Red serge frocks were introduced at about the same time, and during the Mutiny a khaki uniform was permitted for undress wear in hot weather.

ARTILLERY 1857—1861

The Bengal Horse Artillery went into action in full dress at the outbreak of the Mutiny, but soon shed much of it en route. Plate 84 shows the artillery in white helmets with white pugris, white shell jackets and white trousers, although as the artist, G F Atkinson, explained in the caption, they gradually exchanged white for the 'all-prevailing mud colour'. Individual officers are pictured in peaked forage caps swathed with white pugris, white tunics (in some cases with white frogging across the front), and white pouch-belts. Dark blue or white stable jackets were also frequently worn.

The Bengal Foot Artillery followed the example of the Royal Artillery by introducing fur caps and tunics in 1856. A photograph of 2nd Lieutenant J N Mark shows him in an Albert shako, dark blue tunic, with red facings and gold embroidery on collar and cuffs, and white pouch-belt and waistbelt.

In the Madras Horse Artillery, the wicker helmet and khaki clothing were officially approved for summer wear on service in 1858, and a regulation of 1859 stated that the officers' khaki tunics should have six loops down the front. In 1861 they were ordered to revert to white.

The Madras Foot Artillery were also authorised, in 1857, to adopt the busby and tunic. The National Army Museum has an example of the busby, of RA pattern with the inscription 'Madras Artillery' on the grenade plume holder.

A photograph of the Bombay Horse Artillery taken during the Mutiny (plate 85) shows them wearing an assortment of head-dress in white or drab, loose fitting white tunics without any adornment, and white overalls.

The Bombay Foot Artillery adopted busby and tunic in 1858.

MUTINEERS

In the early stages of the Mutiny, the rebel sepoys retained their scarlet uniforms. The print of the defence of Arrah house (plate 75) shows the mutineers in forage caps, full dress jackets and white trousers. In the background can be seen a full battalion drawn up, still carrying its colours. The Atkinson drawings of rebel trooper and artilleryman (plate 86) show that cavalry and artillery also retained many features of their British uniform.

However, from the point of view of comfort, and to stress their opposition to the British system, most reverted to native dress, with British accoutrements and weapons as the only indication of their former loyalty. Atkinson's print of 'Mutinous sepoys' (plate 87) shows the mutineers clothed almost entirely in white, with turbans or skull caps, white jackets or shirts, and white doti, the traditional Indian netherwear of a strip of cloth wound around the loins. Their cartouche belts, pouches and waistbelts are still of British pattern.

RESULTS OF THE MUTINY

On 1 November 1858 Queen Victoria assumed the government of India. Hitherto the East India Company had been the instrument through which the British Government ruled India. Since 1784 a cabinet minister, the President of the Board of Trade for India, had exercised political control over the Company's affairs and, by 1834, the Company had ceased to have any trading function. The mutiny provided the Government with the opportunity to complete the transfer of authority. The Governor-General, Lord Canning, became the first Viceroy to govern British India in the name of the Queen, and in London a Secretary of State for India was appointed. With territorial annexation almost at an end, the British were able to concentrate on imposing sound

Plate 87. Mutinous sepoys. Lithograph after Captain George Francklin Atkinson, c 1857.

administration, and due caution was shown in the introduction of further social reforms.

On the military side, it was apparent that the British could only remain in India for so long as they were backed by effective military power, and to that end it was laid down that the strength of the British Army should not fall below 80,000, and that every major garrison should include British troops in the proportion of at least one to three. In practice, the British strength averaged out at 65,000 and the strength of the native armies was accordingly reduced to 135,000.

The East India Company's European regiments were transferred to the British Army:

ARTILLERY

All artillery was transferred to the Royal Artillery, apart from five mountain batteries of the Punjab Irregular Force and four batteries of the Hyderabad Contingent.

After the reorganisations and reductions of the presidential armies, the number of regiments in each was as follows (see below).

The system under which British officers were attached to individual regiments was altered, because regimental cadres were not large enough the bear the uneven strain imposed by the absence of officers on staff appointments and in civil employ.

Instead, each presidency maintained a common officer roll or 'Staff Corps', from which officers were attached to individual regiments.

The distinction in nomenclature and style of dress between regular and irregular corps was abolished, and the best features of both systems were adopted.

CAVALRY

Title	Became
1st Bengal European Cavalry	19th Hussars
2nd Bengal European Cavalry	20th Hussars (later 21st Lancers)
3rd Bengal European Cavalry	21st Hussars

INFANTRY

Title	Became
1st Bengal Fusiliers	101st Regiment (later 1st Royal Munster Fus)
1st Madras Fusiliers	102nd Regiment (later 1st Royal Dublin Fus)
1st Bombay Fusiliers	103rd Regiment (later 2nd Royal Dublin Fus)
2nd Bengal Fusiliers	104th Regiment (later 2nd Royal Munster Fus)
2nd Madras Light Infantry	105th Regiment (later 2nd Yorkshire LI)
2nd Bombay Light Infantry	106th Regiment (later 2nd Durham LI)
3rd Bengal Light Infantry	107th Regiment (later 2nd Royal Sussex Regt)
3rd Madras Infantry	108th Regiment (later 2nd Royal Inniskilling Fus)
3rd Bombay Infantry	109th Regiment (later 2nd Leinster Regt)

	Cavalry Regiments	Artillery Batteries	Sappers and Miners	Infantry Regiments
Bengal	19	—	1	49
Madras	4	—	1	40
Bombay	7	—	1	30
Punjab Frontier Force	6	5	—	12
Hyderabad	4	4	—	6
Other Local Corps	2	—	—	5
Total	42	9	3	142

4
Soldiers of the Queen
1861–1903

After 1861 the extensive reforms of the Indian Army, carried through as a result of the Mutiny, were given time to work out in practice, and it was hoped that emphasis on good administration would reconcile Indian public opinion to British rule. The hope was that, if the Indian Army had to face an invader, it would at least have a peaceful country behind it. However, the first occasion on which the Indian Army went into action in any great strength, the 2nd Afghan War of 1878–80, showed up many defects. As a result, an army commission was set up by Lord Lytton to recommend ways in which the efficiency of the Army could be improved.

Its main recommendation, the abolition of the separate presidency armies, met with so much opposition and so many alternative schemes that the suggestion was put to one side. Several regiments were disbanded, particularly in Madras, where there was increasing difficulty in recruiting. The regiments disbanded were:

Bengal Cavalry	16th and 17th
Bengal Infantry	34th, 35th, 36th, 37th, 41st
Madras Infantry	34th to 41st
Bombay Cavalry	3rd Scinde Horse, 2nd S Mahratta Horse, 2nd Poona Horse
Bombay Infantry	6th, 11th, 15th, 18th

To compensate, there was an increase in the establishment of the surviving regiments.

Although there was opposition to the concept of one Indian Army, it was agreed to pool various administrative services, including finance, commissariat, ordnance and transport. In 1886, the Punjab Frontier Force was transferred from the control of the Government of Punjab to that of the Commander-in-Chief, India. In the same year, infantry battalions were linked, two or three at a time,

according to the British system introduced by Cardwell in 1881. This was combined with a system of reserve liability by which, in times of emergency, trained soldiers continued to be available for call-up after their service with the colours had finished.

In 1895 the abolition of the presidency armies was finally agreed, and the Army of India was divided into four commands, each headed by a lieutenant-general. These commands were:

Punjab, including North-West Frontier and Punjab Frontier Force
Bengal
Madras, including Burma
Bombay, including Sind, Quetta and Aden.

A number of units remained directly under the Government of India. These were the:

Hyderabad Contingent
Central India House
Malwa Bhil Corps
Bhopal Battalion
Deoli Irregular Force
Erinpura Irregular Force
Meywar Bhil Corps
Mharwara Battalion

The Government also had three other sources of reinforcement at its disposal.

Police. The police were set up under civil authority, with responsibility for the maintenance of law and order. However, in the frontier areas, there were also police battalions, run on military lines, and many of these eventually became part of the army.

Volunteer Forces. These were recruited from the British and Anglo-Indian communities. They numbered over 30,000 and were organised into light horse, garrison artillery and rifle volunteer regiments. The railway battalions had particular responsibility for the protection of the 28,000 miles of railway, which were of vital importance to the defence of India.

State Forces. Most Indian princes still maintained their own military forces, and these totalled some 93,000. On the whole, they were poorly equipped and trained. However, the princes also provided some 18,000 Imperial Service troops, trained under the supervision of a British inspecting staff, and available for service with the Indian Army at home or overseas.

Plate 88. British and native officers of the Viceroy's Bodyguard, c 1870.

As part of the British Government's strategy of allocating a 'sphere of influence' to the Government of India, the Indian Army was involved in a number of campaigns in the Far East, Burma and East Africa during the second half of the nineteenth century.

2ND CHINA WAR 1857–1860

A wave of anti-foreign frenzy led to the seizure of the British ship *Arrow* and the closure of the port of Canton and, early in 1857, troops were sent from England and India to deal with this. Although the outbreak of the Mutiny necessitated the diversion of some of the regiments to India, sufficient troops were left to retake Canton in January 1858. After a year of fruitless negotiation with the Chinese, an attempt was made, in June 1859, to capture the Taku forts guarding the approaches to Tientsin and Pekin, but the attack was repulsed.

For this phase of the war, the honour CHINA 1858–1859 was awarded to three Bengal NI regiments, the 47th, 65th and 70th. Their absence from India during the Mutiny ensured their survival, and in 1861 they became the 7th, 10th and 11th regiments.

In 1860 a larger Anglo-French force was assembled at Hong Kong, and in August the Taku forts were successfully stormed. After defeating the Chinese at Palikao, the allies occupied Pekin. The Chinese agreed to abide by the Treaty of Tientsin, by which more Chinese ports were opened to foreign trade.

The battle honours TAKU FORTS and PEKIN were awarded to the 1st Sikh Irregular Cavalry, Fane's Horse (later 19th Lancers), Madras Sappers and Miners, and two regiments of Punjab Infantry, later the 20th and 23rd Pioneers.

Some Indian regiments were attached to Captain Charles Gordon's 'Ever-Victorious Army' which helped the new Chinese Government quell the Taiping rebellion, and the

Plate 89. 6th Bengal Cavalry. Watercolour by Orlando Norie, c 1870.

honour CHINA 1860–1862 was awarded to the Regiment of Ludhiana, the 11th and 19th (later 22nd and 27th) Punjab Infantry and the 5th Bombay Light Infantry.

3RD CHINA WAR 1900

The Indian Army was involved in further operations in China, in 1900, during the uprising of the Boxers, a secret society dedicated to the expulsion of foreigners from China, who received tacit support from the Dowager Empress, Tsz'e Hsi. In June, the British embassy in Pekin asked for troops to be sent to protect foreigners there. An international force set out from the coast, but was turned back by the Chinese near Tientsin. In Pekin the German ambassador was murdered and the legations were besieged. In July, a larger force under General Sir Alfred Gaselee, which included British, Russian and US troops captured Tientsin and pressed on to relieve Pekin after a siege of 55 days. British troops remained in Pekin for a year and garrisons remained in Canton and Shanghai until World War 2.

The regiments which took part in the relief of the legations were awarded the honour PEKIN 1900. These were the 1st Bengal Lancers, 7th and 24th Bengal Infantry, and 51st Sikhs. All other regiments involved in the campaign, including two cavalry, and fifteen infantry, regiments were awarded the honour CHINA 1900.

3RD BURMA WAR 1885–1887

Burma came into prominence again, after the accession of King Thibaw in 1878. Internal order broke down under his rule, he interfered with British trade and signed an agreement with the French. In retaliation, the British assembled an amphibious force of 19,000 troops under General Prendergast, which moved up the Irrawaddy and, against little resistance, took Mandalay. King Thibaw was deposed and the whole of Burma was annexed. However, fighting continued in the mountains of Burma for many years.

The honour BURMA 1885–1887 was awarded to a total of forty-two regiments from all three presidencies, and also to four mountain batteries.

ABYSSINIA 1868

King Theodore of Abyssinia had imprisoned the British consul and the delegation sent to negotiate for his release. The British declared war and an army of some 32,000 troops under Sir Robert Napier was sent from India. They landed at Annesley Bay, fought their way inland and captured the stronghold at Magdala where King Theodore committed suicide. Having released the hostages, the expedition returned to India. The honour ABYSSINIA was awarded to thirteen regiments and a mountain battery, mostly from Bombay.

105

Plate 90. The Indian Contingent engaged with the British forces, in the Egyptian Campaign, 1882. Chromolithograph after Orlando Norie.

Plate 91. Types of the Bengal Army, c 1890. Chromolithograph after Lieutenant A C Lovett.

Plate 92. The Madras Army and Troops under the Government of India, 1893. Chromolithograph after Lieutenant A C Lovett.

Plate 93. Types of the Bombay Army, 1888. Chromolithograph after Lieutenant A C Lovett.

Plate 94. *British officers of the 12th Bengal Cavalry, in review order A, review order B, and undress, c 1875.*

EGYPT 1882

In 1878 the Russians had defeated the Turks and were at the gates of Constantinople, and trouble was brewing once again in Afghanistan. In order to forestall any threat to the recently opened Suez Canal, Indian troops were moved to Malta and Cyprus (plate 99) but were not called upon to fight. The Suez Canal also led to increasing involvement by the French and British in Egyptian affairs. Local reaction, led by Arabi Pasha came to a head in June 1882 with the massacre of Europeans in Alexandria. This was followed by the bombardment of the town by a British fleet in

Plate 95. *A sowar of the 18th Bengal Lancers in China, 1900, wearing khaki drill field service order.*

reprisal. In August, a force under Sir Garnet Wolseley was landed at Ismailia. Three weeks later, at Tel el Kebir, Wolseley launched a night attack which caught the Egyptians by surprise and they were routed. Arabi Pasha surrendered, a British agent was appointed in Cairo and the Egyptian Army was reorganised under British officers.

The Indian regiments involved, (plate 90) the 2nd, 6th and 13th Bengal Cavalry, Madras Sappers and Miners, 7th and 20th Bengal Infantry and 29th Bombay Infantry were awarded the honours TEL EL KEBIR and EGYPT 1882.

1ST SUDAN WAR 1884—1885

Britain now found herself involved in the Sudan, where the Mahdi had proclaimed himself and had launched a dervish revolt. An Egyptian force under Hicks Pasha was annihilated at Kordofan in November 1883, and General Gordon, sent to evacuate Egyptian garrisons from the Sudan was trapped, and later killed, in Khartoum. On the Red Sea coast, the Mahdi's lieutenant, Osman Digna had had some success at the expense of local Egyptian forces. In the Spring of 1884, therefore, a force under General Graham was sent to Suakin, and while the force gained local victories over the dervishes at El Teb, Tamai and Tofrek, the mobility of the enemy prevented any decisive outcome.

The Indian regiments in Graham's force, the 9th Bengal Cavalry, Madras Sappers and Miners, 15th and 17th Bengal Infantry and the 28th Bombay Infantry were awarded the honours SUAKIN 1885 and (except for the Madras Sappers and Miners) TOFREK.

BRITISH EAST AFRICA 1896—1901

Operations against the slave traders of Zanzibar and East Africa led to the award of the battle honour BRITISH EAST AFRICA to four Bombay regiments, the 24th (1896), 27th (1897–1899), 4th (1898) and 16th (1901).

NORTH WEST FRONTIER 1861—1903

The main preoccupation of the Indian Army

Plate 96. British officers of the 3rd Punjab Cavalry, in various orders of dress, c 1900.

during this period was the North-West Frontier. There were two main elements to consider. First there was the conflict of local interests. Much as nature abhors a vacuum, so the Government of British India could not countenance anarchy within its territory, and objected to any on its borders. But, to the tribesmen of the North-West Frontier, independence, and adherence to their own laws and no one else's, had been a way of life for centuries. The second element was the steady expansion of the Russian empire into Central Asia during the 1860s and 1870s, which brought Russia to the borders of Afghanistan, and enabled them, in the British view, to threaten India.

2ND AFGHAN WAR 1878—1880

Matters came to a head in 1878 when the Amir of Afghanistan, Sher Ali, showed favour to the Russians by accepting their mission while refusing to accept British envoys. The British declared war and mustered a powerful force, which seized the frontier passes, the Khyber, the Kurram and the Bolan, and defeated Sher Ali's army at Peiwar Kotal. Sher Ali fled, his son Yakub Khan made

peace, and accepted a British resident at Kabul. So the army began to withdraw back into India.

Two honours were awarded for this phase, ALI MASJID, the fortress at the entrance to the Khyber pass and PEIWAR KOTAL on the Kurram Pass.

However, in September 1879, the resident, Sir Louis Cavagnari and his escort of Guides were massacred, and the Afghans rose in revolt. In reprisal, a force under Sir F Roberts marched from Kandahar to Kabul, defeating

Plate 97. Havildar and jemedar of the Guides Cavalry, c 1900. Photograph by James Burke.

Plate 98. Colonel Walter Fane, 19th Bengal Lancers (Fane's Horse), c 1865. Oil painting, artist unknown.

Plate 99. 10th Bengal Lancers in Malta, 1878. Oil painting by G Gianni.

the Afghan Army at Charasiah, just outside the capital. Kabul was taken without further trouble, but the Afghans rallied to a call for a holy war against the British and besieged Roberts' force which had withdrawn to Sherpur, an entrenched position just outside the city. An attempt to storm the position failed and the besieging forces were dispersed. The regiments of Roberts' force were awarded the honours CHARASIAH and KABUL 1879.

It was deemed advisable for the British Army to be seen in other parts of the country and, in March 1880, Sir D Stewart set out with a force of 7,000 from Kandahar. He defeated the Afghans in several engagements, the most notable being AHMAD KHEL, near Ghazni, which was later awarded as a battle honour.

In June 1880, Ayub Khan, brother of Yakub Khan, laid claim to the throne and marched from Herat to Kandahar. A small British force sent to intercept him was massacred at Maiwand and Ayub Khan laid siege to Kandahar. Roberts reacted quickly. He marched from Kabul with 10,000 men and covered the 313 miles to Kandahar in twenty-two days. Ayub Khan's army was routed on 1 September and KANDAHAR 1880 became a further entry on the roll of battle honours.

A pro-British government under Abdur Rahman was established and the British left Afghanistan in 1881.

In addition to the individual honours described above, all the regiments involved in the war received the general honour AFGHANISTAN with various combinations of dates, 1878–1879, 1878–1880 or 1879–1880.

CHITRAL 1895 AND PUNJAB FRONTIER 1897

Operations against dissident tribesmen on the North-West Frontier were too numerous to recount in detail, and description has been limited to the few actions which attracted battle honours. In 1893 a new frontier was agreed between Afghanistan and India, and the area on India's side was brought under British control by the creation of the N W Frontier Province. This extension of British influence led to major outbreaks of fighting in 1895 and 1897.

Chitral, a state on the western edge of Kashmir, came into prominence in 1895, when its ruler was murdered by a rival claimant and the small British garrison, composed of a company of the 14th Sikhs, was besieged. After seven weeks, the 32nd Sikh

110

Plate 100. Captain John Watson, 1st Punjab Cavalry, c 1865. Tinted photograph.

Plate 101. 5th Punjab Cavalry, c 1880. Watercolour by Orlando Norie.

Pioneers fought their way through from Gilgit to reinforce the garrison and they were followed shortly after by a strong force under Sir Robert Low.

The 14th Sikhs were awarded the unique honour DEFENCE OF CHITRAL, while the 32nd and the regiments of Low's force received the honour CHITRAL.

In 1897, calls for a holy war against the infidel led to a more-or-less coordinated attack by tribesmen all along the frontier. Major incidents occurred in the Tochi Valley, at Malakand in the Swat Valley, in the Peshawar Valley with an incursion of Mohmands, and in the Khyber Pass. The first three operations led to the award of the general honour PUNJAB FRONTIER. The honour MALAKAND was also awarded to the regiments involved in the defence of the camp in the Malakand Pass in July 1897 and in its relief.

The attacks by the Afridis on the forts along the approaches to the Khyber Pass were the most dangerous of this series of uprisings. The gallant defence of Fort Gulistan on the Samana Ridge by a small detachment of the 36th Sikhs, who held out for several days against 10,000 tribesmen before being overrun, was commemorated by the award of the honour

SAMANA. To face these attacks, the British assembled over 35,000 troops under Sir William Lockhart. The entrance to the Tirah Valley at Dargai was stormed in October 1897 and the Afridi territory was occupied until the following April. The regiments involved in this operation received the honour TIRAH.

TIBET 1904

One last attempt at expansion by British India, the invasion of Tibet in 1904, should be noted, although the campaign attracted no battle honours.

There had been border disputes between Tibet and the British protectorate of Sikkim, and the British also feared Russian influence in Tibet. A frontier commission was set up in July 1903, but when that failed, a mission under Colonel Francis Younghusband, with a strong military escort, entered Tibet in January 1904. Against some opposition, which was easily brushed aside, the expedition reached Lhasa. Younghusband imposed an indemnity (later reduced by the British Government), installed a trade agent and withdrew, having caused a storm of opposition at home.

1861	*Pre 1861*	*Changes 1861–1903*
1st	1st Irregular	1896 Lancers 1899 Duke of York's
2nd	2nd Irregular	1890 Lancers
3rd	4th Irregular	1901 Skinner's Horse
4th	6th Irregular	1890 Lancers
5th	7th Irregular	
6th	8th Irregular	1883 Prince of Wales's
7th	17th Irregular	1900 Lancers
8th	18th Irregular	1900 Lancers
9th	1st Hodson's	1886 Lancers
10th	2nd Hodson's	1874 Lancers 1878 Duke of Cambridge's Own
11th	1st Sikh Irregular	1864 Lancers 1876 Prince of Wales's
12th	2nd Sikh Irregular	
13th	4th Sikh Irregular	1864 Lancers 1884 Duke of Connaught's
14th	Murray's Jat Horse	1864 Lancers
15th	Cureton's Multanis	1890 Lancers
16th	Rohilcund Horse	1882 disbanded 1885 raised 1900 Lancers
17th	Muttra/Robart's	1882 disbanded 1885 raised 1900 Lancers
18th	Mahratta	1885 Lancers
19th	Fane's	1864 Lancers

Battle honours	*Regiments granted award*		
ABYSSINIA (1868)	10th, 12th	CHARASIAH (1879)	12th, 14th
AFGHANISTAN 1878–1880	1st, 3rd, 4th, 5th, 8th, 10th, 11th, 12th, 13th, 14th, 15th, 17th, 18th 19th	KABUL (1879)	12th, 14th
		AHMAD KHEL (1880)	19th
ALI MASJID (1878)	11th	KANDAHAR (1880)	3rd
PEIWAR KOTAL (1878)	12th	EGYPT 1882	2nd, 6th, 13th

1903 title		Uniform details coat/facings/lace
	1870	yellow/red/gold
1st Duke of York's Own Lancers (Skinner's Horse)	1879	yellow/black/gold
2nd Lancers (Gardner's Horse)	1861	emerald green/—/silver
	1870	emerald green/red/silver
	1882	emerald green/red/gold
	1887	blue/light blue/—
3rd Skinner's Horse	1870	scarlet/blue/silver
	1874	scarlet/blue/gold
	1881	drab
	1891	blue/yellow/gold
4th Lancers	1861	scarlet/blue/gold
5th Cavalry	1870	scarlet/blue/gold
6th Prince of Wales's Cavalry	1870	blue/red/gold
	1898	blue/scarlet/gold
7th Hariana Lancers		red/dark blue/gold
8th Lancers		blue/scarlet/gold
9th Hodson's Horse	1870	blue/red/gold
	1887	blue/white/gold
10th Duke of Cambridge's Own Lancers (Hodson's Horse)	1870	blue/red/gold
11th Prince of Wales's Lancers (Probyn's Horse)	1870	blue/scarlet/gold
12th Cavalry		blue/blue/gold
13th Duke of Connaught's Lancers (Watson's Horse)		dark blue/scarlet/gold
14th Murray's Jat Lancers		dark blue/scarlet/gold
15th Lancers (Cureton's Multanis)	1870	rifle green/scarlet/gold
	1886	blue/scarlet/gold
	pre 1882	green/red/gold
	post 1885	blue/blue/gold
16th Cavalry		
	pre 1882	blue/red/gold
	post 1885	blue/white/gold
17th Cavalry		
18th Tiwana Lancers	1870	red/blue/gold
	1901	red/white/gold
19th Lancers (Fane's Horse)	1861	French grey/—/gold
	1870	dark blue/red/gold
	1874	dark blue/scarlet/silver
	1878	dark blue/light blue/silver
	1895	dark blue/French grey/gold

TEL EL KEBIR (1882)	2nd, 6th, 13th	TIRAH (1897–1898)	18th
SUAKIN 1885	9th	PUNJAB FRONTIER (1897–1898)	3rd, 6th, 11th, 13th, 18th
BURMA 1885–1887	7th		
CHITRAL (1895)	9th, 11th	PEKIN (1900)	1st
MALAKAND (1897)	11th	CHINA (1900)	16th

Plate 102. An officer of the 4th (Prince of Wales's) Madras Cavalry, c 1885.

Plate 103. Lieutenant-Colonel A W H Hornsby Drake, 1st Madras Lancers, 1893. Oil painting by W E Miller.

GOVERNOR-GENERAL'S BODYGUARD
1861—1903

Although Lord Canning formally adopted the title of Viceroy and Governor-General of India in 1858, the Bodyguard was referred to in the official army list as Governor-General's up to 1947. The title 'Viceroy's Bodyguard' is found in use in the 1860s and by the 1880s the cypher 'VCBG' appeared on appointments. The uniform of 1870, which hardly changed until the turn of the century, is shown in plate 88. British officers wore a white helmet, scarlet hussar tunic with dark blue facings and gold loops, white breeches and black Napoleon boots. Native ranks wore a blue and gold turban, red alkaluk decorated with gold lace, crimson and gold girdle, blue pyjamas and dark blue shabraque.

BENGAL CAVALRY 1861—1903

The dress of the newly reorganised Bengal Cavalry was laid down, in some detail, in regulations issued in 1863. The eight irregular cavalry regiments which survived the Mutiny were the senior regiments of the new organisation, and were allowed to retain certain traditional features,, notably the alkaluk.

British officers (plates 89 and 98) wore a grey felt helmet, with fittings of lace colour and a plume, in review order. The senior eight regiments wore an alkaluk, the remainder a cavalry tunic of regimental colour with collar and cuffs of facing colour and four rows of black cord hanging loose 'as in the French staff jacket', pouch-belt and waistbelt were of regimental lace, with a black leather pouch. Overalls were blue, except for regiments with green clothing who had green overalls.

Undress (plate 94) included a forage cap, patrol jacket of dark blue with black lace and six black cord loops or a short stable jacket, also worn as a mess jacket. Overalls were blue. Later orders allowed green patrol jackets and overalls for the 2nd and 15th regiments.

Native officers of the senior eight regiments wore a pugri and alkaluk, the remainder (plate 99) wore kurtas (described as loose frock) with piping of facing colour, chain mail

on the shoulder and sky blue or white pyjamas. Sowars wore serge alkaluks or kurtas
for winter, and white 'American drill' for
summer.

In 1864, five regiments (10th, 11th, 13th,
14th and 19th) were converted to lancers. The
next detailed regulations, issued in 1874, laid
down separate distinctions for them. The 1874
regulations specified the following orders of
dress

Review order A	European style
Review order B	Indian style
Drill order	dismounted duties
Marching order A	European style
Marching order B	Indian style
Field day order	
Drill order	
Undress	dismounted duties
Mess order	

As a general rule, the B uniforms were worn
when parading with the Indian ranks, and the
A uniforms were worn when away from the
regiment. Review order A included a white
cork helmet with gilt spike, a cavalry tunic
with five gold or silver loops for the senior
eight regiments, a lancer jacket for the five
lancer regiments, a cavalry tunic with five
black cord loops for the remainder. Pouch-
belts and swordbelts were of regimental lace,
the lancer regiments having a central silk train
of facing colour. Sabretaches and pouches
were of cloth of facing colour, except for the
lancers who had a silver pouch flap. Lancers
wore a crimson and gold girdle; all wore white

Plate 104. 2nd Madras Lancers, c 1897. Naik, havildar and
subedar major in review order. Photograph by Frederick Bremner.

cloth pantaloons and black Napoleon boots.

Review order B included a lungi, kurta
(with no mention of alkaluks for the older
regiments) and cummerbund.

Marching order A included the review order
helmet with drab cover, patrol jacket of regimental colour with five black loops, pouch-belt,
waistbelt and sabretache all plain.

Marching order B included turban, cummerbund and loose kurta of regimental pattern. The other orders of dress were variants
on the above; undress including a forage cap.
Mess order required a stable jacket, now
retained only for this purpose. Badges of rank
were worn on the collar until the early 1880s
when they were transferred to the shoulder
strap (first specified in the 1886 regulations).

As other regiments were converted to lancers, they altered their uniforms accordingly:

Date	Regiment
1885	18th
1886	9th
1890	2nd, 4th, 15th
1896	1st
1900	7th, 8th, 16th, 17th

The only regiments, therefore, never to
serve as lancers were the 3rd, 5th, 6th and
12th. In review order A, some regiments wore
lancer jackets with full plastrons, others only
with lapels turned back.
The regiments were divided as follows on this
point:

Full plastron

1st	14th
8th	15th
10th	18th (to 1901, then
11th	lapels only)
13th	

Lapels only

2nd	16th
4th	17th
7th	18th (after 1901)
9th	19th

Khaki kurtas (plate 95) were introduced,
gradually, for summer marching order, first
for native officers and sowars, and later for
British officers. The only Bengal Cavalry regiment to wear a drab review order jacket was

Plate 105. *Lieutenant-Colonel Cecil D'Urban de la Touche, 1st Poona Horse, c 1880.*

the 3rd, who adopted it in 1881 but changed to blue in 1891.

PUNJAB CAVALRY 1861—1903

The Guides Cavalry followed their own style of uniform, and did not conform to the general pattern of the cavalry of the Punjab Irregular Force. Early regulations (Punjab Irregular Force Dress Regulations 1865) merely note that British officers were to be dressed as the infantry, with necessary modifications for the cavalry branch. A watercolour in the India Office Library of Sir Harry Lumsden reviewing the Guides shows the native ranks in drab turbans and alkaluks.

The 1886 regulations provided more detail. British officers were to wear a white helmet with blue and gold pugri, cavalry tunic with red velvet facings and drab lace, five drab loops down the front, brown leather equipment, silver pouch flap, and drab overalls with double drab stripe and red welts. In 1896 the regiment was ordered to equip as lancers, but

PUNJAB CAVALRY 1861—1903

Title	Changes 1861–1903	Uniform details coat/facings/lace		1903 title
Guides	1874 Queen's Own	1871	drab/red piping/drab	
		1888	drab/red/drab	Queen's Own Corps of Guides (FF)
1st	1890 Prince Albert Victor's Own	1861	blue/silver	
		1868	blue/red/gold	21st Pavo Cavalry (FF)
2nd		1861	red/—/gold	22nd Cavalry (FF)
		1870	red/dark blue/gold	(Sam Browne's from 1904)
3rd		1861	blue/—/silver	
		1868	blue/red/gold	23rd Cavalry (FF)
4th		1870	green/scarlet/gold	disbanded 1882
5th		1870	green/scarlet/gold	25th Cavalry (FF)

Battle honours	Date of action	Date of award	Regiments granted award
ALI MASJID	1878	1881	Guides
CHARASIAH	1879	1881	5th Punjab
KABUL 1879		1881	Guides, 5th Punjab
AHMED KHEL	1880	1881	1st, 2nd Punjab
KANDAHAR 1880		1881	3rd Punjab
AFGHANISTAN 1878—1880		1881	Guides, 1st, 2nd, 5th Punjab
AFGHANISTAN 1879—1880		1881	3rd Punjab
CHITRAL	1895	1897	Guides
MALAKAND	1897	1897	Guides
PUNJAB FRONTIER	1897	1897	Guides

the only difference in dress was the addition of pickers to the pouch-belt. British officers of Guides Cavalry never adopted the kurta.

Native officers wore a blue and gold pugri over a red khulla, drab kurta, with red collar and cuffs, and three drab braids down the front, shoulder chains and red cummerbund. Plate 97 shows a native officer and havildar in field service order, with khaki drill kurtas, brown equipment, red cummerbunds and dark blue puttees.

The five cavalry regiments of the Punjab Irregular Force were instructed to conform to the 1863 regulations for the 'new' Bengal regiments, with certain modifications, which included the use of the letters 'PIF' on accoutrements.

In review order A, British officers (plates 100 and 101) wore black helmets, with silver or gilt fittings and detachable plumes, blue for the 2nd, green and red for the 5th, and black for the remainder. British officers also wore cavalry tunics and facings of regimental colours with five loops down the front, black before 1874, gold after, although some regiments (2nd and 4th) had adopted gold loops before. Swordbelts were worn under the tunic. Pouches and sabretaches were faced with cloth of regimental colour.

Review order B, worn with native ranks, included lungi, kurta of regimental colour, red cummerbund and white breeches. The wide variety of uniforms required by a British officer is shown in plate 96, this included marching order (white helmet, dark blue frock with shoulder chains, Bedford cord breeches),

Plate 106. British officers of the 1st Bombay Light Cavalry, c 1875.

field service order (khaki drill helmet, frock and breeches) and undress (forage cap, dark blue frock and overalls).

Native officers wore the alkaluk until the early 1880s, the 2nd continuing to do so until the turn of the century. By then the remainder wore kurtas with facings of regimental colour and gold lace. Native officers of the 1st Punjab Cavalry had the unusual distinction of wearing three black cord loops across the front of their kurta. All wore red cummerbunds, white breeches and boots.

The sowars followed a similar pattern, with Bedford cord breeches and black boots.

MADRAS CAVALRY 1861—1903

The Madras Bodyguard (plate 92) wore scarlet, with dark blue facings and gold lace. British officers wore a hussar-pattern uniform similiar to the Viceroy's Bodyguard. Native ranks wore a blue and gold lungi, scarlet alkaluk with gold lace, scarlet cummerbund, white breeches and boots.

MADRAS CAVALRY 1861—1903

Title	Changes 1861–1903		Uniform details coat/facings/lace	1903 title
	1897	Governor's Bodyguard	scarlet/dark blue/gold	
1st	1886	1st Madras Lancers	French grey/buff/silver	26th Light Cavalry
2nd	1886	2nd Madras Lancers	French grey/buff/silver	27th Light Cavalry
3rd	1891	3rd Madras Lancers	French grey/buff/silver	28th Light Cavalry
4th	1876	Prince of Wales's	French grey/buff/silver	
	1876		French grey/scarlet/silver	disbanded 1891

Battle honours	Date of award	Regiments granted award
AFGHANISTAN 1879—1880	1881	1st
BURMA 1885—1887	1891	2nd

Plate 107. British and native officers of the Hyderabad Contingent Cavalry, c 1870.

On the basis of photographic evidence, it appears that the pre-Mutiny British officers dress uniform continued in use after the Mutiny, with the British 1855-pattern sloping shako. The official post-Mutiny British officer's dress uniform (plate 102) included a white helmet, with silver fittings and small regimental pugri, French-grey hussar tunic

Plate 108. Uniform of Lieutenant-Colonel E A L Stotherd, 4th Lancers Hyderabad Contingent, c 1900.

Plate 109. A sowar of the Central India Horse, c 1895. Water-colour by Lieutenant A C Lovett.

with buff facings and silver lace, silver pouch-belt, with dark blue silk train, silver fittings and pouch flap, and sky blue overalls with double silver or white stripe. In 1876 the 4th became Prince of Wales's and adopted red facings. They were disbanded in 1891.

In 1886, the 1st and 2nd were converted to lancers. They adopted a French grey lancer tunic (plate 103) with buff facings, a full lancer plastron and silver lace. In 1891 the 3rd also became lancers, and with the disbandment of the 4th, hussar uniform was no longer worn.

Native officers and sowars had adopted the hussar tunic during the Mutiny, but after 1861 they 'went irregular' (plate 104) and wore pugris of blue, French grey and white. They also wore French grey alkaluks, with silver or white lace, and buff facings. Equipment was buff, altered to dark brown in 1878. Overalls were sky blue with double white stripe, and cavalry boots or puttees were worn. The alkaluk remained in use until the 1903 reorganisation. In 1883 khaki blouses were introduced for field service order.

BOMBAY CAVALRY 1861—1903

The Governor-General's Bodyguard (plate 93) wore scarlet with dark blue facings and gold lace. British officers wore a lancer-pattern full dress including white helmet with white and gold pugri, scarlet lancer tunic with half-lapel, crimson and gold girdle, white breeches and boots. Native ranks wore a white and gold turban, scarlet lancer tunic with dark blue facings and yellow lace (the lapels opened to the waist in an unusual fashion), scarlet and yellow girdle.

In the post-Mutiny reorganisation, the 1st Bombay Lancers reverted to light cavalry status, and for a time the three old Light Cavalry regiments followed much the same pattern. The hussar tunic (plate 105) was adopted by British and native officers after the Mutiny, coloured French grey with white facings and silver lace. In undress they wore a loose blouse of regimental colour (plate 106). The sowars wore a French grey blouse, a tunic length version of the alkaluk, lungi and cummerbund. The overalls and breeches for all ranks were blue, with double silver or white stripe.

Plate 110. 2nd Bombay Lancers, review order, c 1890. Chromolithograph after Richard Simkin.

Plate 111 (left). Native officer and sepoy of the 10th Bengal Native Infantry, in field service order, c 1870. Watercolour by Gavin Dring Crawford. Plate 112 (right). Sepoy of the 14th Sikhs, in review order, 1886. Watercolour by Lieutenant A C Lovett.

Title Changes 1861–1903	Uniform details coat/facings/lace	1903 title
Governor-General's Bodyguard		
1863 raised		
1895 reorganised	scarlet/dark blue/gold	Governor-General's Bodyguard
1st	1861 French grey/white/silver	
1880 Lancers	1878 French grey/blue/silver	
1890 Duke of Connaught's Own	1883 dark green/scarlet/gold	31st Duke of Connaught's Lancers
2nd	1861 French grey/white/silver	
1883 Lancers	1883 dark green/white/gold	32nd Lancers
3rd	1861 French grey/white/silver	
1876 Queen's Own	1876 (scarlet facings) 1883 dark green/scarlet/gold	33rd Queen's Own Light Cavalry
1st Poona Horse	1861 dark green/red/gold	
1885 4th Bombay Cavalry (Poona Horse)	1888 dark green/light green/gold 1889 dark green/French grey/gold	
1890 Prince Albert Victor's Own		34th Prince Albert Victor's Own Poona Horse
1st Scinde Horse	1861 dark green/—/silver	
1885 5th Bombay Cavalry (Jacob-Ka-Risallah)	1882 dark green/scarlet/gold	
1888 5th Bombay Cavalry (Scinde Horse)	1888 dark green/white/gold	
2nd Scinde Horse	1861 dark green/—/silver	35th Scinde Horse
1885 6th Bombay Cavalry (Jacob-Ka-Risallah)	1870 dark green/—/gold 1882 dark green/scarlet/gold	
1888 6th Bombay Cavalry (Jacob's Horse)	1888 dark green/primrose/gold	36th Jacob's Horse
1885 7th Bombay Cavalry (Jacob-ka-Risallah)	1861 dark green/buff/gold	
1886 (Baluch Horse)	1898 khaki	
1890 Lancers		37th Lancers (Baluch Horse)
Gujerat Irregular Horse	dark green/white/gold	disbanded 1865
Southern Mahratta Horse		disbanded 1865
3rd Scinde Horse	dark green/scarlet/gold	disbanded 1882
2nd Southern Mahratta Horse		disbanded 1882
2nd Poona Horse		disbanded 1882
4th Scinde Horse		disbanded 1861
3rd Southern Mahratta Horse		disbanded 1861
2nd Gujerat Horse		disbanded 1861

Battle honours	Date of action	Date of award	Regiments granted award
ABYSSINIA	1868	1869	3rd, 3rd Scinde
KANDAHAR 1880		1881	3rd, 4th
AFGHANISTAN 1878—1879		1881	5th
AFGHANISTAN 1878—1880		1881	3rd Scinde
AFGHANISTAN 1879—1880		1881	2nd, 3rd, 4th, 6th
BURMAH 1885—1887		1891	1st
CHINA 1900		1903	3rd

In 1880 the 1st became lancers, and the 2nd became lancers in 1883. The first three regiments altered their uniform colour to dark green with gold lace, in line with the former irregular cavalry regiments which had become the 4th to 7th regiments.

The Bombay Army Dress Regulations for 1884 summarised the uniform changes. British officers in review order B wore a helmet with lungi or pugri, a dark green blouse with gilt shoulder chains (the 1st and 2nd having red piping on the seams), red cummerbund, buckskin breeches and knee boots. Sabretaches were no longer worn. Review order A was, for the 1st and 2nd, a dark green lancer tunic with scarlet or white collar and cuffs, gold lace and crimson and gold girdle. The 3rd wore a dragoon-pattern tunic with scarlet collar and cuffs, gold lace and gold shoulder cords. All three wore dark green overalls with double gold stripes. Drill order included a white helmet with spike, green serge blouse with steel shoulder chains, Bedford cord breeches and dark green puttees. In addition, the British officer had an undress patrol jacket, dark green with five rows of black cord loops, and dark green overalls with gold lace stripe; There was also a stable jacket, increasingly worn only for mess, and a khaki blouse.

Native officers and sowars (plate 110) followed a similar outline, with black leather equipment, red cummerbunds, natural linen pyjamas, and boots or dark green puttees.

The remaining Bombay Cavalry regiments followed the same general rules, replacing the dark green hussar jacket, worn from the late 1850s, with the dragoon tunic worn by the 3rd. The 1st and 2nd Sind Horse retained their helmets until the 1880s.

In 1890 the 7th Bombay Cavalry became lancers and adopted a review order of drab with buff facings and gold lace, red cummerbund, brown leather equipment and drab breeches. From the 1880s, in field service order, all ranks wore a khaki blouse with red cummerbund, drab breeches and dark green puttees (plate 93, left hand figure). In 1901 the 4th changed their uniform colour to blue, and following the 1903 reorganisation, the other Bombay Cavalry regiments did the same.

Plate 113. Gurkha officers of the 1st Gurkha Light Infantry Regiment (late 66th Bengal Native Infantry), c 1870.

HYDERABAD CONTINGENT CAVALRY
1861—1903

The four cavalry regiments of the Hyderabad Contingent had green as their predominant colour. Plate 107 shows that, even in the

Plate 114. Lance-Naik Sher Khan, 26th Punjabis, in drab review order, 1902.

121

HYDERABAD CONTINGENT CAVALRY 1861–1903

1861 title	1890 title	1903 title		Uniform details coat/facings/lace	
1st Cavalry	1st Lancers	20th Deccan Horse		1861	green/white/gold
2nd Cavalry	2nd Lancers	29th Lancers (Deccan Horse)	*all regiments*	1870	rifle green/white/gold
3rd Cavalry	3rd Lancers	disbanded		1883	rifle green/red/gold
4th Cavalry	4th Lancers	30th Lancers (Gordon's Horse)		1890	rifle green/white/gold

Battle honour	Date of award	Regiment granted award
BURMA 1885–1887	1891	3rd

1870s, British and native officers wore practically the same uniform as they did in the 1840s, with a red and gold twisted turban, and green alkaluk heavily decorated with gold lace. The only modern item is a pouch-belt of gold lace with a red train and silver pickers. Photographs show that this uniform was still in use as late as 1884.

The new uniform was described in the 1886 regulations. British officers wore a white helmet with dark blue and gold pugri, a green hussar tunic with gold lace, gold lace pouch-belt with red train, white breeches or green overalls with double gold stripe, and a green patrol jacket with black braid down the front and on the seams. In review order B, British officers wore a dark green kurta with gold lace. Native ranks followed the same pattern with a blue lungi and brown pyjamas.

In 1890, all the regiments were converted to lancers, and British officers adopted a dark green lancer tunic (plate 108) with white facings, gold lace pouch-belt with white train and silver pouch flap, and gold and white girdle. Somewhat surprisingly a contemporary picture (plate 92) shows the dress of the native ranks to be dark blue, with blue lungi, short blue blouse with red cummerbund, light drab breeches and blue puttees.

The regiments were back in green by the time of the 1901 regulations. Native officers wore a dark green lungi, a dark green kurta, with gold lace and silver shoulder chains, red cummerbund, white breeches and black boots. Sowars wore a similar pattern uniform with brown equipment and dark green puttees.

CENTRAL INDIA HORSE 1861–1903

The Central India Horse were adopted after the Mutiny as regiments under the Government of India (plate 92). From their early days, they based their organisation on the Corps of Guides, and adopted their drab uniform, which they always retained (plate 109).

The 1868 regulations specified that British officers were to wear maroon velvet helmets with scarlet plumes (altered in 1886 to drab

CENTRAL INDIA HORSE 1861–1903

1861 title	1903 title	Uniform details coat/facings/lace
1st Central India Horse (formerly Mayne's Horse)	38th Central India Horse	drab/maroon/gold
2nd Central India Horse (formerly Beatson's Horse)	39th Central India Horse	drab/maroon/gold

Battle honours	Date of award	Regiment granted award
KANDAHAR 1880	1881	1st
AFGHANISTAN 1879–1880	1881	1st
PUNJAB FRONTIER 1897	1899	1st

with blue and gold pugri and spike), drab
hussar tunic, with maroon facings, drab lace
and gold lace cords, gold lace pouch-belt with
maroon train and pouch-flap (later altered to
silver), and white breeches or drab overalls.

Native officers wore a blue turban with
white and yellow stripes, drab serge kurta with
gold lace, scarlet cummerbund, yellow pyjamas and boots or red puttees.

BENGAL INFANTRY 1861—1903

The reorganisation of the Bengal Infantry after
the Mutiny retained twelve of the old regular
NI regiments, and brought into the line a
number of old Bengal local corps (13th to
22nd), fourteen of the Punjab regiments (23rd
to 36th), and other levies raised during the
Mutiny (37th to 45th). The old Gurkha regiments, initially included in the line were, a
few months later, removed and formed into a
grouping of their own.

The uniform colour of the new Bengal Infantry remained predominantly scarlet. Although
the new Punjab regiments had mostly worn
drab when first raised, only six of these (20th,
21st, 23rd, 25th, 26th and 27th) retained that
colour. Gurkha regiments not in the main list,
wore dark green, as did the 39th Garhwalis
when raised in 1890.

*Plate 115. Rifleman Chanda Singh Gurung, 4th Gurkha (Rifle)
Regiment, c 1895. Watercolour by Lieutenant A C Lovett.*

*Plate 116. 5th Gurkha (Rifle) Regiment on manoeuvres, in field
service order, 1882.*

123

Title	Formed from	Changes 1861-1903	1903 title	date	Uniform details coat/facings
					red/lemon yellow
1st	21st Native Infantry		1st Brahmans	1886	red/white
2nd	31st Native Infantry	1861 2nd Bengal Light Infantry			
		1876 Queen's Own	2nd (Queen's Own) Rajput		red/buff
		1897 Rajput	Light Infantry	1879	red/blue
3rd	32nd Native Infantry		3rd Brahmans		red/black
4th	33rd Native Infantry	1890 Prince Albert Victor's	4th Prince Albert		
		1897 Rajput	Victor's Rajputs		red/black
5th	42nd Light Infantry	1861 Light Infantry	5th Light Infantry		red/yellow
6th	43rd Light Infantry	1861 Light Infantry			red/pea green
		1897 Jat	6th Jat Light Infantry	1887	red/white
7th	47th Native Infantry	1883 Duke of Connaught's Own	7th Duke of Connaught's		
		1893 Rajput	Own Rajputs		red/yellow
8th	59th Native Infantry	1897 Rajput	8th Rajputs		red/saxon green
				1888	red/white
9th	63rd Native Infantry	1894 (Gurkha Rifle) Regiment	9th Gurkha Rifles		green/black
10th	65th Native Infantry	1897 Jat	10th Jats		red/yellow
11th	70th Native Infantry	1897 Rajput	11th Rajputs		red/yellow
12th	Kelat-i-Ghilzai Regt	1864 (The Kelat-i-Ghilzai)	12th Pioneers (The Kelat-i-Ghilzai Regiment)		red/white
13th	Shakhawati Battalion	1884 (Shakhawati Regiment)	13th Rajputs (The Shekhawati Regiment)		red/dark blue
14th	Regiment of Ferozepore	1864 (The Ferozepore) 1885 Sikhs	14th Ferozepore Sikhs		red/yellow
15th	Regiment of Ludhiana	1864 (Ludhiana) 1885 Sikhs	15th Ludhiana Sikhs		red/green
16th	Regiment of Lucknow	1864 (The Lucknow) 1897 Rajput	16th Rajputs (The Lucknow Regiment)		red/white
17th	Loyal Purbeah Regiment	1864 (Loyal Purbeah)	17th The Loyal Regiment		red/white
18th	Calcutta Native Militia Alipore Regiment	1864 (Alipore Regiment) 1885 Alipore dropped	18th Infantry		red/black
19th	7th Punjab Regiment	1864 (Punjab)	19th Punjabis		red/dark blue
20th	8th Punjab Regiment	1864 (Punjab) 1883 (Duke of Cambridge's Own)	20th (Duke of Cambridge's Own Infantry) (Brownlow's Punjabis)		drab/green
21st	9th Punjab Infantry	1864 (Punjab)	21st Punjabis		drab/red
22nd	11th Punjab Regiment	1864 (Punjab)	22nd Punjabis	1886	red/blue
23rd	15th Punjab Infantry	1864 (Punjab) (Pioneers) 1901 23rd Punjab Pioneers	23rd Sikh Pioneers		drab/chocolate
24th	16th Punjab Infantry	1864 (Punjab)	24th Punjabis		red/white
25th	17th Punjab Infantry	1864 (Punjab)	25th Punjabis		drab/white

Title	Formed from	Changes 1861-1903	1903 title	date	Uniform details coat/facings
26th	18th Punjab Infantry	1864 (Punjab)	26th Punjabis		drab/red
27th	19th Punjab Infantry (Rawalpindi)	1864 (Punjab)	27th Punjabis		drab/red
28th	20th Punjab Infantry (Ferozepore)	1864 (Punjab)	28th Punjabis		red/dark green
29th	21st Punjab Infantry	1864 (Punjab)	29th Punjabis	1886	red/light blue red/blue
30th	22nd Punjab Infantry	1864 (Punjab)	30th Punjabis	1886	red/buff red/white
31st	23rd Punjab Infantry (Cortlandt's Levy)	1864 (Punjab)	31st Punjabis	1886	red/green red/white
32nd	24th Punjab Infantry (Pioneers)	1864 (Punjab)/(Pioneers)	32nd Sikh Pioneers		red/dark blue
33rd	Allahabad Levy	1864 (Allahabad) 1885 Allahabad dropped 1890 Punjabi	33rd Punjabis		red/white
34th	Fatehgarh Levy	1864 (Fatehgarh) 1887 34th (Punjab) Pioneers	disbanded 1882 34th Sikh Pioneers		red/white red/dark blue
35th	Mynpoorie Levy	1864 (Mynpoorie) 1887 35th (Sikh) Regt	disbanded 1882 35th Sikhs		red/white red/yellow
36th	Bareilly Levy	1864 (Bareilly) 1887 36th (Sikh) Regt	disbanded 1882 36th Sikhs		red/blue red/yellow
37th	Meerut Levy	1864 (Meerut) 1887 37th (Dogra) Regt	disbanded 1882 37th Dogras		red/white red/yellow
38th	Agra Levy	1864 (Agra) 1890 (Dogra)	38th Dogras	1892	red/dark blue red/yellow
39th	Aligarh Levy	1864 (Aligarh) 1890 39th (The Garhwali) Regt	disbanded 1890 39th Garhwalis		red/dark blue dark green/black
40th	Shajenpur Levy	1864 (Shajehanpur) 1890 (Baluch) 1892 (Pathan)	40th Pathans	1892	red/white drab/green
41st	Sipni Contingent	1864 (Gwalior) 1900 41st (Dogra) Regt	disbanded 1882 41st Dogras		red/cavalry grey red/yellow
42nd	Cuttack Legion/1st Assam Light Infantry	1885 (Assam) 1886 42nd Gurkha Light Infantry 1891 42nd Gurkha (Rifle) Regt	6th Gurkha Rifles		dark green/black
43rd	Assam Sebundy Corps/ 2nd Assam Light Infantry	1864 (Assam) 1886 43rd Gurkha Light Infantry 1891 43rd Gurkha (Rifle) Regt	7th Gurkha Rifles		dark green/black
44th	Sylhet Light Infantry	1864 (Sylhet) 1886 44th Gurkha Light Infantry 1891 44th Gurkha (Rifle) Regt	8th Gurkha Rifles		dark green/black
45th	Bengal Military Police	1864 (Rattray's Sikh) 1900 46th (Punjab) Regt 1901 47th (Sikhs) Regt 1901 48th Infantry (Pioneers)	45th Rattray's Sikhs 46th Punjabis 47th Sikhs 48th Pioneers	1870	drab/blue red/buff drab/green red/yellow red/emerald green

Pre 1861	Changes 1861-1903	1903 number	Uniform details coat/facings
66th Gurkha LI	1861 1st Gurkha LI Regt		red/white
	1891 1st Gurkha (Rifle) Regt	1st	1886 green/red
Sirmoor Rifle Regt	1861 2nd Gurkha Regt		
	1864 (Sirmoor Rifles)		
	1876 Prince of Wales's Own	2nd	green/red
Kamaon Bn	1861 3rd Gurkha Regt		
	1864 (Kamaon)		
	1887 Kamaon dropped	3rd	green/black
Extra Gurkha Regt	1861 4th Gurkha Regt		
	1891 4th Gurkha (Rifle) Regt	4th	green/black
25th Punjab Inf/ Hazara Gurkha Bn	1861 5th Gurkha Regt		
	1887 5th Gurkha (Rifle) Regt	5th	green/black
Cuttack Legion/ Assam LI	1861 42nd Bengal NI		
	1885 (Assam)		
	1886 42nd Gurkha LI		
	1891 42nd Gurkha (Rifle) Regt	6th	green/black
Assam Sebundy Corps/ 2nd Assam LI	1861 43rd Bengal NI		
	1864 (Assam)		
	1886 43rd Gurkha LI		
	1891 43rd Gurkha (Rifle) Regt	7th	green/black
Sylhet LI	1861 44th Bengal NI		
	1864 (Sylhet)		
	1886 44th Gurkha LI		
	1891 44th Gurkha (Rifle) Regt	8th	green/black
63rd Bengal NI	1861 9th Bengal NI		red/yellow
	1894 9th Gurkha (Rifle) Regt	9th	green/black
	1890 1st Regt Burma Inf		
	1891 10th (1st Burma Bn) Madras Inf		
	1892 10th (1st Burma Rifles) Madras Inf		
	1895 10th Regt (1st Burma Gurkha Rifles) Madras Inf	10th	green/black

Plate 117. Riflemen of the 7th Gurkha Rifles in field service order, with Gurkha hats and khaki drill shorts, c 1905.

Plate 118. Lieutenant-Colonel T Higginson, 1st Punjab Infantry, in review order, c 1897. Photograph by Maull and Fox.

Battle honours	Date of action	Date of award	Regiments granted award
CHINA 1858–1859		1892	7th, 10th, 11th
CHINA 1860–1862		1892	15th, 22nd, 27th
TAKU FORTS	1860	1862	20th, 23rd
PEKIN	1860	1862	20th, 23rd
ABYSSINIA	1868	1869	21st, 23rd
ALI MASJID	1878	1881	6th, 14th, 20th, 27th, 45th, GR 4th
PEIWAR KOTAL	1878	1881	23rd, 29th
CHARASIAH	1879	1881	23rd, 28th
KABUL 1879		1881	23rd, 28th, GR 2nd, 4th
AHMAD KHEL	1880	1881	15th, 19th, 25th, GR 3rd
KANDAHAR 1880		1881	15th, 23rd, 24th, 25th, GR 2nd, 4th
AFGHANISTAN 1878–1879		1881	6th, 12th, 14th, 26th, Mharwara (44th)
AFGHANISTAN 1878–1880		1881	11th, 15th, 19th, 20th, 21st, 23rd, 24th, 25th, 27th, 28th, 29th, 32nd, 39th, 45th, GR 1st, 2nd, 3rd, 4th
AFGHANISTAN 1879–1880		1881	2nd, 3rd, 4th, 5th, 8th, 9th, 13th, 16th, 17th, 22nd, 30th, 31st, Deoli (42nd)
TEL EL KEBIR	1882	1883	7th, 20th
EGYPT 1882		1882	7th, 20th
SUAKIN 1885		1885	15th, 17th
TOFREK	1885	1886	15th, 17th
BURMA 1885–1887		1891	1st, 2nd, 4th, 5th, 10th, 11th, 12th, 16th, 18th, 26th, 27th, 33rd, GR 3rd, 6th, 8th
DEFENCE OF CHITRAL	1895	1897	14th
CHITRAL	1895	1897	13th, 15th, 23rd, 25th, 29th, 30th, 32nd, 34th, 37th, GR 3rd, 4th
MALAKAND	1897	1897	24th, 31st, 35th, 38th, 45th
SAMANA	1897	1899	6th
TIRAH	1897	1899	15th, 30th, 36th, GR 1st, 2nd, 3rd, 4th
PUNJAB FRONTIER	1897	1899	12th, 15th, 20th, 22nd, 24th, 30th, 31st, 34th, 35th, 36th, 37th, 38th, 39th, 45th, GR 1st, 2nd, 3rd, 4th, 9th
PEKIN 1900		1903	7th, 24th
CHINA 1900		1903	2nd, 6th, 14th, 20th, 34th, GR 4th

Those British officers dressed in red, followed closely the uniforms of British line regiments, while those in drab and dark green followed the British rifle regiment pattern of uniform. At first the British shako was retained. However by 1864 wicker helmets 'of Ellwood pattern', with an air pipe crest to give ventilation, and covered in white or drab, had been approved for ordinary duties, to be worn with a pugri of the same colour as the other ranks' turban. By the late 1860s a helmet in white, drab or dark green cloth, with spike, pugri and regimental badge had been adopted for general wear, and remained in use thereafter. The full-dress tunic was scarlet, with collar and cuffs of facing colour and gold lace, worn with a crimson shoulder sash, buff swordbelt and dark blue trousers with narrow red stripe. After 1881 the collar was stiffened and heightened, and badges of rank were transferred from the collar to twisted gold shoulder cords. British officers, of regiments clothed in dark green or drab, wore a rifle pattern tunic with collar and cuffs of facing colour, and black or drab lace loops down the front, black or brown leather pouch-belt, pouch with bronze or silver badge, and green or drab overalls with drab piping.

Undress for British officers included a plain helmet and a loose fitting tunic of regimental

Plate 119. *The Queen's Own Corps of Guides (Infantry), 1897. Sepoy in cold weather drill order, subedar in review order, lance-naik and havildar in hot weather drill order. Photograph by F Bremner.*

colour, with collar and cuffs of facing colour but without gold lace embellishments. The khaki frock was already in use, for field service order, by the time the 2nd Afghan War started (1878–1880), and was officially approved for use in 1885.

Native ranks generally followed a different pattern. Turbans were approved for use in 1860, but many regiments, notably the Gurkhas, never adopted the turban, and several line regiments retained the Kilmarnock cap into the 1890s. In 1863, the so-called 'zouave' jacket was introduced for native ranks (plate 111). It bore little resemblance to the short jacket worn by the French zouaves, but was a scarlet tunic with a panel of facing colour down the front, edged with white piping. Collar, shoulder straps and cuffs were of facing colour, with the regimental number on the shoulder straps and three-button slash cuffs. In the early pattern, the lower skirts of the tunic were cut away in a curve (plate 113) but by the 1890s (plate 112), they had been squared off. In illustrations from that time native officers are shown wearing both the British officers' pattern tunic and the zouave jacket. Indianisation was carried a stage further by the introduction, in 1869, of baggy knickerbocker trousers in dark blue with red piping on the seam, worn in review order with white gaiters, and in other orders of dress with drab puttees or bare legs. Equipment was buff until 1879 when brown equipment was officially authorised.

Native ranks of regiments dressed in drab (plate 114), wore a plain drab tunic with collar, shoulder straps and pointed cuffs of facing colour, brown equipment and drab knickerbockers and puttees. Prior to the 1880s, field service order (plate 111) comprised a drab turban, scarlet frock, dark blue knickerbockers and drab puttees. With the introduction of khaki, all regiments in field service order wore khaki turbans, khaki collarless blouses or short kurtas buttoning to the waist, brown equipment, khaki drill knickerbockers and gaiters or puttees.

From 1864, the 23rd and 32nd were designated pioneers, and they were joined in 1887 by the 34th, and in 1901 by the 48th. They wore normal infantry dress with the addition of extra tools and equipment, and wore crossed axes as their regimental badges.

GURKHA RIFLE REGIMENTS 1861–1903

In 1861, four Gurkha regiments were brought into the line and then, shortly after, formed into a separate grouping of their own, numbered 1st to 4th, with the 5th coming from the Hazara Gurkha battalion of the Punjab Irregular Force. Between 1886 and 1895 a further five regiments formally adopted the Gurkha title taking the sequence to 10 by 1903.

The 1st remained clothed as normal Bengal NI (plate 113) until 1886 when, with some

Plate 120. *8th Madras Infantry, 1897. Subedar, havildar, sepoy and naik in review order. Photograph by F Bremner.*

128

reluctance, they changed to dark green with red facings.

British officers wore a rifle green helmet with green pugri and bronzed fittings, a rifle pattern tunic with black collar and cuffs, black braid, and five black loops down the front, black patent-leather pouch-belt and pouch with bronzed fittings, and rifle green trousers with black stripe. Native ranks (plate 115) wore a rifle green kilmarnock cap with the regimental number on the front, dark green zouave jacket with dark green front panel, until the 1890s, when they were replaced by a plain single-breasted tunic. Black leather waistbelt with silver snake-hook fitting, kukri suspended in a black leather frog on the right hip, dark green knickerbockers and dark green puttees or black leather gaiters.

Drab kilmarnock caps and jackets for field service order were introduced in the early 1880s, worn at first with dark green trousers and puttees (plate 116), and later worn with khaki drill trousers and dark green or khaki puttees. By 1900 (plate 117), they wore a slouch or 'Kashmir' hat, khaki jacket with black equipment, khaki shorts and puttees.

PUNJAB INFANTRY 1861–1903

1851–1865	Punjab Irregular Force
1865–1901	Punjab Frontier Force
1901	'Frontier Force' dropped from title
1903	(Frontier Force) restored

The Sikh and Punjab regiments of the Punjab Irregular Force, later the Punjab Frontier Force all wore drab uniforms, except the 1st Punjab (plate 118) who wore green but conformed in other respects. British officers wore a drab helmet and pugri with silver fittings, drab rifle pattern tunic with collar and cuffs of facing colour, brown leather pouch-belt and pouch, with silver badges, and drab overalls with drab stripe. Undress included a drab frock coat with collar and pointed cuffs of facing colour. Native ranks (plate 122) wore a drab turban, drab jacket with collar, shoulder strap, pointed cuffs and piping of facing colour, brown equipment; drab knickerbockers and brown gaiters or drab puttees. In field service order (plate 119), native ranks wore a

Plate 121. 1st Madras Pioneers, Burma, c 1890. All ranks in field service order.

khaki blouse in place of the tunic. In winter they wore a fur-lined poshteen. A photograph from 1886 shows this blouse with collar and cuffs of facing colour, but by the 1890s, collar and cuffs were plain.

MADRAS INFANTRY 1861–1903

In 1864, four regiments were disbanded, the 42nd, 43rd and 44th as the most junior and the 18th for misconduct. In the same year, flank companies (light, grenadier and rifle companies) were abolished. Reductions in the size of the army, following the recommendations of the Lytton Committee in 1882, led to the disbandment of the 34th to 41st regiments. Madras regiments were experiencing increasing difficulty in recruiting, owing to the increasing availability of alternative employment.

The prevalent attitude towards the Madras Army was expressed by Sir Frederick Roberts, who had been a long time advocate of a unified Indian Army and who was appointed Commander-in-Chief Madras in 1880. He concluded that long periods of peace made the southern Indian soft, and that Madras regiments could not be employed outside the limits of Southern India. On the other hand, because they were better educated, they were more suitable for the technical arms, Roberts had a high opinion of the Madras Sappers and Miners and backed his views by converting the 1st and 4th Regiments to Pioneers in 1883. The 21st were made Pioneers in 1891.

In 1885 Roberts became C-in-C Bengal with supervisory powers over the armies of the

Plate 122. Sepoys of the 3rd Punjab Infantry in field service order and drab review order, 1879. Watercolour by C R Woodthorpe.

Plate 123. 1st Burma Rifles (later 10th Gurkha Rifles). Riflemen in field service marching order.

PUNJAB INFANTRY 1861—1903

Title	Uniform details coat/facings/lace	Changes 1861–1903	1903 title
Guides (Queen's Own, from 1876)	drab/drab/drab	1870 red piping 1882 red facings	Queen's Own Corps of Guides (FF)
SIKH INFANTRY			
1st	drab/yellow/drab		51st Sikhs (FF)
2nd or Hill Regiment	drab/black/drab	1870 drab lace, red piping 1882 red facings	52nd Sikhs (FF)
3rd	drab/yellow/drab	1870 drab/red/drab	53rd Sikhs (FF)
4th	drab/dark green/drab	1888 drab/emerald green/drab	54th Sikhs (FF)
PUNJAB			
1st	green/green/black	1870 red piping	55th Coke's Rifles (FF)
2nd	drab/black/drab		56th Infantry (FF)
3rd	drab/green/green	1870 green piping	disbanded 1882
4th	drab/French grey/drab	1870 khaki/Prussian blue/drab 1898 drab/Prussian blue/drab	57th Wilde's Rifles (FF)
5th	drab/green/drab		58th Vaughan's Rifles (FF)
6th*	red/green/drab	1870 drab/red/drab	59th Scinde Rifles (FF)

*Motto: 'Ready Aye Ready'

130

Battle honours	Date of action	Date of award	Regiments granted award
ALI MASJID	1878	1881	Guides, 1st Sikh
PEIWAR KOTAL	1878	1881	2nd, 5th Punjab
KABUL 1879		1881	Guides, 3rd Sikh, 5th Punjab
CHARASIAH	1879	1881	5th Punjab
KANDAHAR 1880		1881	2nd, 3rd Sikh
AFGHANISTAN 1878—1879		1881	1st Sikh, 1st, 2nd Punjab
AFGHANISTAN 1878—1880		1881	Guides, 2nd Sikh, 5th Punjab
AFGHANISTAN 1879—1880		1881	3rd Sikh, 4th Punjab
CHITRAL	1895	1897	Guides, 4th Sikh
MALAKAND	1897	1897	Guides
TIRAM	1897	1899	3rd Sikh, 2nd Punjab
PUNJAB FRONTIER	1897	1899	Guides, 3rd Sikh, 2nd Punjab
PEKIN 1900		1903	1st Sikh
CHINA 1900		1903	4th Punjab

MADRAS INFANTRY 1861—1903

		Uniform		
1861 title	Changes 1861–1903	all coats red, all lace gold, unless stated		1903 title
		facings 1861	facings 1882	
1st	1883 (Pioneers)	white	white	61st Pioneers
2nd		green	green	62nd Punjabis
3rd	Palamcottah Light Infantry	green	green	63rd Palamcottah Light Infantry
4th	1883 (Pioneers)	orange	yellow 1895 white	64th Pioneers
5th		black	yellow	65th Carnatic Infantry
6th		buff	white	66th Punjabis
7th		sky blue	yellow	67th Punjabis
8th	1902 8th Gurkhas	yellow	white green/black	disbanded 1902
9th		gosling green	dark green	69th Punjabis
10th		red	yellow	disbanded 1891
	1890 1st Regt Burma Infantry 1891 10th (1st Burma Bn) Madras Infantry 1892 10th (1st Burma Rifles) Madras Infantry 1895 10th (1st Burma Gurkha Rifles) Madras Infantry	green/black/black		10th Gurkha Rifles
11th	1902 11th Coorg Infantry	dark green	green	71st Coorg Rifles disbanded 1904
12th		pale buff	white	
	1890 2nd Burma Bn 1901 12th Burma Infantry	drab/white/drab		72nd Punjabis

		Uniform		
		all coats red, all lace gold, unless stated		
1861 title	*Changes 1861–1903*	*facings 1861*	*facings 1882*	*1903 title*
13th		white	white	73rd Carnatic Infantry
14th		buff	white	74th Punjabis
15th		orange	yellow	75th Carnatic Infantry
16th		black	yellow	76th Punjabis
17th		white	white	
	1902 1st Moplah Rifles	green/red/black		77th Moplah Rifles disbanded 1907
18th		red	—	disbanded 1864
19th		sky blue	yellow	79th Carnatic Infantry
20th		green	green	80th Carnatic Infantry
21st	1891 (Pioneers)	pale buff	white	81st Pioneers
22nd		buff	white	82nd Punjabis
23rd	Wallajahabad Light Infantry	green	green	83rd Wallajahabad Light Infantry
24th		green	green	84th Punjabis
25th		green	green	
	1902 2nd Moplah Rifles	green/red/black		78th Moplah Rifles disbanded 1907
26th		green	green	86th Carnatic Infantry
27th		black	yellow	87th Punjabis
28th		black	yellow	88th Carnatic Infantry
29th		white	white	
	1893 7th Burma Bn 1901 29th Burma Infantry	drab/blue/drab		89th Punjabis
30th		white	white	
	1893 5th Burma Bn	drab/black/drab		90th Punjabis
31st	Trichinopoly Light Infantry 1893 6th Burma Bn 1901 31st Burma Light Infantry	dark green drab/cherry/drab	green	91st Punjabis (Light Infantry)
32nd		pale yellow	yellow	
	1891 4th Burma Bn 1901 32nd Burma Infantry	drab/white/drab		92nd Punjabis
33rd		black	yellow	
	1891 3rd Burma Bn 1902 33rd Burma Infantry	drab/yellow/drab		93rd Burma Infantry
34th	Chicacole Light Infantry	dark green		disbanded 1882
35th		pale buff		disbanded 1882
36th	Nundy Regiment	pale buff		disbanded 1882
37th	Grenadier Regiment	blue		disbanded 1882
38th		buff		disbanded 1882
39th		dark green		disbanded 1882
40th		dark green		disbanded 1882
41st		deep green		disbanded 1882

42nd to 52nd Madras Native Infantry were disbanded between 1862–1864

Battle honours	Date of action	Date of award	Regiments granted honour
AFGHANISTAN 1878—1880		1881	21st, 30th
AFGHANISTAN 1879—1880		1881	1st, 4th, 15th
BURMA 1885—1887		1891	1st, 3rd, 5th, 12th, 13th, 14th, 15th, 16th, 17th, 21st, 23rd, 25th, 26th, 27th, 30th
TIRAH	1897	1899	21st
PUNJAB FRONTIER	1897	1899	21st
CHINA 1900		1903	1st, 3rd, 28th, 31st

other presidencies, and he set out on a policy of substituting men of the more warlike and hardy races of the north-west for existing races, in all three armies.

Until the introduction of Burma Battalions in the 1890s, all Madras Infantry wore scarlet. British officers followed the same pattern of uniform as Bengal Infantry, dressed in red. They were permitted drab or white uniforms for summer wear, as early as 1859, although these did not come into general use until the early 1880s. Native ranks, from 1861 to 1883, wore a single breasted scarlet tunic with collar, shoulder straps and cuffs of regimental facing colour, edged with white piping. They had buff equipment, and wore dark blue trousers with red welt. Light Infantry regiments and rifle companies (until their abolition in 1875) wore black equipment. Native officers' badges of rank were worn on the right breast of the tunic, a crown for the subedar-major, crossed swords for the subedar and a single sword for the jemedar. In 1881, badges of rank were altered to silver crown or stars worn on shoulder cords.

In 1883, a zouave jacket like that of the Bengal Infantry was introduced (plate 120). The uniform then comprised a drab turban, scarlet zouave jacket with collar, shoulder straps, panel down front and slash cuffs of facing colour, brown equipment, dark blue knickerbockers with red welt, and drab gaiters or puttees. Service in Burma, in the early 1880s, hastened the use of khaki for summer wear and for field service order for Madras Infantry. Plate 121 shows a group of the 1st Pioneers in Burma. They wear khaki turbans, khaki blouses buttoning to the waist, brown leather equipment, khaki knickerbockers and

puttees. A native officer wears a shorter khaki tunic, similar to that worn by the British officers. The pioneer regiments (1st and 4th from 1883, and 24th from 1891) wore normal infantry uniform with the addition of extra tools to their equipment.

Plate 124. Jemedar of the 2nd Bombay Grenadier Regiment, c 1878.

Plate 125. 16th Bombay Infantry, c 1888. Naik and havildar in review order, sepoy in field service order, British officer and subedar in review order, British officer and drummer in field service order. Watercolour by R W Wymer.

The Burma battalions, recruited from Sikhs and Gurkhas, wore drab in all orders of dress (plate 123). Facing colours were given, but it is not clear whether there was a full dress version of the drab uniform, like that worn by the Punjab regiments. Those shown in plate 123 are dressed like Gurkhas, with khaki kilmarnocks, khaki blouses with black equipment, khaki knickerbockers and dark puttees.

HYDERABAD CONTINGENT INFANTRY
1861—1903

1861 title	1903 title
1st Infantry Hyderabad Contingent	94th Russell's Infantry
2nd Infantry Hyderabad Contingent	95th Russell's Infantry
3rd Infantry Hyderabad Contingent	96th Berar Infantry
4th Infantry Hyderabad Contingent	97th Deccan Infantry
5th Infantry Hyderabad Contingent	98th Infantry
6th Infantry Hyderabad Contingent	99th Deccan Infantry

Battle honours	Date of award	Regiments granted award
BURMA	1891	2nd, 3rd
CHINA	1903	5th

The six infantry regiments of the Hyderabad Contingent followed the same pattern of uniform as the Madras Infantry, and all wore scarlet uniforms with dark green facings and gold lace.

BOMBAY INFANTRY 1861—1903

After the heavy involvement of the armies of all three presidencies in the 2nd Afghan War,

134

Plate 126. *29th Bombay Native Infantry (Duke of Connaught's Own Baluchis). Field firing, in marching order, c 1890. Chromolithograph after Richard Simkin.*

and as a result of the recommendations of the Lytton Council, four Bombay Infantry regiments, the 6th, 11th, 15th and 18th, and the 3rd Sind Horse, were disbanded. In 1889 the 23rd and 25th regiments became rifles, linking with the 4th who had been rifles since 1841. The Bombay Infantry included three types of regiment, line, rifle and Baluchi.

The line were dressed in scarlet, and kept, throughout the period, to a plain single-breasted tunic, ignoring the zouave jacket introduced elsewhere. British officers followed the same pattern as the British Army and other presidencies. Native officers (plate 124) followed the style of the British officers very closely, apart from the turban. Native ranks adopted the tunic as early as 1856, and by 1861 all the native ranks were clothed in a

turban and a tunic which closely followed the undress tunic of the British infantry. In 1880 this was replaced by a new pattern tunic (plate 125), which had collar and shoulder straps of facing colour, but not cuffs, which usually remained plain. The 1st Bombay Grenadiers retained their unusual distinction of wearing grenades on the collar. Equipment was white and then brown. Dark blue knickerbockers, with red welt and white gaiters were worn. Khaki field-service order, introduced at about the same time, included khaki tunic, knicker-bockers and gaiters.

The rifle regiments were the 4th from 1861, and the 23rd and 25th from 1890. All wore rifle green, with red facings and black braid. British officers wore a dark green helmet, rifle pattern tunic, with black patent leather

135

Title	Changes 1861–1903	Uniform details coat/facings/lace	1903 title
1st Grenadier Regiment		red/white/gold	101st Grenadiers
2nd Grenadier Regiment	1876 Prince of Wales's	red/white/gold	102nd Prince of Wales's Own Grenadiers
3rd	1871 Light Infantry	red/sky blue/gold 1888 red/blue/gold 1895 red/black/gold	103rd Mahratta Light Infantry
4th or Rifle Corps		green/red/black	104th Wellesley's Rifles
5th Light Infantry		red/black/gold	105th Mahratta Light Infantry
6th		red/black/gold	disbanded 1882
7th	1900 (Pioneers)	red/white/gold	107th Pioneers
8th		red/white/gold	108th Infantry
9th		red/black/gold	109th Infantry
10th	1871 Light	red/black/gold	110th Mahratta Light Infantry
11th		red/buff/gold	disbanded 1882
12th		red/buff/gold 1884 red/yellow/gold	112th Infantry
13th		red/buff/gold 1882 red/yellow/gold	113th Infantry
14th		red/buff/gold 1882 red/yellow/gold	114th Mahrattas
15th		red/buff/gold	disbanded 1882
16th		red/buff/gold 1882 red/yellow/gold	116th Mahrattas
17th		red/yellow/gold	117th Mahrattas
18th		red/yellow/gold	disbanded 1882
19th		red/yellow/gold	119th Infantry (The Mooltan Regiment)
20th		red/yellow/gold	120th Rajputana Infantry
21st (Marine Battalion)		red/green/gold	121st Pioneers
22nd		red/green/gold	122nd Rajputana Infantry
23rd Light Infantry	1889 Rifles	red/green/gold 1890 green/red/black	123rd Outram's Rifles
24th	1891 (Baluchistan) 1895 Duchess of Connaught's Own	red/green/gold 1891 drab/red/gold	124th Duchess of Connaught's Baluchistan Infantry
25th	1889 Rifles	red/yellow/gold 1890 green/red/black	125th Napier's Rifles
26th	1892 (Baluchistan)	red/light buff/gold 1890 drab/red	126th Baluchistan Regiment
27th 1st Baluch Regiment	1871 Light Infantry	green/red/black	127th Baluch Light Infantry
28th	1888 (Pioneers)	red/yellow/gold	128th Pioneers
29th 2nd Baluch Battalion	1883 (Duke of Connaught's Own	green/red/black	129th Duke of Connaught's Own Baluchis
30th Jacob's Rifles	1881 3rd Baluch Battalion	green/red/black	130th Baluchis

Battle honours	Date of action	Date of award	Regiments granted award
CHINA 1860–1862		1892	5th
ABYSSINIA	1868	1869	2nd, 3rd, 10th, 18th, 21st, 25th, 27th
KANDAHAR 1880		1881	1st, 4th, 19th, 28th, 29th
AFGHANISTAN 1878–1880		1881	1st, 19th, 29th, 30th
AFGHANISTAN 1879–1880		1881	4th, 5th, 8th 9th 10th, 13th, 16th, 23rd, 24th, 27th, 28th
TEL EL KEBIR	1882	1883	29th
EGYPT 1882		1882	29th
SUAKIN 1885		1885	28th
TOFREK	1885	1886	28th
BURMA 1885–1887		1891	1st, 5th, 7th, 23rd, 25th, 27th
TIRAH	1897	1899	28th
PUNJAB FRONTIER	1897	1899	28th
BRITISH EAST AFRICA	1896	1901	24th
BRITISH EAST AFRICA	1897–1899	1901	27th
BRITISH EAST AFRICA	1898	1901	4th
CHINA 1900		1903	22nd, 26th, 30th
BRITISH EAST AFRICA	1901	1905	16th

pouch-belt and pouch, and dark green over-alls. Native ranks wore a dark green frock with red piping down the front and pointed red cuffs.

The original Baluchi regiments, the 27th, 29th and 30th wore (plate 126) a dark green turban, dark green tunic with red collar, cuffs and piping on seams, brown leather equipment, red knickerbockers and white gaiters. British officers wore rifle-pattern uniform with red facings, brown leather pouch-belt with silver ornaments and red overalls.

In 1891 the 24th and 26th were also converted to Baluchi regiments, but were dressed in drab rather than dark green. British officers wore a drab infantry-pattern tunic rather than the rifle pattern, with red collar and cuffs and gold lace, brown leather pouch-belt and pouch. Native ranks wore a drab turban, drab tunic with red facings and piping down front, drab knickerbockers and white gaiters.

ARTILLERY

Apart from the artillery of the Hyderabad Contingent, all native artillery was disbanded after the mutiny, except mountain batteries retained for use on the North-West Frontier. By 1903, there were the following:

No. 1 Kohat Mountain Battery
No. 2 Derajat Mountain Battery
No. 3 Peshawar Mountain Battery
No. 4 Hazara Mountain Battery
No. 5 Bombay Mountain Battery (Quetta)
No. 6 Bombay Mountain Battery (Jullundar)
No. 7 Bengal Mountain Battery (Gujerat)
No. 8 Bengal Mountain Battery (Lahore)
No. 9 Native Mountain Battery (Murree)
No. 10 Native Mountain Battery (Abbotabad)

British officers wore a white helmet with gilt ball and fittings, dark blue tunic with red facings and gold lace, RA pattern pouch-belt and swordbelt, and dark blue trousers with red stripe.

Native ranks (plate 93) wore a red turban (except No. 1 Battery who wore drab). They also wore a blue tunic red collar with yellow grenade, with collar, shoulder straps and cuffs edged in yellow piping, brown leather equipment, blue knickerbockers with broad red stripe and dark blue puttees.

The Hyderabad Contingent retained their artillery until 1903, but adhered very closely to

Royal Artillery dress regulations. Native officers wore a blue pugri with gold stripes and a gold khulla, dark blue knickerbrockers with broad red stripe and dark blue puttees.

SAPPERS AND MINERS

British officers followed the uniform of the Royal Engineers, with a white helmet, a scarlet tunic with black facings and gold lace, and dark blue trousers with red stripe. Native ranks wore a dark blue pugri with red and yellow stripes, a red tunic with dark blue facings and yellow cord, brown leather equipment and dark blue knickerbockers and puttees. Prior to 1887, British and native officers wore a blue serge frock with gold braid for undress. After that, khaki was taken into use.

Native ranks of the Madras Sappers and Miners (plate 127) had distinctive head-dress. Native officers wore a bulky gold and blue turban, and the other ranks wore a dark blue fez, with a narrow red turban around the lower edge.

Plate 127. Queen's Own Madras Sappers and Miners, 1897. Jemedar and sapper in review order, sapper in drill order, colour havildar in marching order. Photograph by F Bremner.

5

Kitchener's Army
1903–1922

In 1902, Lord Kitchener took over as Commander-in-Chief, India, and, despite considerable differences with the Viceroy, Lord Curzon, carried through many far-reaching reforms during his six years in the post.

Kitchener completed the unification of the Indian Army, which had begun in 1895. He abolished the system by which British officers were part of an Indian Staff Corps, as the fact that they were not actually staff but were regimental officers caused confusion, and he returned to the pre-1861 system whereby officer's were gazetted direct to regiments of the Indian Army. Cavalry and Infantry regiments were numbered in one sequence, and references to their former presidential affiliations were dropped.

In the cavalry, the Bengal regiments retained their old numbers up to 19, Punjab regiments took numbers 21 to 25, Madras 26 to 28 and Bombay 31 to 37. The Hyderabad Cavalry were reduced from four regiments to three, and filled gaps, taking the numbers 20, 29 and 30, while the Central India Horse took 38 and 39. The infantry were formed in a similar manner, with Bengal taking 1 to 48, Punjab 51 to 59, Madras 61 to 93, Hyderabad 94 to 99 and Bombay 101 to 130.

While the 61st to 93rd were formed from Madras regiments, the policy advocated by Lord Roberts of replacing old Madras regiments with regiments of Punjabis was continued. In the 1903 reorganisation, three Madras regiments, the 5th, 8th and 11th were disbanded, and a further 15 were converted to Punjabis. In 1907, the 17th and 25th, which had become the 77th and 78th Moplah Rifles, were disbanded.

Kitchener established certain important principles regarding the role and use of the Indian Army. Its main function was defined as the defence of the North-West Frontier rather than internal security. He organised the Army in peacetime into the corps and divisions in which it would fight in wartime, and insisted that all units should be equally capable of carrying out the roles of an army in the field. To that end, he wished to change the existing distribution of military stations, to keep wartime formations reasonably close together in peacetime. However, financial restrictions prevented him from carrying out all his proposals, and, by 1908, the army had been divided into a Northern Army of five divisions and three brigades, and a Southern Army of four divisions, also the Burma Division and the Aden Brigade. This allowed for a field army of 152,000, including nine divisions and eight cavalry brigades, and an internal security force of over 80,000.

1914–1918

THE INDIAN ARMY
IN WORLD WAR I

The Indian Army of 1914 was not prepared for a major war outside India. Although it was supposed to provide up to two divisions for overseas expeditions, no forces had been specifically earmarked or organised for this purpose.

The Army was short of modern equipment, particularly machine-guns and it was largely equipped with secondhand British Army weapons. There were no plans for any substantial expansion in the size of the army.

Nevertheless, between 1914 and 1918, over 1·3 million men served, and from a strength of 155,000 at the outbreak of war, the army had risen to 573,000 by the armistice.

When war was declared, without hesitation, all shades of Indian opinion supported the British cause, so there was no shortage of recruits for the regular army. In addition, the Imperial Service Troops (the old Indian state forces) were offered for service by the Indian princes, to be paid for out of state funds, and over 20,000, including fifteen cavalry regiments, thirteen infantry battalions, three Camel corps, two mountain batteries, and other supporting services, served.

On 8 August 1914, two infantry divisions, the 3rd (Lahore) and 7th (Meerut), and the

Plate 128. King's Indian Orderly Officers, 1911. 30th Lancers, 26th Light Cavalry, 5th Cavalry, 51st Sikhs and 32nd Mountain Battery.

Plate 129. British officers of the 11th (KEO) Lancers (Probyn's Horse), in review order, 1907.

4th (Secunderabad) Cavalry Brigade were mobilised. Within two weeks they had left Karachi, and they landed at Marseilles on 26 September 1914. The first regiment, the 129th Baluchis, went into action on 30 October during the battle of Ypres. The German advance was halted at heavy cost to the Lahore Division.

The Indian Corps was heavily involved at Festubert in December 1914, and at 2nd Ypres in March 1915, where they faced gas for the first time. They were involved at Festubert again in September 1915 and at Loos in September 1915. By late 1915, Kitchener's new divisions began to arrive from Britain. It was decided that the Indian Corps would be better deployed against Turkey in the Middle East, and in November it was withdrawn from the line, sailing from Marseilles to Egypt.

The Secunderabad and Sialkot cavalry brigades remained on the Western front. They took part in the Battle of the Somme in July 1916, and in October were expanded to form the 4th and 5th cavalry divisions. They saw further action in 1917, notably at Cambrai, where they played a valuable part as a mobile reserve during the German counter-attacks.

Britain's main reliance on the Indian Army came in the Middle East. Of prime importance, was the defence of the Suez Canal, essential to the communications of the Empire. This was threatened when Turkey came into the war as allies to Germany. There were also vital British interests to defend in Arabia; in particular, the passage through the Red Sea, and oil supplies from the Persian Gulf. Finally, in East Africa, there was the German Colony of Tanganyika to be liquidated. In all these areas, the Indian Army was well placed to help. Once Turkey had entered the war, the Indian Army Command was given prime responsibility for operations against Turkey and two pincer thrusts, one through the Gulf and Mesopotamia, the other through Gallipoli were mounted, to squeeze Turkey out of the war.

The first priority, however, was the security of the Suez Canal and of the main British base in Egypt, from which operations were mounted to Gallipoli, Palestine and Arabia.

Operations in Mesopotamia began in October 1914, when the 6th (Poona) Division landed in Iraq, and the following month captured Basra. Early in 1915, the British force was increased to two divisions and a cavalry brigade. After beating off some Turkish counter-attacks, one force, under Major-General C V F Townshend, was sent up the Tigris and another was sent in parallel along the Euphrates. Townshend occupied Amara in June and after waiting for reinforcements, went on to take Kut el Amara by storm in September.

Despite misgivings, and difficulties over supplies which could only come by river boat, Townshend pressed on towards Baghdad.

However, at Ctesiphon he came up against a powerful Turkish force, which he could not dislodge, and eventually his losses were so great that he was forced to retire to Kut. The Turks followed up and by late December 1915, Townshend's force had been surrounded in Kut. The siege lasted until April 1916 when he surrendered.

For months, the India Army Command and the War Office debated whether to withdraw from the area, and at last, in December 1916, General Sir F S Maude, with his army built up to 166,000 men, advanced along the Tigris. Kut was retaken in February, and after several days fighting, Indian troops entered Baghdad on 11 March 1917. In the autumn Maude prepared to resume the advance towards the oilfields of Mosul, but he died, and with the growing intensity of operations in Palestine, further offensive action on the Mesopotamian front was curtailed, and many Indian units were transferred to Allenby's army. In October 1918, with Turkey's collapse imminent, a force was hurriedly sent to secure the Mosul oilfields.

Turkish forces made a determined attack on the Suez Canal, early in 1915, but it was successfully beaten off. This was their last attempt, and Egypt was coming into its own as a base for offensive operations. The most daring of these was the landing on the Gallipoli Peninsula. Success there would probably have led to the elimination of Turkey from the war, and would certainly have given great support and encouragement to Russia. However, faulty planning, the lack of surprise and

hardy resistance by the Turks led to failure. The original landings in April 1915 and a further offensive in August were both held. Evacuation was decided upon in November, and successfully carried out in January 1916. The Indian Army was represented on this operation by the 29th Infantry Brigade.

In Arabia, the peacetime garrisons at Aden and Bahrein were reinforced, and successfully held off Turkish attacks. They became bases from which guerilla operations against the Turks could be sustained, most notably by T E Lawrence who organised Arab resistance to the Turks and led them to the gates of Damascus.

During 1916, the British gradually extended the Suez Canal defences into the Sinai Desert, encountering some Turkish resistance as they went. Eventually, in January 1917, the Sinai Peninsula was cleared of Turkish troops and plans were approved to extend the advance into Palestine. However, two British offensives on the Gaza positions in March and April 1917 failed, and General Sir Edmund Allenby was appointed to command. He took time to build up reinforcements and only in October 1917 did he feel ready to continue. His army included the 3rd Lahore Division, the 7th Meerut Division and two independent brigades, the 20th and 49th Indian Infantry Brigades.

At the 3rd Battle of Gaza, Allenby successfully turned the Turkish position and pressed on against strong resistance. After bitter fighting in the Judean Hills, he entered Jerusalem on 9th December. With the western front

Plate 131. British officers of Indian Cavalry, c 1908. 5th Cavalry, 23rd Cavalry, 17th Cavalry, 26th Light Cavalry, 11th Lancers. Daffadar of the 4th Cavalry, jemedar of the 16th Cavalry. Watercolour by Major A C Lovett.

Plate 132. Queen's Own Corps of Guides, c 1908. Sepoy of the Guides Infantry, jemedar of the Guides Cavalry. Watercolour by Major A C Lovett.

Plate 133. 31st Lancers, sowar in field service order, c 1908. Watercolour by Major A C Lovett.

Plate 134. Punjab Regiments, c 1908. The 24th, 67th, 29th, 21st, 25th, 28th, 93rd, 74th, 87th, 76th, 69th, 84th, 72nd and 91st. Watercolour by Major A C Lovett.

Plate 135. Rajputana Regiments, c 1908. The 113th, 104th, 119th, 123rd, 109th, 112th and 122nd. Watercolour by Major A C Lovett.

in crisis, he then lost many of his formations, which were gradually replaced by Indian units, many of which were transferred from the Mesopotamian front. When, in September 1918, Allenby resumed his offensive, Indian troops formed the greater part of his army. At the battle of Megiddo, the Turkish Army was decisively defeated and in the following month, three Turkish armies were destroyed. On 30 October 1918, Turkey capitulated.

In East Africa, German interests were defended by the brilliant von Lettow Vorbeck who kept superior British and Indian forces at bay for four years before surrendering after the armistice of November 1918.

Plate 136. 51st Sikhs, c 1905. Havildar in field service order, sepoy in drab review order, sepoy in winter drill order, sepoy in summer drill order.

INDIAN CAVALRY 1903—1922

1903 title (and changes 1903–1922)	Pre 1903 title	Uniform details coat/facings/lace	1922 amalgamation title with	
1st Duke of York's Own Lancers (Skinner's Horse)	1st Bengal	yellow/black/gold	3rd	1st Duke of York's Own Skinner's Horse
2nd Lancers (Gardner's Horse)	2nd Bengal	blue/light blue/gold	4th	2nd Lancers (Gardner's Horse)
3rd Skinner's Horse	3rd Bengal	blue/yellow/gold	1st	1st Duke of York's Own Skinner's Horse
4th Lancers 1904 4th Cavalry	4th Bengal	scarlet/blue/gold	2nd	2nd Lancers (Gardner's Horse)
5th Cavalry	5th Bengal	scarlet/blue/gold	8th	3rd Cavalry
6th Prince of Wales's Cavalry 1906 6th King Edward's Own Cavalry	6th Bengal	blue/scarlet/gold	7th	18th King Edward's Own Cavalry
7th Hariana Lancers	7th Bengal	red/dark blue/gold	6th	18th King Edward's Own Cavalry
8th Lancers 1904 8th Cavalry	8th Bengal	blue/scarlet/gold	5th	3rd Cavalry
9th Hodson's Horse	9th Bengal	blue/white/gold	10th	4th Duke of Cambridge's Own Hodson's Horse
10th Duke of Cambridge's Own Lancers (Hodson's Horse)	10th Bengal	blue/scarlet/gold	9th	4th Duke of Cambridge's Own Hodson's Horse
11th Prince of Wales's Own Lancers (Probyn's Horse) 1905 11th King Edward's Own Lancers (Probyn's Horse)	11th Bengal	blue/scarlet/gold	12th	5th King Edward's Own Probyn's Horse

1903 title (and changes 1903–1922)	Pre 1903 title	Uniform details coat/facings/lace	1922 amalgamation title with	
12th Cavalry	12th Bengal	blue/blue/gold	11th	5th King Edward's Own Probyn's Horse
13th Duke of Connaught's Lancers (Watson's Horse)	13th Bengal	dark blue/scarlet/silver	16th	6th Duke of Connaught's Lancers (Watson's Horse)
14th Murray's Jat Lancers	14th Bengal	dark blue/scarlet/gold	15th	20th Lancers
15th Lancers (Cureton's Multanis)	15th Bengal	blue/scarlet/gold	14th	20th Lancers
16th Cavalry	16th Bengal	blue/blue/gold	13th	6th Duke of Connaught's Lancers (Watson's Horse)
17th Cavalry	17th Bengal	blue/white/gold	37th	15th Lancers
18th Tiwana Lancers 1906 Prince of Wales's Own 1910 King George's Own	18th Bengal	red/white/gold	19th	19th King George's Own Lancers
19th Lancers (Fane's Horse)	19th Bengal	blue/French grey/silver	18th	19th King George's Own Lancers
20th Deccan Horse	1st Hyderabad	rifle green/white/gold	29th	9th Royal Deccan Horse
Queen's Own Corps of Guides 1911 Queen Victoria's Own Corps of Guides Frontier Force (Lumsden's)	Guides	drab/red/silver	—	10th Queen Victoria's Own Corps of Guides Cavalry (Frontier Force)
21st Prince Albert Victor's Own Cavalry (Frontier Force)	1st Punjab	blue/scarlet/gold	23rd	11th Prince Albert Victor's Own Cavalry (Frontier Force)
22nd Cavalry (Frontier Force) 1904 22nd Sam Browne's Cavalry (FF)	2nd Punjab	scarlet/blue/gold	25th	12th Cavalry (Frontier Force)
23rd Cavalry (Frontier Force)	3rd Punjab	blue/scarlet/gold	21st	11th Prince Albert Victor's Own Cavalry (Frontier Force)
25th Cavalry (Frontier Force)	5th Punjab	dark green/scarlet/gold	22nd	12th Cavalry (Frontier Force)
26th Light Cavalry 1906 Prince of Wales's Own 1910 King George's Own	1st Madras	French grey/buff/silver	30th	8th King George's Own Light Cavalry
27th Light Cavalry	2nd Madras	French grey/buff/silver		16th Light Cavalry
28th Light Cavalry	3rd Madras	French grey/buff/silver		7th Light Cavalry
29th Lancers (Deccan Horse)	2nd Hyderabad	rifle green/white/gold	20th	9th Royal Deccan Horse
30th Lancers (Gordon's Horse)	4th Hyderabad	rifle green/white/gold	26th	8th King George's Own Light Cavalry
31st Duke of Connaught's Lancers	1st Bombay	dark blue/scarlet/gold	32nd	13th Duke of Connaught's Own Lancers
32nd Lancers	2nd Bombay	dark blue/white/gold	31st	13th Duke of Connaught's Own Lancers
33rd Queen's Own Light Cavalry 1911 Queen Victoria's Own	3rd Bombay	dark blue/scarlet/gold	34th	17th Queen Victoria's Own Poona Horse

1903 title (and changes 1903–1922)	Pre 1903 title	Uniform details coat/facings/lace	1922 amalgamation title with	
34th Prince Albert Victor's Own Poona Horse	4th Bombay	dark blue/French grey/gold	33rd	17th Queen Victoria's Own Poona Horse
35th Scinde Horse	5th Bombay	dark blue/white/gold	36th	14th Prince of Wales's Own Scinde Horse
36th Jacob's Horse	6th Bombay	dark blue/primrose/gold	35th	14th Prince of Wales's Own Scinde Horse
37th Lancers (Baluch Horse)	7th Bombay	khaki/buff/gold	17th	15th Lancers
38th Central India Horse 1906 Prince of Wales's Own 1910 King George's Own	1st Central India	drab/maroon/gold	39th	21st King George's Own Central India Horse
39th Central India Horse 1906 Prince of Wales's Own 1910 King George's Own	2nd Central India	drab/maroon/gold	38th	21st King George's Own Central India Horse
1918 40th Cavalry				disbanded 1921
1918 41st Cavalry				disbanded 1921
1918 42nd Cavalry				disbanded 1921
1918 43rd Cavalry				disbanded 1919
1918 44th Cavalry				disbanded 1919
1918 45th Cavalry				disbanded 1919
1918 46th Cavalry (formerly Alwar Lancers)				disbanded 1919

The uniform for the Viceroy's Bodyguard was altered in 1897. British officers wore a white helmet, a scarlet tunic with blue cuffs, white piping and eight rows of scarlet mohair (five above the girdle and three below), and a crimson and gold girdle. Native ranks wore a blue and gold lungi, a scarlet frock coat with dark blue facings and gold lace (the dark blue piping and buttons on the front forming a shape like a lancer plastron), white breeches and black boots.

Bengal Cavalry were little affected by the 1903 reorganisation, retaining their pre-1903 numbers, and apart from a few minor details there was little change in their uniform. Official attempts to reduce the expense of British officers' uniform resulted in trouser stripes being altered from silver or gold to regimental facing colour, and Napoleon-style boots being replaced by knee boots.

The 1913 dress regulations stated that review order A (European as opposed to Indian style) was optional, but it is doubtful if much notice was paid, although in two regiments, the 4th and 14th, British officers never wore Indian style uniform.

In 1904, two further regiments, the 4th and 8th, reverted from lancers to cavalry, but, as with similar earlier changes, they continued to wear lancer features in their uniform. By 1914 most regiments had changed their embroidered pouches for silver. The other trend to be noted in full dress, was the tendency for the officers kurta (plate 129) to become more elaborate and heavily decorated, each regiment developing its own particular style. The appointment of royal colonels-in-chief became more common after 1900, and often led to the incorporation of royal cyphers, the Prince of Wales' feathers, or other monograms into uniform embellishments.

The Punjab Cavalry regiments took the numbers 21 to 25 (less 24, the 4th Punjab Cavalry were disbanded in 1881 and not replaced). The Guides Cavalry remained without number outside the main sequence,

Plate 137. 1/8th Gurkha Rifles, 1914. Bandsmen and subedar in review order, Gurkha officer and Gurkha in field service order, Gurkha in mufti. Watercolour by Richard Simkin.

Plate 138. 'A Rearguard Action'. 4th Gurkha Rifles in action on the North-West Frontier, c 1908. Watercolour by Major A C Lovett.

Plate 139. *Sowar of Indian Cavalry in France, 1915. Water-colour by J Berne Bellecoeur.*

appearing in the Army List after the 39th Central India Horse. There was little change in their uniform after 1903, apart from the general trends noted above. British officers of the 23rd did not wear Indian style uniform.

The three remaining Madras regiments took the numbers 26, 27 and 28. British officers (plate 131) who never wore Indian dress, did not alter their uniform. The Indian ranks finally discontinued the alkaluk and adopted the kurta, in conformity with the rest of the cavalry, although they retained their distinctive French grey colour, with plain collar and cuffs. They also wore shoulder chains, a red cummerbund, brown leather equipment, sky blue overalls, with double white stripe, and black puttees. Native officers (plate 128) wore a dress kurta heavily embellished with silver lace and embroidery.

Plate 140. *Indian ranks of Hodson's Horse on patrol near Vraignes, France, April 1917.*

The Hyderabad Contingent now became part of the Indian Army. Of the cavalry regiments, the 3rd was disbanded and the 1st, 2nd and 4th took the numbers 20, 29 and 30 respectively. The 20th became the Deccan Horse, losing their lancer status. The British officers discontinued lancer uniform and wore Indian dress, including the blue and gold lungi, green kurta with gold lace, shoulder chains on white cloth, gold lace pouch-belt with white train and silver pickers, gilt pouch flap, red cummerbund and white pantaloons. British officers of the 29th and 30th continued to wear lancer uniform, the 29th having a full plastron, the 30th having lapels only. They also wore Indian dress, as the 20th, except that the kurta had white collar and cuffs. Indian ranks changed little from the previous period.

The Bombay Cavalry took the numbers 31 to 37. As noted in chapter 4, the 4th had changed their uniform from green to blue, and after 1903 the remaining regiments did the same, except for the 37th who continued to wear the drab they had adopted in 1890. British officers wore a dark blue lungi and red khulla, dark blue kurta with collar and cuffs of facing colour, shoulder chains, a gold lace pouch-belt with silver pouch flap, gold lancer cap lines, a red cummerbund, white breeches and boots. The lancer regiments wore piping of facing colour along the seams.

Some regiments retained their old green full-dress for dismounted duties. Others adopted a new dark blue uniform. Indian ranks wore a similar blue kurta, with plain collar and cuffs, shoulder chains of facing colour, and piping of facing colour on seams, brown leather equipment, red cummerbund, white breeches and dark blue puttees.

British officers of the 35th adopted a dragoon version of the dismounted full dress, with white helmet, dark blue tunic with white collar, cuffs and piping, gold pouch-belt and waistbelt with red silk train, and dark blue overalls with double white stripe.

In the 36th, British officers adopted a hot-weather full dress of dark blue lungi, khaki kurta, full dress pouch-belt and waistbelt, red cummerbund, khaki breeches and brown boots. In the 37th the British officer's full dress was white helmet, dark blue lancer tunic with

Plate 141. British and Indian officers of the 129th Baluchis, in field service order, shortly before embarkation for France, 1914.

salmon pink collar, full plastron and cuffs, shoulder chains and dark blue overalls with double salmon-pink stripes. Their mounted full dress was a blue and gold lungi over a khaki khulla, khaki kurta with plain collar and cuffs edged in gold lace, shoulder chains on dark blue cloth, brown Sam Browne belt over a red cummerbund, brown leather pouch-belt edged in silver chain with silver whistle and silver pouch flap, khaki breeches and brown boots. Sowars wore a similar uniform, with khaki pugri and khulla, khaki kurta with shoulder chains, brown leather equipment, red cummerbund, khaki breeches and puttees.

The two regiments of the Central India Horse became the 38th and 39th in the new

sequence. British officers continued to wear a dismounted full dress of drab hussar tunic with maroon facings. The only changes were the shape of the helmet and the addition of silver pickers to the pouch-belt. Native officers wore a blue and white lungi, drab kurta with plain collar and cuffs heavily embroidered with gold, gold lace pouch-belt and waistbelt with maroon train, red cummerbund, white breeches and brown boots. The sowars had a kurta with a distinctive pleated front, with red piping around the edges.

To summarise what an Indian cavalry regiment might have worn prior to 1914, the following is an extract from the Regimental Standing Orders of the 8th Cavalry for 1910:

	Order	Weather	Head-dress	Uniform
British officers				
Mounted	review	cold	lungi	kurta
		hot	khaki helmet	khaki jacket
	undress	cold	white helmet	blue serge jacket
		hot	khaki helmet	khaki jacket
	drill	both	khaki helmet	khaki jacket
	field service	both	khaki helmet	khaki jacket (with equipment)

	Order	Weather	Head-dress	Uniform
Dismounted	review	cold	as mounted or white helmet	full dress tunic
		hot	white helmet	white jacket
	undress	cold	as mounted	
		hot	white helmet	white jacket
	drill	both	khaki helmet	khaki jacket
	mess	cold	forage cap	coloured mess jacket
		hot	field service cap	white mess jacket
Indian ranks	review	cold	coloured lungi	coloured kurta
		hot	coloured lungi	khaki kurta
	drill	cold	coloured lungi	khaki kurta
		hot	khaki lungi	khaki kurta
	field service	as drill, with addition of equipment		

INDIAN INFANTRY 1903—1922

Pre 1903	1903 title (and changes 1903–1922)	1922 amalgamation title	See p 124 for uniform details, except
1st Bengal	1st Brahmans	4th/1st Punjab Regiment	
2nd Bengal	2nd (Queen's Own) Rajput Light Infantry 1911 2nd Queen Victoria's Own Rajput Light Infantry	1st (Queen Victoria's Own) Light Infantry Bn, 7th Rajput Regiment	
3rd Bengal	3rd Brahmans	disbanded 1922	
4th Bengal	4th Prince Albert Victor's Rajputs	2nd Bn (Prince Albert Victor's) 7th Rajput Regiment	
5th Bengal	5th Light Infantry	disbanded 1922	
6th Bengal	6th Jat Light Infantry	1st Royal Bn (Light Infantry) 9th Jat Regiment	
7th Bengal	7th Duke of Connaught's Own Rajputs	3rd Bn (Duke of Connaught's Own) 7th Rajput Regiment	
8th Bengal	8th Rajputs	4th/7th Rajput Regiment	
Bhopal Levy	9th Bhopal Infantry	4th Bn (Bhopal) 16th Punjab Regiment	1905 yellow facings drab/chocolate
10th Bengal	10th Jats	3rd/9th Jat Regiment	
11th Bengal	11th Rajputs	5th/7th Rajput Regiment	1905 yellow facings 1908 black facings
12th Bengal	12th Pioneers (The Kelat-i-Ghilzai Regiment)	2nd Bn 2nd Bombay Pioneers (Kelat-i-Ghilzai)	
13th Bengal	13th Rajputs (The Shekhawati Regiment)	10th (Shekhawati) Bn 6th Rajputana Rifles	
14th Bengal	14th Ferozepore Sikhs 1906 Prince of Wales's Own 1910 (King George's Own)	1st Bn (King George's Own) (Ferozepore Sikhs) 11th Sikh Regiment	

Pre 1903	1903 title (and changes 1903–1922)	1922 amalgamation title	See p 124 for uniform details, except
15th Bengal	15 Ludhiana Sikhs	2nd Bn (Ludhiana Sikhs) 11th Sikh Regiment	
16th Bengal	16th Rajputs (The Lucknow Regiment)	10th Bn (The Lucknow Regiment) 7th Rajput Regiment	
17th Bengal	17th The Loyal Regiment	disbanded 1922	
18th Bengal	18th Infantry	4th/9th Jat Regiment	
19th Bengal	19th Punjabis	1st/14th Punjab Regiment	
20th Bengal	20th Duke of Cambridge's Own Infantry (Brownlow's Punjabis)	2nd Bn (Duke of Cambridge's Own) (Brownlow's) 14th Punjab Regiment	
21st Bengal	21st Punjabis	10th/14th Punjab Regiment	
22nd Bengal	22nd Punjabis	3rd/14th Punjab Regiment	
23rd Bengal	23rd Sikh Pioneers	1st/3rd Sikh Pioneers	
24th Bengal	24th Punjabis	4th/14th Punjab Regiment	
25th Bengal	25th Punjabis	1st/15th Punjab Regiment	
26th Bengal	26th Punjabis	2nd/15th Punjab Regiment	
27th Bengal	27th Punjabis	3rd/15th Punjab Regiment	
28th Bengal	28th Punjabis	4th/15th Punjab Regiment	
29th Bengal	29th Punjabis	10th/15th Punjab Regiment	
30th Bengal	30th Punjabis	1st/16th Punjab Regiment	
31st Bengal	31st Punjabis	2nd/16th Punjab Regiment	
32nd Bengal	32nd Sikh Pioneers	2nd/3rd Sikh Pioneers	1905 drab/green
33rd Bengal	33rd Punjabis	3rd/16th Punjab Regiment	
34th Bengal	34th Sikh Pioneers 1921 34th Royal Sikh Pioneers	3rd Royal Bn 3rd Sikh Pioneers	
35th Bengal	35th Sikhs	10th/11th Sikh Regiment	
36th Bengal	36th Sikhs	4th/11th Sikh Regiment	
37th Bengal	37th Dogras 1921 37th (Prince of Wales's Own) Dogras	1st Bn (Prince of Wales's Own) 17th Dogra Regiment	
38th Bengal	38th Dogras	2nd/17th Dogra Regiment	
39th Bengal	39th Garhwal Rifles	18th Garhwal Rifles	
40th Bengal	40th Pathans	5th/14th Punjab Regiment	
41st Bengal	41st Dogras 1st Bn 2nd Bn	3rd/17th Dogra Regiment 10th/17th Dogra Regiment	
Deoli Irregular Force	42nd Deoli Regiment	disbanded 1922	
Erinpoorah Irregular Force	43rd Erinpura Infantry	disbanded 1922	
Mharwara Battalion	44th Mharwara Regiment	disbanded 1922	
45th Bengal	45th Rattrays Sikhs	3rd Bn (Rattray's Sikhs) 11th Sikh Regiment	
46th Bengal	46th Punjabis	10th/16th Punjab Regiment	

Pre 1903	1903 title (and changes 1903–1922)	1922 amalgamation title	See p 125 for uniform details, except
47th Bengal	47th Sikhs 1921 47th Duke of Connaught's Own Sikhs	5th Bn (Duke of Connaught's Own) 11th Sikh Regiment	
48th Bengal	48th Pioneers	4th/2nd Bombay Pioneers	
	1917 49th Bengalis	disbanded 1922	
	1917 4/39th Garhwal Rifles		
	1917 4/39th Kumaon Rifles	1922 att 9th Jat Regiment	
	1918 1/50th Kumaon Rifles	1923 att 19th Hyderabad Regiment	
Guides	Queen's Own Corps of Guides		See p 130
	1911 Queen Victoria's Own Corps of Guides Frontier Force (Lumsden's) Infantry	5th Bn (Queen Victoria's Own Corps of Guides) 12th Frontier Force Regiment	
1st Sikh	51st Sikhs (FF) 1921 The Prince of Wales's Own	1st Bn (Prince of Wales's Own) 12th Frontier Force Regiment	
2nd Sikh	52nd Sikhs (FF)	2nd Bn (Sikhs) 12th Frontier Force Regiment	
3rd Sikh	53rd Sikhs (FF)	3rd Bn (Sikhs) 12th Frontier Force Regiment	
4th Sikhs	54th Sikhs (FF)	4th Bn (Sikhs) 12th Frontier Force Regiment	
1st Punjab	55th Coke's Rifles (FF)	1st Bn (Coke's) 13th Frontier Force Rifles	
2nd Punjab	56th Infantry (FF)	2nd/13th Frontier Force Rifles	
4th Punjab	57th Wilde's Rifles (FF)	4th Bn (Wilde's) 13th Frontier Force Rifles	
5th Punjab	58th Vaughan's Rifles (FF)	5th/13th Frontier Force Rifles	
6th Punjab	59th Scinde Rifles (FF) 1921 59th Royal Scinde Rifles (FF)	6th Royal Bn 13th Frontier Force Rifles	
1st Madras	61st Pioneers 1906 Prince of Wales's Own 1910 King George's Own	1st/1st Madras Pioneers (King George's Own)	red/white
2nd Madras	62nd Punjabis	1st/1st Punjab Regiment	red/green
3rd Madras	63rd Palamcottah Light Infantry	disbanded 1922	red/emerald green
4th Madras	64th Pioneers	2nd/1st Madras Pioneers	red/white
5th Madras	65th Carnatic Infantry	disbanded 1904	red/yellow
6th Madras	66th Punjabis	2nd/1st Punjab Regiment	red/green
7th Madras	67th Punjabis	1st/2nd Punjab Regiment	red/green
9th Madras	69th Punjabis	2nd/2nd Punjab Regiment	red/green
	1917 70th Burma Rifles	20th Burma Rifles	
11th Madras	71st Coorg Rifles	disbanded 1904	green/red
	1917 71st Punjabis	disbanded 1922	
12th Madras	72nd Punjabis	3rd/2nd Punjab Regiment	drab/white
13th Madras	73rd Carnatic Infantry	1st/3rd Madras Regiment	red/white
14th Madras	74th Punjabis	4th/2nd Punjab Regiment	red/yellow
15th Madras	75th Carnatic Infantry	2nd/3rd Madras Regiment	red/yellow

Pre 1903	1903 title (and changes 1903–1922)	1922 amalgamation title	See p 134 for uniform details, except
16th Madras	76th Punjabis	3rd/1st Punjab Regiment	red/green
17th Madras	77th Moplah Rifles	disbanded 1907	green/red
25th Madras	78th Moplah Rifles	disbanded 1907	red/green
19th Madras	79th Carnatic Infantry	3rd/3rd Madras Regiment	red/yellow
20th Madras	80th Carnatic Infantry	disbanded 1922	red/green
21st Madras	81st Pioneers	10th/1st Madras Pioneers	red/white
22nd Madras	82nd Punjabis	5th/1st Punjab Regiment	red/white
23rd Madras	83rd Wallajahabad Light Infantry	4th/3rd Madras Regiment (disbanded 1923)	red/green
24th Madras	84th Punjabis	10th/1st Punjab Regiment	red/green
	1917 Burma Bn		
	1918 85th Burma Rifles		
	1921 Kachin China Bn		
	1921 3rd Bn 70th (Kachin) Rifles	3rd/20th Burma Rifles	
26th Madras	86th Carnatic Infantry	10th/3rd Madras Regiment	red/green
27th Madras	87th Punjabis	5th/2nd Punjab Regiment	red/green
28th Madras	88th Carnatic Infantry	disbanded 1922	red/yellow
29th Madras	89th Punjabis	1st/8th Punjab Regiment	drab/blue
30th Madras	90th Punjabis	2nd/8th Punjab Regiment	drab/black
31st Madras	91st Punjabis (Light Infantry)	3rd/8th Punjab Regiment	drab/cherry
32nd Madras	92nd Punjabis 1921 (The Prince of Wales's Own)	4th Bn (Prince of Wales's Own) 8th Punjab Regiment	drab/white
33rd Madras	93rd Burma Infantry	5th (Burma) Bn 8th Punjab Regiment	drab/yellow
1st Hyderabad	94th Russell's Infantry	1st Bn (Russell's) 19th Hyderabad Regiment	
2nd Hyderabad	95th Russell's Infantry	10th Bn (Russell's) 19th Hyderabad Regiment	
3rd Hyderabad	96th Berar Infantry	2nd Bn (Berar) 19th Hyderabad Regiment	
4th Hyderabad	97th Deccan Infantry	3rd/19th Hyderabad Regiment	
5th Hyderabad	98th Infantry	4th/19th Hyderabad Regiment	
6th Hyderabad	99th Deccan Infantry	5th/19th Hyderabad Regiment	
1st Bombay	101st Grenadiers	1st/4th Bombay Grenadiers	
2nd Bombay	102nd Prince of Wales's Own Grenadiers 1906 King Edward's Own	2nd Bn (King Edward's Own) 4th Bombay Grenadiers	See p 136
3rd Bombay	103rd Mahratta Light Infantry	1st/5th Mahratta Light Infantry	
4th Bombay	104th Wellesley's Rifles	1st Bn (Wellesley's) 6th Rajputana Rifles	
5th Bombay	105th Mahratta Light Infantry	2nd/5th Mahratta Light Infantry	1904 drab/red
	1904 106th Mazara Pioneers	4th Hazara Pioneers	
7th Bombay	107th Pioneers	1st/2nd Bombay Pioneers	
8th Bombay	108th Infantry	3rd/4th Bombay Grenadiers	

Pre 1903	1903 title (and changes 1903–1922)	1922 amalgamation title	See p 136 for uniform details, except
9th Bombay	109th Infantry	4th/4th Bombay Grenadiers	
10th Bombay	110th Mahratta Light Infantry	3rd/5th Mahratta Light Infantry	
	1917 111th Mahrattas	disbanded 1922	
12th Bombay	112th Infantry	5th/4th Bombay Grenadiers	
13th Bombay	113th Infantry	10th/4th Bombay Grenadiers	
14th Bombay	114th Mahrattas	10th/5th Mahratta Light Infantry	
16th Bombay	116th Mahrattas	4th/5th Mahratta Light Infantry	
17th Bombay	117th Mahrattas 1921 117th Royal Mahrattas	5th Royal Bn 5th Mahratta Light Infantry	
19th Bombay	119th Infantry (The Mooltan Regiment)	2nd Bn (Mooltan Regiment) 9th Jat Regiment	
20th Bombay	120th Rajputana Infantry 1921 Prince of Wales's Own	2nd Bn (Prince of Wales's Own) 6th Rajputana Rifles	
21st Bombay	121st Pioneers	10th (Marine) Bn 2nd Bombay Pioneers	red/white
22nd Bombay	122nd Rajputana Infantry	3rd/6th Rajputana Rifles	
23rd Bombay	123rd Outram's Rifles	4th Bn (Outram's) 6th Rajputana Rifles	
24th Bombay	124th Duchess of Connaught's Own Baluchistan Infantry	1st Bn (Duchess of Connaught's Own) 10th Baluch Regiment	
25th Bombay	125th Napier's Rifles	5th Bn (Napier's) 6th Rajputana Rifles	
26th Bombay	126th Baluchistan Regiment	2nd/10th Baluch Regiment	
27th Bombay	127th Baluch Light Infantry 1909 Princess of Wales's Own 1910 Queen Mary's Own	3rd Bn (Queen Mary's Own) 10th Baluch Regiment	
28th Bombay	128th Pioneers	3rd/2nd Bombay Pioneers	red/white
29th Bombay	129th Duke of Connaught's Own Baluchis	4th Bn (Duke of Connaught's Own) 10th Baluch Regiment	
30th Bombay	130th Baluchis 1906 Prince of Wales's Own 1910 King George's Own	5th Bn (King George's Own) (Jacob's Rifles) 10th Baluch Regiment	

Indian Infantry Regiments raised during World War I

	1916 131st United Provinces Regiment	disbanded 1919	
	1918 133rd Regiment	disbanded 1919	
	1918 140th Patiala Regiment	disbanded 1919	
	1918 141st Bikanir Infantry	disbanded 1919	
	1918 142nd Jodhpur Infantry	disbanded 1919	
	1918 143rd Narsingh (Dholpur) Infantry	disbanded 1919	

1918 144th Bharatpur Infantry	disbanded 1919
1918 145th Alwar (Jai Paltan)	disbanded 1919
1918 150th Indian Infantry	disbanded 1919
1918 151st Sikh Infantry	disbanded 1919
1918 152nd Punjabis	disbanded 1919
1918 153rd Punjab Infantry	disbanded 1919
1918 154th Indian Infantry	disbanded 1919
1918 155th Indian Pioneers	disbanded 1919
1918 156th Indian Infantry	disbanded 1919

GURKHA RIFLE REGIMENTS
1903–1922

1903 title	*Changes 1903–1922*
1st Gurkha Rifles (The Malaun Regiment)	1906 1st Prince of Wales's Own Gurkha Rifles (The Malaun Regiment)
	1910 1st King George's Own Gurkha Rifles (The Malaun Regiment)
2nd (Prince of Wales's Own) Gurkha Regiment (The Sirmoor Rifles)	1906 2nd King Edward's Own Gurkha Rifles (The Sirmoor Regiment)
3rd Gurkha Rifles	1907 3rd The Queen's Own Gurkha Rifles
	1908 3rd Queen Alexandra's Own Gurkha Rifles
4th Gurkha Rifles	
5th Gurkha Rifles Frontier Force	
6th Gurkha Rifles	
7th Gurkha Rifles	1907 2/8th Gurkha Rifles
8th Gurkha Rifles	
9th Gurkha Rifles	
10th Gurkha Rifles	1907 the 2/10th Gurkha Rifles became 7th Gurkha Rifles

Uniform

The 1903 reorganisation left the uniform of the Bengal infantry, like that of the Bengal cavalry, relatively unaffected. British officers of regiments in scarlet, followed British infantry uniform and, after 1901, wore a crimson sash around the waist instead of over the shoulder, and followed general Indian Army custom in changing the shape of their helmets.

The major change was in the dress of the Indian ranks, particularly the abolition of the zouave jacket, although judging by the frequency with which it is still worn in those watercolours by A C Lovett drawn before 1911, for the book *Armies of India*, it would appear that the jacket was retained by many regiments for ceremonial occasions (plate 134). Native officers either wore a full dress tunic of a similar pattern to a British officer's, or they wore an officer's version of the new Indian other ranks' uniform. This was a red or green blouse, collarless, buttoned to the waist and almost of knee length. It was piped in facing colour around the neck, down the front on either side of the buttons and on the pointed cuff. The uniform included a cummerbund of facing colour, dark blue (or dark green) knickerbockers with a red welt and white gaiters or dark blue or green puttees.

In regiments dressed in drab, Indian ranks continued to wear the single breasted tunic, with collar, cuffs and piping of facing colour,

Plate 142. 39th Garhwal Rifles, in France, 1915.

as before (plate 134). In some regiments Indian officers wore the same rifle-pattern tunic with brown pouch-belt as did the British officers.

The Frontier Force infantry took the numbers 51 to 59, in the 1903 list, but since all but the 59th were dressed in dark green or drab, they were not affected by the changes.

The Madras regiments which kept their association with Madras, retained the pre-1903 zouave jacket and were virtually unchanged. The regiments, which bore the title 'Carnatic Infantry', were the 63rd, 65th, 73rd, 75th, 79th, 80th, 83rd, 86th and 88th, while the 61st, 64th and 81st formed the Madras Pioneer regiments.

The other former Madras regiments, which had become Punjabis (plate 134), followed the pattern of the Bengal infantry, and, if dressed in scarlet, adopted a tunic with collar, cuffs and piping of facing colour.

Three other regiments were introduced into the Madras section of the line, but proved short-lived. The 71st Coorg Rifles wore a red fez, and a dark green uniform with red facings.

The 77th and 78th Moplah Rifles wore green, faced with scarlet, and scarlet faced with green, respectively.

The Hyderabad Contingent formed numbers 94 to 99 in the new organisation, and all wore scarlet with dark green facings. They changed from the zouave jacket to a scarlet blouse with dark green turban, dark green piping and cummerbund, dark blue knickerbockers with red welts and dark green puttees. According to the 1913 regulations, Indian officers of the 95th, 97th and 99th wore the blouse and those of the 96th and 98th wore tunics.

The Bombay Infantry (plate 135), numbered 101 to 130, all adopted the blouse, whether clothed in scarlet, green or drab. In some regiments Indian officers wore the blouse in others, the tunic. The 124th, for example, had a drab pugri with red khulla, drab blouse with red shoulder straps and piping, red cummerbund with blue and white stripes, red knickerbockers and white gaiters.

The Gurkhas (plate 137), now, at last, settled into a 1st to 10th sequence, changed

Plate 143. Havildar of the 89th Punjabis, in the Middle East, 1918.

their uniform very little from that worn before 1903, and the 1913 regulations followed the details given in the 1901 regulations. Probably the most noticeable change was the adoption, after the Delhi Durbar of 1911, of white helmets in lieu of black, worn in full dress with black lines.

Standing orders, of infantry regiments of the period, are consistent in laying down the following orders of dress:

	Order	Weather	Head-dress	Uniform
British officers	review	cold	white helmet	coloured dress jacket
		hot	khaki helmet	khaki jacket
	drill	cold	white helmet	coloured dress jacket
		hot	khaki helmet	khaki jacket
	Dismounted functions (away from other ranks)	hot	white helmet	white patrol jacket
	field service		khaki helmet	khaki jacket, with equipment
Indian ranks	review	cold	coloured turban	coloured blouse
		hot	khaki turban	khaki blouse
	drill	cold	coloured turban	coloured blouse
		hot	khaki turban	khaki blouse
	field day	hot	as drill, with pouches and waterbottle	
	field service	hot	as drill, with full equipment	

Plate 144. Indian Army, Palestine, 1917. 123rd Outram's Rifles, 121st Pioneers, Mysore Lancers (Imperial Service Troops), 1st KGO Sappers and Miners, Bearer Corps. Watercolour by A E Haswell Miller.

SERVICE DRESS

We have seen earlier how drab uniform first appeared in India (chapter 2), and how it became widely accepted for wear on active service, at first unofficially, during the Indian Mutiny, then gradually achieving official acceptance, so that by the early 1880s, all Indian regiments wore khaki on service. Three other elements of uniform, which also became widely accepted, should be noted. The Sam Browne belt was developed by General Sir Sam Browne VC after he lost an arm in the Mutiny. Having difficulty, thereafter, in managing his sword, he wanted a belt which would hold both sword and pistol safely, whether the wearer was mounted or dismounted. His belt was the prototype of an item which has been taken up by the armies of the world, and is today accepted as a symbol of rank and authority. The introduction of shoulder chains was discussed in chapter 3. By 1900, they were

widely worn by mounted regiments, in both ceremonial and service dress. Puttees were the third element and the use of these grew extensively during the second half of the nineteenth century. They were strips of cloth, originally introduced from the Himalayas, and used in lieu of gaiters by both mounted and dismounted troops. Although they required some expertise to wear smartly, they were comfortable and cheap. There was a parallel development in equipment, from pipeclayed buff to brown leather to webbing, but this will be considered separately for cavalry and infantry.

One feature of field service order was the degree of standardisation involved. In order to provide some regimental distinction, particularly for native ranks, regimental cap badges and shoulder titles were introduced. Prior to 1914, the native ranks did not normally wear

MOUNTAIN BATTERY OFFICER
(PANJABI MUHAMMADAN)

CAVALRY OFFICER
(PANJABI MUHAMMADAN)

INFANTRY OFFICER (DOGRA RAJPUT)

OFFICER, BALUCH LIGHT INFANTRY

Plates 145. Our Indian Army, 1918.
Top: Indian officers of mountain artillery, cavalry, infantry (Dogras) and Baluch Light Infantry.
Bottom: Indian other ranks of Sikh Infantry, Jat Infantry, Frontier Force Infantry and Punjabi Infantry.
Coloured lithographs after W Luker.

NAIK, SIKH INFANTRY

SEPOY, JAT INFANTRY

HAVILDAR, FRONTIER FORCE
(PANJABI MUHAMMADAN)

LANCE-NAIK, PANJABIS
(PANJABI MUHAMMADAN)

159

regimental badges, although there were exceptions in some regiments. In most regiments native ranks were identified by shoulder titles, in brass, worn on khaki-drill shoulder straps. Those British officers having the peaked forage cap for undress, had regimental cap badges of the British pattern.

Cavalry

By the early 1900s, field service order for cavalry had settled into a pattern, which was to see them through World War I with little change. In India and the Middle East, the essential features for British officers were, the broad brimmed solar topee or turban, khaki drill tunic, open at the collar and worn with white shirt and black tie, or khaki shirt and tie, khaki drill breeches and brown boots. The tunic was cut long in the skirt with four patch pockets, each regiment having its own particular style. The officers also wore a Sam Browne belt, with sword frog and, if required, a pistol holster and ammunition pouch.

Standing Orders of the 8th Cavalry give field service marching order as khaki helmet, khaki jacket with shoulder chains, khaki shirt and tie, Sam Browne belt, haversack, field glasses, revolver and holster, cord breeches and field boots.

Indian ranks (plate 136) wore a khaki turban, a khaki drill blouse, buttoning to the waist and with long skirts, khaki breeches and puttees. In peacetime, cummerbunds were worn, but these were usually left off on service, because of their vivid colours. Equipment was brown leather. At the end of the 19th century, many regiments had adopted the Mackenzie equipment (plate 104), consisting of a waist-belt with ammunition pouches, braces with cartridge pockets down the front, and a sword frog. However by the 1900s, this had been largely replaced by an ordinary Sam Browne. The Sam Browne was worn by all ranks, with, if ammunition was required, a leather bandolier of the British 1903 ninety-round pattern. To this, could be added a waterbottle with narrow leather strips or a bayonet and scabbard (plate 133).

At first, those regiments serving on the Western front during World War I wore khaki, with the pugri, serge kurta with shoulder chains and cummerbund (plate 139). The cummerbund was soon discontinued, but pugri and kurtas were worn until the steel helmet was introduced in 1915. Eventually, the regiments changed to home-pattern serge (plate 140). British officers wore the peaked forage cap, serge jacket with badges of rank on the shoulder strap, and khaki stock, later changed to shirt and tie. Eventually changes of officer became so frequent, that few officers were dressed alike, and slacks, ammunition boots and gumboots, or anything sensible and comfortable, became accepted in the trenches. Indian ranks remained more regimental in their appearance, although they also had to make do with issue clothing from Britain.

In the Middle East, the pre-war field service order proved appropriate without much change being necessary. In very hot weather, jackets were discarded and shirt-sleeves worn. In the winter, officers wore home-pattern caps and serge jackets.

Infantry

British officers (plate 141) wore a helmet, peaked forage cap or turban, khaki drill jacket with patch pockets, Sam Browne (some rifle and light infantry regiments had double braces), khaki drill breeches, and puttees or brown field boots. In Gurkha or Garhwali regiments where shorts were worn by the men, the junior British officers also sometimes wore shorts (plate 138). Indian officers (plate 145) wore a turban, and either a khaki jacket similar to the one used by British officers, or a blouse with patch pockets below as well as above the belt. In field service order, officers wore the sword frog, pistol holster, ammunition pouch and binocular case.

Indian other ranks (plate 136) wore a khaki turban, khaki blouse with buttons to the waist, two patch pockets and regimental shoulder title on shoulder strap, khaki knickerbockers and puttees. Gurkha or Garhwali regiments (plates 137 and 138) wore a khaki slouch hat, short khaki drill jacket, buttoning the whole way down, and khaki shorts. Shorts were not popular with other Indian regiments, although they were sometimes worn in the later stages of the war (plate 143).

Equipment was of the British 1903 pattern, introduced after the Boer War. This lasted in British service only until the introduction of web equipment in 1908, but it remained in use in the Indian Army throughout World War I. It comprised a brown leather waistbelt with plain brass buckle, up to four cartridge pouches, a 50-round bandolier, worn over the left shoulder, a canvas haversack, with webbing shoulder strap and webbing harness for greatcoat and blanket, with shoulder straps fastening to the belt in front, and a steadying strap in the rear.

Regiments serving on the Western front in 1914–1915 retained their own head-dress and the 1903 equipment, but were issued with standard British-pattern khaki serge service dress (plate 142). In the Middle East, they continued to wear Indian-pattern khaki drill (plate 143).

Plate 146. The King's Indian Orderly Officers, 1919. 6th Light Infantry, 24th Punjabis, 76th Punjabis, 21st Cavalry and 14th Lancers.

6
Towards Independence 1922–1947

Events in India between 1918 and 1939 were increasingly dominated by demands for independence or at least dominion status. Remarkably though, the Indian Army remained largely insulated from the political upheavals and unrest which these demands produced, and maintained its family spirit and loyalty to its British officers. At the same time, there was a realisation that if political independence was granted, then the army must become self-sufficient, and there had to be Indian officers with the ability and training to take over its command.

In 1919 the Esher Committee on the future of the Indian Army recommended an improved command system, better balance between teeth arms and services, improvement of equipment and a machinery for reinforcement and expansion in war. It also anticipated the eventual removal of British troops from India and the replacement of British officers by Indian officers. To this end, the Prince of Wales's Royal Military College was opened at Dehra Dun, to give a public-school type education to Indians considered suitable for commissioning, and twenty places were reserved for Indians at the Royal Military Academy Woolwich and the Royal Military College at Sandhurst.

Because it was not yet considered appropriate that British officers should serve under the command of Indian officers, eight units were selected for Indianisation. These were:

7th Light Cavalry
16th Light Cavalry
2/1 Punjab Regiment
2/3 Madras Pioneers
5/5 Mahratta Light Infantry
1/7 Rajput Regiment
1/14 Punjab Regiment
4/19 Hyderabad Regiment

Later the 3rd Cavalry, 3/10 Baluch Regiment, 4/12 Frontier Force Regiment and 6/13 Frontier Force Rifles were added. The plan was that Indian officers should be posted in at the bottom and British officers wasted out through promotion or retirement.

The Sandhurst experiment was not a great success, as the Indian cadets were measured against British cadets with a very different background and so, in 1932, the Indian Military Academy at Dehra Dun was opened and by 1938 was commissioning fifty-six Indian officers a year. In October 1939, out of 4,000 officers of the Indian Army, 400 were Indian. By 1945 there were 8,000 out of 42,000.

An officer of the Indian Army could hold one of a number of different types of commission:

BO   British Officer, expatriate officer holding a commission in His Majesty's Land Forces.

KCIO   King's Commission Indian Officer, trained at the RMA or RMC, holding the same commission as the BO, up to 1934.

ICO   Indian Commissioned Officer, holding a commission in His Majesty's Indian Land Forces, trained at the IMA after 1934.

ECO   British officer holding an emergency commission in HM's Land Forces.

IECO   Indian officer holding an emergency commission in HM's Indian Land Forces.

VCO   Viceroy's Commissioned Officer, Indian officer holding a commission in HM's Indian Land Forces, issued by the Viceroy of India. He was commissioned from the ranks and junior to all officers holding a King's commission. Prior to 1934, they were known as Indian officers.

Other recommendations from the Esher Committee were carried out by Lord Rawlinson, the Commander-in-Chief. He divided the Army into four commands, Northern, Eastern, Western and Southern, each under a Lieutenant-General. In 1922 the single battalion regiments of infantry were combined into large regiments of four or five battalions each, with one battalion becoming the 10th or train-

Plate 147. The King's Indian Orderly Officers, 1924. 3/14 Punjab Regiment, 3rd Cavalry, 20th Lancers, 4/13 Frontier Force Rifles, 5/12 Frontier Force Regiment.

ing battalion. The ten Gurkha regiments retained their two-battalion system, without training battalions. In the cavalry, the sillidar system, whereby the soldier provided his own horse and equipment in return for a grant from the government, was abolished. The Indian Territorial Force was formed in 1920 for home defence. It was open to Indians and provided the 11th Bn of each infantry regiment. The Auxiliary Force (India) (AFI), open to Europeans and Anglo-Indians only, continued with its particular role of internal security.

The difficult economic climate of the 1930s led to reductions in British troops in India, from 75,000 to 57,000, and in the Indian Army from 159,000 to 140,000. This led to the disbandment of the whole of the 3rd Madras Regiment, several battalions of other regiments, the four pioneer regiments and the transfer of three cavalry regiments to a training role.

By 1938, it was apparent that the Indian Army required modernisation, and the growing threat of war introduced a note of urgency. In 1938–1939 the Chatfield Committee recommended a programme of modernisation and mechanisation over the following five years. This was only just beginning to take effect when war broke out.

At the outbreak of war, the Army in India had three roles:

1 A field army of four divisions and four cavalry brigades to guard against invasion by or through Afghanistan.

2 Frontier brigades to keep peace on the N W Frontier.

3 Internal Security brigades to keep peace within India.

Although there were no operational headquarters above Brigade, four district headquarters were designated as divisional headquarters on mobilisation. These were:

Rawalpindi District—1st Indian Division

163

Plate 148. King's Indian Orderly Officers 1937. Top row: 12th Cavalry (FF), 20th Lancers. Bottom row: 5th (KEO) Probyn's Horse, 13th DCO Lancers and 15th Lancers.

Quetta District—2nd Indian Division
Meerut District—3rd Indian Division
Deccan District—4th Indian Division

Frontier brigades in Peshawar, Kohat and Waziristan districts were named after their respective territorial area (eg Landi Kotal Brigade). Internal security brigades had their own particular areas, eg Lahore Brigade Area. The field army brigades were responsible for internal security in their respective areas.

In infantry and cavalry brigades, it was usual to have one British infantry battalion or cavalry regiment. All artillery was British, except one regiment, the 1st Indian Field Regiment, formed in 1935, and the mountain batteries, normally allocated to the NW Frontier on attachment for particular operations.

Throughout the period between the wars, the Indian Army was continually involved in operations on the North-West Frontier. World War I had no sooner ended, than Afghanistan, encouraged by revolutionary outbreaks in the Punjab, decided that it was an opportune time to invade. However, the 3rd Afghan War lasted for only a few months, and after the Afghan Army had been repulsed, in the Khyber Pass and at Thal in the Kurram Valley, an armistice was signed. The aftermath of unrest remained and, that autumn, there was a large scale rising among the Waziri tribes, which saw the use of aircraft for the first time on the frontier. The British decided upon a forward policy and built bases at Razmak and Wana, from which punitive expeditions against the tribesmen could be mounted. Intermittent fighting, particularly against the Waziris and Mohmands, continued well into World War 2 and, for the Indian Army the frontier proved an excellent training ground for field-craft and small scale operations.

THE INDIAN ARMY IN WORLD WAR 2

On 3 September 1939, Britain declared war on Germany. The Viceroy also declared war, on behalf of the Government of India, as he was empowered to do without recourse to Congress, as the question of dominion status for India was still under discussion. The Congress Party of India was opposed to this act, and continued to press for Indian Independence throughout the war. Nevertheless, they sympathised with the war aims of the western powers and were vehemently opposed to fascism. The Indian Army loyally supported the crown throughout the war, apart from the subversion by the Japanese of a number of Indian prisoners of war to form the Indian National Army.

As in World War 1, the scale of India's contribution to the British cause was impressive. In 1939, the Army in India totalled 350,000, of which 61,000 were British troops, 205,000 regular Indian troops and 84,000 auxiliary troops including State Forces,

Plate 149. Hodson's Horse 1938. Indian officers in cold weather review order, hot weather drill order and review order, sowar in review order, daffadars in hot weather and cold weather drill order.

Plate 150. Captain John Smyth VC, 2/11 Sikh Regiment, c 1930, in full dress.

N W Frontier units, Auxiliary Forces (India) and the Indian Territorial Force. The Army had fallen way behind in weapons and equipment, but manpower was less of a problem. The new Indian commissioned officers and the Indianisation of units meant that there was a strong nucleus of professional officers and NCOs on which to expand, and by 1945 India had 2·5 million men under arms.

During the war, the Indian Army was mainly involved in the Middle East and South-East Asia. In the Middle East, the Indian Army played a major, if traditional, role in defending oil supplies and protecting Imperial communications. The Japanese invasion of South-East Asia was different. It represented a direct threat to India from an unexpected direction.

Even before war broke out, the Indian Army was called on to honour her Imperial commitments. In August 1939, the 4th Indian Division was sent to Egypt and an infantry brigade was sent to Malaya.

North Africa 1939–1943

Two Indian divisions, the 4th and 5th, together with several smaller formations, served in North Africa. At first their role was defensive. In August 1940, the Italians invaded British Somaliland, in September the Italians crossed the frontier from Libya into Egypt. However, in December 1940 this threat was removed by Wavell's brilliant counter-riposte with the 4th Indian and 7th Armoured divisions, which destroyed eight Italian divisions.

In January 1941, the British attacked the Italian army in Eritrea and Abyssinia with three divisions from Kenya, and two, the 4th and 5th Indian, from Sudan to the north. The Indian troops defeated the Italians at Agordat, and then pursued them to Keren, where, after severe fighting, the Indian troops broke through in March. Addis Ababa, the Abyssinian capital fell and a month later the Italians surrendered. However, before the end of the campaign, the German Army began to arrive in North Africa. The 4th Indian Division was recalled to the Western Desert in March 1941, after Keren, and the 5th Indian Division followed, after the Italian surrender.

The Germans, under Rommel, had gone quickly into action against the allied forces, who were much reduced by the decision to send help to Greece. In June 1941, 4th Indian took part in operation Battleaxe, an unsuccessful attack on Rommel's position on the Sollum Halfaya passes, the failure of which led

Plate 151. 16th Light Cavalry, 1938. Top: British officers in blue patrol dress, cold weather mess dress, hot weather drill order and hot weather mess dress. Bottom left: cold weather field service order. Bottom right: sowar in cold weather field service order.

Plate 152. 1/13 Frontier Force Rifles, 1929–1939. Bandsmen in full dress, British and Indian officers in review order, havildar in review order, sepoy in walking out dress, naik in hot weather field service order.

Plate 153. 2/16 Punjab Regiment, 1938. Colour party, with havildars and Indian officers in review order.

Plate 154. 3/11 Sikh Regiment, 1938. Indian officers in field service order, mufti and review order.

to the replacement of General Wavell by Sir Claude Auchinleck. Wavell went to India as Commander-in-Chief.

Auchinleck's offensive, operation Crusader, was launched in November 1941, and he drove Rommel back to his starting point at El Agheila. Within a month, the Germans launched a counter-attack which caught the 8th Army off guard, and the British, in their turn, were driven back to the Gazala-Bir Hacheim line. 4th Indian was withdrawn to Egypt to refit and was replaced by 5th Indian. In May 1942, Rommel outflanked Bir Hacheim, captured Tobruk and pursued the British back to El Alamein, where the 4th Indian and 18th Indian infantry brigades were hastily brought into the line. Here, at last, Rommel was halted, but Auchinleck was replaced by Montgomery and returned to India as Commander-in-Chief, replacing Wavell

Plate 155. 2/16 Punjab Regiment, 1938. Sepoys in review order, mufti and field service order.

who became Viceroy. Montgomery prepared methodically for the defeat of the Germans, building up a force of three armoured and seven infantry divisions (including 4th Indian, but not 5th which had left for the Far East). The battle of El Alamein began on 23 October, and raged for twelve days before Montgomery's breakthrough came.

Rommel withdrew, out of Libya into Tunisia. 4th Indian came back into the line here, where its expertise in mountain warfare played an important part in the breakthrough. In April 1943, the 8th Army joined up with the 1st Army, which had fought its way from Algeria, and together they launched the final attack on Tunis.

Early in May, the Axis forces in North Africa surrendered.

Middle East 1941–1942

In 1941, the Germans, as part of their preparations for the invasion of Russia, intensified political pressure on the Middle East oil states of Iraq, Syria and Iran. The protection of oil supplies, and the need for a secure supply route to Russia, led to Allied intervention in all three countries, and the 8th and 10th Indian divisions were involved in the elimination of pro-Nazi regimes.

Italy 1943–1945

In 1939 a decision had been taken that the Indian Army would not be called upon to fight the Germans on the mainland of Europe. However, Indian troops had proved themselves in North Africa, particularly in the mountains of Tunisia in the latter stages of the campaign, where much of the terrain was similar to that which would be encountered in Italy. The Indian Army was, therefore, strongly represented in Italy, with the 4th, 8th and 10th Indian divisions and the 43rd Gurkha Lorried Infantry Brigade.

8th Indian Division, brought in from the Middle East, took part in the fighting to establish a bridgehead in the toe of Italy, and took part in the crossing of the River Sangro, which forced the enemy to abandon a valuable part of their winter line.

Early in 1944, however, the Allies came up against the Gustav line, some 100 miles south of Rome, with the great mountain monastery of Cassino as its key. The Gustav line was not broken until May 1944, when 10th Indian played an important part in forcing a crossing of the River Garigliano. At last the Allies broke through into the Liri Valley and the enemy were driven northward beyond Rome, which fell on 4 June 1944.

The Allies pressed on, despite German delaying actions in the Arno Valley and Chianti Hills, involving mainly 10th Indian. By late August, the Allies encountered the next major German defensive position, the Gothic line, which stretched across Italy to the north of the line Pisa-Florence-Ancona. The allied offensive ground to a halt here, as formations were taken for the invasion of Southern France, and those divisions which were left spent a cold winter in trenches facing the German positions. The final stage of the campaign came in April 1945, when the Argenta Gap was taken and the 8th Army broke out into the Po Valley. On 2 May 1945, the German Armies in Italy surrendered.

Plate 156. 20th Burma Rifles, 1937. Rifleman in field service order.

Far East 1941–1945

On 7 December 1941, the Japanese Navy attacked the US fleet at Pearl Harbour. On the following day, Japanese troops began to land in Thailand and Malaya, and attacked the mainland defences of Hong Kong which included two Indian battalions. After two weeks, the colony surrendered.

The garrison of Malaya included the 9th and 11th Indian divisions in the north of the country. However, the Japanese exploited the lack of jungle training and the inadequate equipment of the British and by 31 January 1942, the Japanese had reached the Straits of Johore and threatened Singapore. Another Indian division, the 18th, landed there, but to no avail, and on 15 February the base surrendered with the loss of 60,000 troops, including 32,000 Indians. Having also occupied Thailand, the Japanese then set their sights on Burma, where the garrison comprised an understrength division, the 1st Burma, which was reinforced in January 1942 by the arrival of the 17th Indian Division. When the Japanese attack came, on 15 January, the only other troops available were the 7th Armoured Brigade and a Chinese division. Rangoon fell on 7 March, and there followed a fighting withdrawal of over 1,000 miles to the Assam border. The Japanese, with their troops exhausted and their supply lines over-extended, halted at the Chindwin river.

In September 1942, the 14th Indian Division launched an attack from Chittagong, along the Arakan coastal region, but the advance was delayed by bad weather, and then beset by a supply problem and the lack of experience of the troops in jungle warfare. Early in 1943, the offensive was halted, and in April a Japanese counter-attack pushed the division back to its starting-point. Also in 1943, the first Chindit operation was carried out by 77th Indian Infantry Brigade. Its object was deep penetration into Japanese held territory, with supply from the air, to carry out various sabotage and disruption tasks. It was not an unqualified success, but did show that with proper training the British could match

169

Plate 157. 7th Gurkha Rifles, 1938. Gurkhas in mufti, hot weather review order, field service order, drill order and cold weather review order.

the Japanese at jungle fighting, and it was a great morale-booster.

Both sides planned offensives for 1944. The British launched the 2nd Arakan offensive in December 1943, with the 5th and 7th Indian divisions. They were halted by strong Japanese positions, and in a counter-offensive, were cut off, but were supplied by air while the 26th Indian attacked and inflicted heavy casualties on the Japanese. The Japanese were forced to retreat and failed in their aim of diverting more British forces from the Imphal area.

In March 1944, the Japanese were ready to launch their main offensive against Imphal, which was intended to defeat the British forces on the border and open the way into India. The British accepted a Japanese outflanking movement which cut off Imphal and its associated stronghold, Kohima. Reinforcements, including the 5th Indian, and supplies were brought in by air while ground troops, notably the 23rd Indian and the 7th Indian, from the Arakan, fought to re-establish contact. The ground forces linked up in June, but the battle

raged on until September, by which time, the Japanese, exhausted and having lost the best part of five divisions, were forced out of the hills back into the Chindwin Valley.

Meanwhile, in March-August 1944, further Chindit operations were carried out, using five infantry brigades, on separate operations behind the Japanese lines. Some linked up with the Chinese forces in the north of Burma, and cleared much of Kachin State of Japanese.

In December 1944, the third Arakan offensive was launched by 25th Indian and 82nd West African and, on this occasion, the important

Plate 158. OPPOSITE TOP: 2nd Bombay Pioneers, c 1925. Sepoys of the 128th, in field service order, subedar of the 48th and sepoy of the 107th in full dress, sepoys of the 121st and 12th in field service order. Watercolour by C L P Lawson.

Plate 159. OPPOSITE BOTTOM: Madras Sappers and Miners opening the gates of Fort Dufferin after the fall of Mandalay, 20th March 1945. Watercolour by Mary Sheldon.

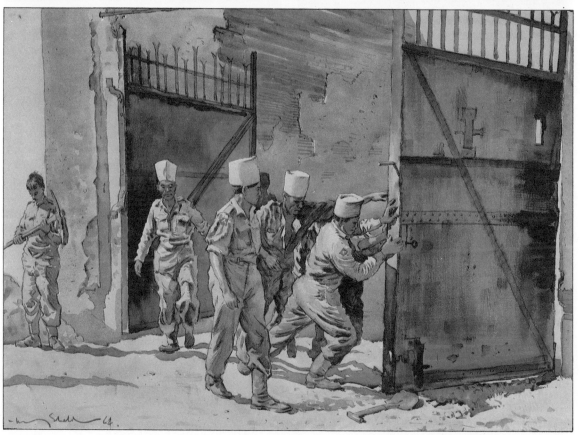

171

Plate 160. The Jungle green drill uniform of an officer of the 18th Cavalry, 1944.

Plate 161. Havildar of the 2/4th Gurkha Rifles in battle dress, 1943. Charcoal drawing by C G Borroman.

coastal airfields were taken. At the same time, the main 14th Army crossed the Chindwin and closed up on the Irrawaddy. Here, in a brilliant piece of deception, Slim managed to convince the Japanese that his main crossing would be near Mandalay, which drew their main forces to that area when, in fact, 4th Corps, with 7th and 17th Indian, were sent over 100 miles further south, to cross near Meiktilia. Both Mandalay and Meiktilia were taken during March 1945, and 14th Army pressed on towards Rangoon. They were just beaten by an air/sea operation against Rangoon, when a Gurkha parachute battalion attacked the coastal defences and the 26th Indian were landed from the sea. The Japanese abandoned Rangoon, and withdrew towards Thailand. As 12th Army pursued them, and preparations were made for the invasion of Singapore, the atomic bomb was dropped on Hiroshima on 6 August 1945,

followed a few days later by another atomic bomb on Nagasaki, and, on the 14th August, Japan surrendered. 'The Indian Army... met the Japanese around Imphal on equal terms and beat them decisively; then it hunted the enemy out of Central Burma and into the sea...'

After the surrender of Germany and Japan, Indian troops were involved in many places as occupying forces, or to restore law and order. In December 1944, 4th Indian were sent to Greece where they remained until December 1946. Indian troops also served in Malaya, Thailand, Indo-China and Indonesia.

In 1946, 10,000 Indian troops, including the 268th Indian Infantry Brigade, went to Japan as part of the British Commonwealth Occupying Force. In the Middle East, Indian troops remained in Egypt, Palestine, Iran and Iraq until 1947.

Plate 162. Indian ranks of the 19th King George V's Own Lancers, Secunderabad, 1944.

Meanwhile, in 1946, the British Government agreed to the independence of India, but the Muslim league demanded a separate state of Pakistan. In 1947, Vice-Admiral Lord Louis Mountbatten was appointed Viceroy with powers to bring independence by June 1948. After negotiations, he recommended partition and brought forward the date to August 1947. After 200 years of service to the British, the old Indian Army had come to an end. The two new states were to have independent armies, and the existing army and its equipment was to be split on a 3:1 basis. However, the way in which classes and religions were mixed in individual regiments caused difficulties, and in many cases, squadrons or companies of a regiment allocated to one country left to join a regiment allocated to the other. After partition there were widespread massacres as Hindu and Moslem populations migrated to their respective countries, but religious fanaticism was notably absent in the army and the transfer was carried out in the best possible spirit.

The Gurkha regiments were a special case, as they were recruited not from India but from the independent kingdom of Nepal. It was decided that the arrangement should continue, with both Britain and India, with the result that after partition, four regiments transferred to the British Army, and six remained with the Indian Army. This arrangement still continues.

The regiments of the present armies of India and Pakistan trace their succession from regiments of the old Indian Army and jealously guard their traditions, battle honours and trophies. Many still maintain close links with their former British officers.

INDIAN CAVALRY 1922–1947

In order to facilitate recruiting and recruit training, the twenty-one cavalry regiments were formed into seven consecutive groups of three regiments each. The 1923 Army List gave blue as the uniform colour for the whole cavalry with the following facings.

Group I   primrose yellow
Group II   scarlet
Group III French grey
Group IV   blue
Group V   scarlet
Group VI   French grey
Group VII blue

While this was, at first, observed in the colour of the mess jacket, in full dress (which was by now only worn for rare ceremonial occasions), regiments adhered to the old full dress of the senior of each pair of regiments.

INDIAN CAVALRY 1922—1947

Pre 1922 title	1922 title
1st Horse	
3rd Horse	1st Duke of York's Own Skinner's Horse
2nd Lancers	
4th Lancers	2nd Lancers (Gardner's Horse)
5th Cavalry	
8th Cavalry	3rd Cavalry
9th Horse	
10th Lancers	4th Duke of Cambridge's Own Hodson's Horse
11th Lancers	
12th Cavalry	5th King Edward's Own Probyn's Horse
13th Lancers	
16th Cavalry	6th Duke of Connaught's Own Lancers
28th Light Cavalry	7th Light Cavalry
26th Light Cavalry	
30th Lancers	8th King George's Own Light Cavalry
20th Horse	
29th Lancers	9th Royal Deccan Horse
Guides	10th Queen Victoria's Own Corps of Guides Cavalry (FF)
21st Cavalry	
23rd Cavalry	11th Prince Albert Victor's Own Cavalry (FF)
22nd Cavalry	
23rd Cavalry	12th Cavalry (FF)
31st Lancers	
32nd Lancers	13th Duke of Connaught's Own Bombay Lancers
35th Horse	
36th Horse	14th Prince of Wales's Own Scinde Horse
17th Cavalry	
37th Lancers	15th Lancers
27th Light Cavalry	16th Light Cavalry
33rd Cavalry	
34th Horse	17th Queen Victoria's Own Poona Horse
6th Cavalry	
7th Lancers	18th King Edward's Own Cavalry
18th Lancers	
19th Lancers	19th King George's Own Lancers
14th Lancers	
15th Lancers	20th Lancers
38th Horse	
39th Horse	21st King George's Own Central India Horse

Changes 1922–1947	Group	Uniform details (coat/facings) 1922	Changes 1922–1947	Allocated to (1947)
1927 Skinner's Horse (1st Duke of York's Own)	I	blue/primrose	1928 yellow/black	India
1935 2nd Royal Lancers (Gardner's Horse)		blue/primrose	1931 blue/light blue	India
		blue/primrose		India
1927 Hodson's Horse (4th Duke of Cambridge's Own Lancers)	II	blue/scarlet		India
1927 Probyn's Horse (5th King Edward's Own Lancers) 1936 (.. King Edward VII's Own ..)		blue/scarlet		Pakistan
1924 6th Duke of Connaught's Own Lancers (Watson's Horse)		blue/scarlet		Pakistan
	III	blue/French grey		India
1937 8th King George V's Own Light Cavalry		blue/French grey		India
1927 The Royal Deccan Horse (9th Horse)		blue/French grey	1928 rifle green/white	India
1927 The Guides Cavalry (10th) (Queen's Victoria's Own FF)	IV	blue/blue	1931 drab/red	Pakistan
1927 Prince Albert Victor's Own Cavalry (FF)		blue/blue	1928 blue/scarlet	Pakistan
1927 Sam Browne's Cavalry (12th FF) 1936 training regiment		blue/blue	1931 scarlet/blue	Pakistan
1927 13th Duke of Connaught's Own Lancers	V	blue/scarlet		Pakistan
1927 The Scinde Horse (14th Prince of Wales's Own)		blue/scarlet		India
1937 training regiment 1940 amalgamated with 12th Cavalry		blue/scarlet	1928 blue/buff	Pakistan
	VI	blue/French grey		India
1927 The Poona Horse (17th Queen Victoria's Own Cavalry)		blue/French grey		India
1936 18th King Edward VII's Own Cavalry		blue/French grey		India
1937 19th King George V's Own Lancers	VII	blue/blue	1928 scarlet/white	Pakistan
1937 training regiment		blue/blue	1931 blue/scarlet	India
1927 The Central India Horse (21st King George's Own Horse) 1937 (.. King George V's Own ..)		blue/blue	1928 drab/maroon	India

Probably the best documentation for this last use of full dress, is the series of photographs of the King's Indian Orderly Officers from 1922 to 1939, showing British and Indian officers in full dress (plates 147 and 148).

As time went on, many regiments reverted to their traditional colour for mess dress also, and these changes were officially recognised in the Army List and the Dress Regulations, for example, the 1931 dress regulations note that Skinner's Horse had resumed their traditional mustard yellow colour.

The mess jacket in the early 1920s was dark blue, with roll collar and pointed cuffs of facing colour, worn with a mess vest and a stiff-fronted shirt, dark blue overalls with two stripes of facing colour and Wellington boots. By 1931, the cavalry had reverted to the old style, with high collar and studs down the front.

The normal uniform of Indian cavalry between the wars is summarised in a number of regimental standing orders, and while there are variations from regiment to regiment, a standard pattern evolves which is confirmed by photographs from the time (plates 149 and 151). Regimental distinctions appeared in the lungi and khulla, and in the shoulder titles, cut of jacket, cummerbund, and pouch-belt and pouch.

British officers

Review order: coloured lungi of regimental pattern, a khaki drill kurta or jacket (many regiments had distinctive features, such as shoulder chains on cloth of facing colour or piping around collar, red for Guides Cavalry, or brass olivets in place of buttons, 18th Cavalry), full dress pouch-belt and pouch, full dress waistbelt over cummerbund of regimental colour, breeches, dark brown or black boots.

Drill Order, cold weather: peaked forage cap, khaki drill jacket, Sam Browne belt and khaki drill breeches. Some regiments wore a 'home pattern' khaki serge jacket for wear in cold conditions, and khaki jerseys were often worn in place of the jacket in the late 1930s (see plate 151.)

Drill order, hot weather: khaki drill pith helmet, probably with pugri or flash incor-porating the regimental colour, khaki drill jacket or shirt sleeves, khaki drill or cotton cord breeches, knee boots or puttees and brown ankle boots.

Field service order: as drill order, with addition of equipment, a typical arrangement being

Equipment	Place
revolver and holster	right thigh
compass	left side
cartridge pouch	right side
field glasses	right side
haversack	left side
waterbottle	under left arm

Undress order (for wear in camp or as orderly officer): dark blue forage cap with black peak and band of facing colour, blue serge jacket with shoulder chains, dark blue overalls with double stripe of facing colour, Wellington boots and spurs.

Mess dress, cold weather: forage cap or field service cap, mess jacket and waistcoat of regimental colour, dark blue overalls with double stripe.

Mess dress, hot weather: field service cap, white drill jacket, soft shirt, cummerbund, dark blue or white overalls.

Indian officers followed the same general rules, except that they wore a khaki lungi in place of a helmet and their khaki drill jacket was buttoned to the neck, with a stand and fall collar.

Indian other ranks

Review order: colour lungi, khaki drill kurta with shoulder chains, Sam Browne belt over coloured cummerbund, khaki breeches, khaki puttees and black ankle boots.

Drill order, cold weather: khaki lungi, khaki drill or serge kurta, Sam Browne belt, bandolier, breeches, puttees and ankle boots.

Drill order, hot weather: as cold weather, except for a grey twill collarless shirt in place of the kurta.

Field service order: as for drill order, with added equipment, including bandolier over left shoulder, haversack under right arm and waterbottle under left arm. Khaki jerseys were often worn in cold weather.

As cavalry regiments became mechanised after 1939 (plates 160 and 162), cavalry features were retained for review order only. For training and operations all ranks wore berets with regimental badges (except for Sikhs who retained their turbans). Officers wore slip-on shoulder titles. In other respects, they adopted standard issue British uniform.

INDIAN INFANTRY 1922–1947

1922 title Regt / Bns	Formed from	Uniform details and changes 1922–1947 coat/facings	Allocated to (1947)
1st Punjab Regiment		scarlet/green	Pakistan
1st Bn	62nd Punjabis		
2nd Bn	66th Punjabis		
3rd Bn	76th Punjabis		
4th Bn	1st Brahmans	disbanded 1931	
5th Bn	82nd Punjabis		
10th Bn	84th Punjabis		
2nd Punjab Regiment		scarlet/green	India
1st Bn	1/67th Punjabis		
2nd Bn	69th Punjabis		
3rd Bn	72nd Punjabis		
4th Bn	74th Punjabis	disbanded 1939	
5th Bn	87th Punjabis		
7th Bn	raised 1941		
10th Bn	2/67th Punjabis		
3rd Madras Regiment	disbanded 1923–1928 reraised 1941	scarlet/emerald green	India
1st Bn	73rd Carnatic Infantry		
2nd Bn	75th Carnatic Infantry		
3rd Bn	79th Carnatic Infantry		
4th Bn (Wallajahabad Light Infantry)	83rd Light Infantry		
10th Bn	86th Carnatic Infantry		
4th Bombay Grenadiers 1945–1946 Indian Grenadiers		scarlet/white	India
1st Bn	101st Grenadiers		
2nd Bn (King Edward's Own)	102nd Grenadiers	1936 (King Edward VII's Own)	
3rd Bn	108th Infantry	disbanded 1930	
4th Bn	109th Infantry	disbanded 1930	
5th Bn	112th Infantry	disbanded 1933	
10th Bn	113th Infantry		
5th Mahratta Light Infantry		scarlet/black	India
1st Bn	103rd Light Infantry		
2nd Bn	105th Light Infantry		
3rd Bn	110th Light Infantry		
4th Bn	116th Mahrattas		
5th Royal Bn	117th Mahrattas		
10th Bn	114th Mahrattas		
6th Rajputana Rifles		dark green/scarlet	India
1st Bn (Wellesley's)	104th Rifles		
2nd Bn (Prince of Wales's Own)	120th Infantry		
3rd Bn	122nd Infantry		
4th Bn (Outram's)	123rd Rifles		
5th Bn (Napier's)	125th Rifles		
6th Bn	raised 1940		
10th Bn (Shekhawati)	13th Rajputs		

1922 title Regt Bns	Formed from	Uniform details and changes 1922–1947 coat/facings	Allocated to (1947)
7th Rajput Regiment		scarlet/blue	India
1st Bn (Queen Victoria's Own Light Infantry)	2nd Light Infantry		
2nd Bn (Prince Albert Victor's)	4th Rajputs		
3rd (Duke of Connaught's Own)	7th Rajputs		
4th Bn	8th Rajputs		
5th Bn	11th Rajputs		
10th Bn (The Lucknow Regiment)	16th Rajputs		
8th Punjab Regiment		drab/blue	Pakistan
1st Bn	1/89 Punjabis		
2nd Bn	90th Punjabis		
3rd Bn	91st Punjabis		
4th Bn (Prince of Wales's Own)	92nd Punjabis		
5th Bn (Burma)	93rd Burma Infantry		
10th Bn	2/89 Punjabis		
9th Jat Regiment		scarlet/blue	India
1st Royal Bn (Light Infantry)	1/6th Light Infantry		
2nd Bn (Mooltan Battalion)	119th Infantry		
3rd Bn	10th Jats		
4th Bn	18th Infantry		
10th Baluch Regiment		drab/blue	Pakistan
1st Bn (Duchess of Connaught's Own)	124th Infantry		
2nd Bn	126th Infantry		
3rd Bn (Queen Mary's Own)	127th Light Infantry		
4th Bn (Duke of Connaught's Own)	129th Baluchis		
5th Bn (King George's Own) (Jacob's Rifles)	130th Baluchis		
11th Sikh Regiment		scarlet/yellow	India
1st Bn (King George's Own) (Ferozepore Sikhs)	14th Sikhs		
2nd Bn (Ludhiana Sikhs)	15th Sikhs	1935 2nd (Royal) Bn scarlet/white	
3rd Bn (Rattray's Sikhs)	45th Sikhs		
4th Bn	36th Sikhs		
5th Bn (Duke of Connaught's Own)	47th Sikhs		
7th Bn	raised 1940		
10th Bn	35th Sikhs		
12th Frontier Force Regiment		drab/red	Pakistan
1st Bn (Prince of Wales's Own) (Sikhs)	51st Sikhs		
2nd Bn (Sikhs)	52nd Sikhs		
3rd Bn (Sikhs)	53rd Sikhs	1935 3rd Royal Bn	
4th Bn (Sikhs)	54th Sikhs		
5th Bn (Queen Victoria's Own Corps of Guides)	Guides Infantry		
10th Bn (Queen Victoria's Own Corps of Guides)	Guides Infantry		
13th Frontier Force Rifles		rifle green/scarlet	Pakistan
1st Bn (Coke's)	55th Rifles		
2nd Bn	56th Rifles		
4th Bn (Wilde's)	57th Rifles		
5th Bn	58th Rifles		
6th Royal Bn (Scinde)	59th Rifles		
10th Bn	2/56th Rifles		
14th Punjab Regiment		scarlet/green	Pakistan
1st Bn	19th Punjabis		

1922 title Regt Bns	Formed from	Uniform details and changes 1922–1947 coat/facings	Allocated to (1947)
2nd Bn (Duke of Cambridge's Own) (Brownlow's)	20th Punjabis		
3rd Bn	22nd Punjabis		
4th Bn	24th Punjabis		
5th Bn	40th Pathans	1934 5th Bn (Pathans)	
10th Bn	21st Punjabis		
15th Punjab Regiment		scarlet/buff	Pakistan
1st Bn	25th Punjabis		
2nd Bn	26th Punjabis	drab/scarlet	
3rd Bn	27th Punjabis		
4th Bn	28th Punjabis		
5th Bn	29th Punjabis		
16th Punjab Regiment		scarlet/white	Pakistan
1st Bn	30th Punjabis		
2nd Bn	31st Punjabis		
3rd Bn	33rd Punjabis		
4th Bn (Bhopal)	9th Infantry		
10th Bn	46th Punjabis		
17th Dogra Regiment		scarlet/yellow	India
1st Bn (Prince of Wales's Own)	37th Dogras		
2nd Bn	38th Dogras		
3rd Bn	1/41st Dogras		
4th Bn	raised 1939		
10th Bn	2/41st Dogras		
18th Royal Garhwal Rifles		dark green/black	India
1st Bn	1/39th Rifles		
2nd Bn	2/39th Rifles		
3rd Bn	3/39th Rifles		
10th Bn	4/39th Rifles		
19th Hyderabad Regiment		scarlet/green	India (as Kumaon Regiment)
1945 The Kumaon Regiment			
1st Bn (Russell's)	94th Infantry		
2nd Bn (Berar)	96th Infantry		
3rd Bn	97th Infantry	disbanded 1931	
4th Bn	98th Infantry		
5th Bn	99th Infantry	disbanded 1924	
6th Bn	raised 1941		
1st Kumaon Rifles	1/50th Rifles	rifle green/black	
2nd Kumaon Rifles	2/50th Rifles	disbanded 1923	
10th Bn (Russell's)	95th Infantry		
20th Burma Rifles		rifle green/scarlet	Burma (1937)
1st Bn	1/70th Rifles		
2nd Bn	2/70th Rifles		
3rd Bn (Kachin)	85th Rifles		
4th Bn (Chin)	4/70th Rifles	disbanded 1925	
10th Bn	5/70th Rifles		
Regiments raised 1941–1945			
Bihar Regiment			India
Assam Regiment			India
Mahar Regiment			India
Ajmer Regiment			India
Chamar Regiment			India
Coorg Battalion			India
Lingayat Battalion			India

Gurkha Rifles

1922 title

1st King George's Own (The Malaun Regiment)		1937 King George V's Own	India
2nd King Edward's Own (The Sirmoor Rifles)		1936 King Edward VII's Own	Britain
3rd Queen Alexandra's Own Gurkha Rifles			India
4th Gurkha Rifles		1924 Prince of Wales's Own	India
5th Royal Gurkha Rifles (Frontier Force)			India
6th Gurkha Rifles			Britain
7th Gurkha Rifles			Britain
8th Gurkha Rifles			India
9th Gurkha Rifles			India
10th Gurkha Rifles			Britain

After World War 1 the Indian infantry no longer wore full dress as an official order of dress, but it was still worn for ceremonial occasions away from the regiment, for example, by the King's Indian Orderly Officers and by Coronation contingents (plate 150). The regimental colour was also used for the officer's mess jacket. It was therefore necessary for the authorities to specify the uniform colour selected for each of the new large regiments: these are given in the Army List. The pre-1914 system still applied, so that for regiments dressed in red, the British officer's full dress was the same as that of British line infantry, except for the head-dress, and for regiments dressed in dark green or drab, rifle-pattern full dress was worn.

The main orders of dress of Indian infantry are summarised below. The term 'coloured' refers to the regimental full dress colour, scarlet, green or drab.

British officers (plate 152)

Review order: Wolseley helmet (replaced in the late 1930s by the pith helmet), with pugri and regimental flash or badge, khaki drill jacket, or, in cold weather, service dress jacket, with regimental shoulder titles, brown leather Sam Browne (with two braces, for some rifle and light infantry regiments), or full dress pouch-belt for rifle and drab regiments. Khaki breeches, leather leggings and ankle boots. Rifle regiments wore black leather equipment.

Drill order, cold weather: pith helmet or service dress cap, khaki drill jacket or jersey, Sam Browne, knickerbockers, puttees and brown ankle boots.

Drill order, hot weather: pith helmet or service dress cap, khaki shirt with rank badge and regimental shoulder title, shorts, khaki hosetops (or regimental colour) with regimental flash, short puttees.

Undress order: coloured forage cap, coloured patrol jacket and overalls, full dress sword slings.

Field service order, cold weather: khaki lungi or pith helmet, khaki drill jacket with lanyard and whistle, web equipment, (including haversack on back, with waterbottle, revolver and holster, ammunition pouch and field glass case.

Field service order, hot weather: as for cold weather, but with khaki shirt, shorts, hosetops with regimental flash, puttees and ankle boots. On NW Frontier operations, the silver-grey OR's pattern shirt was usually worn.

Mess dress, cold weather: coloured forage cap, coloured mess jacket and vest, stiff white shirt, coloured overalls and Wellington boots.

Mess dress, hot weather: white drill jacket, soft shirt, coloured cummerbund, coloured or white overalls, Wellington boots and spurs.

Indian officers (plates 153 and 154) wore the same uniform as British officers, except that they wore the lungi in place of the helmet or cap, and their khaki drill jacket was buttoned to the neck with stand and fall collar. In review order they wore knickerbockers and spats. In drill order they wore, as an alternative to the jacket, a blouse buttoning to the waist, with two patch pockets.

Indian other ranks (plates 152, 155 and 156) Review order: coloured or khaki lungi, usually incorporating the regimental badge; khaki drill kurta, later replaced by a long khaki drill jacket, with regimental shoulder titles (in cold weather a thicker serge version might be worn). 1903 brown leather equipment, with waistbelt, ammunition pouches and bayonet frog, khaki knickerbockers

---

ARTILLERY, ENGINEERS, SAPPERS AND MINERS, PIONEERS 1922—1947

		Full dress uniform details coat/facings
Royal Artillery		dark blue/scarlet
	1st to 19th Mountain Batteries	dark blue/scarlet
1935 Indian Artillery, 1st Indian Field Regiment		scarlet/dark blue
1941 Corps of Royal Indian Engineers		scarlet/dark blue
1925 Indian Signals Corps		scarlet/dark blue
Queen Victoria's Own Madras Sappers and Miners	1941 Madras Sappers and Miners Group	
King George's Own Bengal Sappers and Miners	1937 King George V's Own Bengal Sappers and Miners	
	1941 Bengal Sappers and Miners Group	scarlet/dark blue
Royal Bombay Sappers and Miners	1941 Royal Bombay Sappers and Miners Group	
	1946 Bombay Sappers and Miners Group, Royal Indian Engineers	scarlet/dark blue
1st Madras Pioneers	1929 The Corps of Madras Pioneers	
	1933 disbanded	scarlet/white
1st Bn (King George's Own) 61st Pioneers		
2nd Bn 64th Pioneers		
10th Bn 81th Pioneers		
2nd Bombay Pioneers	1929 The Corps of Bombay Pioneers	
	1933 disbanded	scarlet/white
1st Bn 107th Pioneers		
2nd Bn (Kelat-i-Ghilzie) 12th Pioneers		
3rd Bn 128th Pioneers		
4th Bn 48th Pioneers		
10th Bn (Marine Bn) 121st Pioneers		
3rd Sikh Pioneers	1929 The Corps of Sikh Pioneers	
	1933 disbanded	
	1941 reraised as The Sikh Light Infantry	
	1947 India	scarlet/blue
1st Bn 1/23rd Pioneers		
2nd Bn 32nd Pioneers		
3rd Royal Bn 34th Pioneers		
10th Bn 2/23rd Pioneers		
1/4th Hazara Pioneers	1929 Hazara Pioneers	
	1933 disbanded	scarlet/blue

white gaiters or khaki puttees, and black ankle boots.

Drill order, cold weather: as review order, except khaki lungi and puttees rather than gaiters.

Drill order, hot weather: khaki lungi, collarless silver-grey flannel shirt, shorts, hosetops, short puttees, ankle boots.

Field service order, cold weather: khaki lungi, khaki drill jacket or jersey, web equipment, knickerbockers, puttees, boots. The British 1908 pattern web equipment was issued to the Indian Army after World War 1 (plate 156), and lasted well into World War 2. The equipment comprised a 3in. waistbelt, 2in. braces, two cartridge carriers (each with five pouches), bayonet frog, waterbottle and carrier, haversack or valise with supporting straps, entrenching tool and carrier.

Field service order, hot weather: khaki lungi, silver-grey shirt with cloth shoulder titles, web equipment, shorts, hosetops, short puttees, boots.

Gurkha and Garhwali regiments (plate 157) followed similar rules to Indian infantry. British officers wore rifle features, including black equipment and puttees. In field service order, they wore the double felt slouch hat. Gurkha ranks wore the black kilmarnock cap for review and drill order, and the slouch hat for field service order. They also wore black leather or web equipment, dark green puttees and black boots.

ARTILLERY, ENGINEERS, ETC 1922–1947

In general, artillery, engineers and other corps (plate 159) followed infantry dress rules. Pioneers (plate 158), until their disbandment in 1933, followed the general rules of the infantry, with the addition of extra pioneer equipment.

SERVICE DRESS 1939–1945

During the early stages of World War 2, the

Plate 163. Indian officers of 10th Indian Division, in Italy, 1944, wearing battle dress with turbans or berets.

Plate 164. *1st Indian Field Artillery Regiment, in jungle green drill, jungle hat and 1937 pattern web equipment, being inspected by Field-Marshal Sir Claude Auchinleck, 1944.*

pre-war field service order proved eminently suitable for operations in the Middle East, and features such as the woollen jersey were taken up by the British Army. Gradually, however, with the replacement of personnel, uniform became devoid of any regimental, or even national, distinction, and standard British issue items were adopted. Steel helmets replaced pugris, for all but Sikhs, who continued to wear turbans, and Gurkhas who, where possible, preferred their slouch hats. The 1908-pattern web equipment was gradually replaced by the 1937-pattern (plate 161), comprising a narrower web belt, with two large 'basic' pouches, bayonet frog, waterbottle and carrier, small pack, large pack with shoulder straps attaching to the pouches. Web gaiters were available, although many Indians regiments continued to wear short puttees. Officers and tank crews (plate 162) wore brace attachments with revolver holster and ammunition pouch, in addition, officers had binocular case, compass case and an officer's

haversack.

When operations moved to Tunisia and Italy, where cold weather was encountered, the British 1937-pattern battle dress was issued to Indian troops (plate 163).

On the outbreak of war in the Far East, Indian troops who were sent to Malaya wore their khaki drill field service order. This proved unsuitable for jungle operations, and was replaced by British jungle green drill (plate 160 and 164), worn with Gurkha slouch hat, the jungle hat or beret, cellular shirt, web equipment painted or blancoed dark green, long or short jungle green trousers, web gaiters or short puttees and boots.

After the war, some Indian regiments returned to their pre-war ceremonial dress, and restored features such as the lungi, khaki drill jacket, leather belt, knickerbockers and white gaiters. Others adapted and smartened their wartime uniform (plate 165), and wore a beret (in scarlet, green or drab according to their regimental colour), a khaki drill jacket or shirt, 1937-pattern web equipment, khaki drill trousers and boots.

After 1947, many Indian and Pakistan regiments retained features of their British uniform which may still be seen today, particularly in ceremonial dress.

Plate 165. 1st Punjab Regiment, colour party, c 1947.

Glossary

Ranks — Cavalry

Rissaldar Major	Senior Indian officer
Rissaldar	Lieutenant
Jemedar	2nd Lieutenant
Kot Daffadar	Troop sergeant major
Daffadar	Sergeant
Lance-daffadar	Corporal
Acting lance-daffadar	Lance-Corporal
Sowar	Trooper

Ranks — Infantry

Subedar-Major	Senior Indian officer
Subedar	Lieutenant
Jemedar	2nd Lieutenant
Havildar-Major	Sergeant-Major
Havildar	Sergeant
Naik	Corporal
Lance-Naik	Lance-Corporal
Sepoy	Private

Terms used in text

Alkaluk	Long coat reaching to the knees with embroidered bib-shaped front.
Chapplis	Sandals.
Cummerbund	Long waist sash.
Golundauz	Native artillery.
Janghirs	Shorts.
Khulla	Pointed cap worn within the turban by some castes.
Kurta	Long coat reaching to the knees.
Lascar	Camp follower, labourer.
Lungi	Turban, term generally used for cavalry.
Plastron	Panel of facing colour on front of lancer jacket.
Poshteen	Skin coat with fur worn inside.
Pugri	Turban, or cloth wound around helmet.
Puttee	Cloth wound around leg.
Pyjamas	Loose trousers worn by cavalry.
Shabraque	Decorated saddle cloth.
Sillidar	Soldier of irregular cavalry providing his own horse and equipment.
Tarleton	British light dragoon helmet with bearskin crest, 1784–1812.
Turban	Cloth wound into a head-dress.
Zouave jacket	Jacket with panel of facing colour down front.

Index of Indian Regimental Names

This index includes the special names of the regiments listed in the tables throughout the book. It also includes titles of regiments in the following categories which are not included in the book.

Auxiliary Forces (India)
State Forces
Frontier Battalions

The following abbreviations are used:

AF	Auxiliary Forces
Aux	auxiliary
Bde	brigade
Be	Bengal
Bn	battalion
Bo	Bombay
Cav	cavalry
CIH	Central India Horse
Con	contingent
Fen	fencible
Fro	frontier units
Gds	guards
GR	Gurkha Rifles
HCC	Hyderabad Contingent Cavalry
HCI	Hyderabad Contingent Infantry
Hse	horse
Inf	infantry
Irr	irregular
Loc	local
Lt	light
Ma	Madras
Mil	militia
Mtd	mounted
NC	Native Cavalry
NI	Native Infantry
Pio	pioneers
Pol	police
Pu	Punjab
Regt	regiment
Rlwy	railway
S and M	sappers and miners
SF	State Forces
Si	Sikh
Vol	volunteers

The dates given refer either to the date of formation of the regiment, or to the date when the title given was first used.

Aden Rifles, 1917, AF Inf, —.
Agra Levy, 1857, 38 Be Inf, 97.
Agra Vol Rifles 1876, AF Inf, —.
Ajmer Regt, 1941, Inf, 179.
Alexander's Horse, 1857, Be Irr Cav, 93.
Aligarh Levy, 1857, 39 Be Inf, 97.
Allahabad Levy, 1857, 33 Be Inf, 97.
Allahabad Lt Hse, 1890, AF Cav, —.
Allahabad Rifles, 1871, AF Inf, —.
Alwar Inf, 1918, 145 Inf, 155.
Alwar Lancers, 1902, 46 Cav, 146.
Arracan Bn, 1830, Be Lo Inf, 68.
Assam Bengal Rlwy Bn, 1901, AF Inf, —.
Assam Regt, 1941, Inf, 179.
Assam Rifles (1–5), 1917, Pol Bn, —.
Assam Sebundy Corps, 1835, 43 Be NI, 65; 2/8 GR, 155.
Assam Valley Lt Hse, 1891, AF Cav, —.
Baddeley's Frontier Hse, 1814, 4 Be Loc Hse, 19.
Baluch Bn, 1844, 27 Bo NI, 80.
Baluch Hse, 1903, 37 Lan, 146.
Baluchistan Vol Rifles, 1886, AF Inf, —.
Bangalore Bn, 1868, AF Inf, —.
Banaras Infantry, 1826, SF, —.
Bareilly Levy, 1857, 36 Be Inf, 97.
Bareilly Con, 1871, AF Inf, —.

Baria Ranjit Inf, 1909, SF, —.
Baroda Cav, 1886, SF, —.
Baroda Gds, 1886, SF, —.
Barrow's Vol Cav, 1857, AF–Cav, —.
Behar Hse, 1857, AF–Cav, —.
Behar Irr Cav, 1857, Be Irr Cav, 95.
Beatson's Hse, 1858, 2 CIH, 96.
Belooch Bn, 1844, 27 Bo NI, 80.
Benares Hse, 1857, Be Irr Cav, 95.
Benares Levy, 1818, 61 Be NI 28.
Bencoolen Bn, 1822, 15 Be Lo Inf, 68.
Be Mil Pol Bn, 1856, Be Loc Inf, 68; 45 Be Inf, 125.
Bengal–Nagpur Rlwy Bn, 1888, AF Inf, —.
Bengal & WNW Rlwy Bn, 1892, AF–Inf, —.
Bengal Yeomanry Cav, 1857, AF–Cav, 92.
Berar Inf, 1797, 3 HCI, 81.
Bhagalpur Hill Rangers, 1792, 3 Be Loc Inf, 68.
Bharatpur Inf, 1918, 144 Inf, 155.
Bharatpur Jaswant H'hold Inf, 1921, SF, —.
Bhavnagar Lan, 1892, SF, —.
Bhavnagar Inf, 1872, SF, —.

Bhawalpur Inf, 1827, SF, —.
Bhopal Contingent, 1845, Be Irr Con, —.
Bhopal Lan, 1902, SF, —.
Bhopal Inf, 1911, SF, —.
Bhopal Levy, 1858, Be Irr Inf, 97; 9 Inf, 150.
Bihar Lt Hse, 1862, AF Cav, —.
Bihar Regt, 1941, Inf, 179.
Bikanir Camel Corps, 1884, SF, —.
Bikanir Inf, 1918, 141 Inf, 179.
Bikanir Lan, 1884, SF, —.
Bombay, Baroda & Central India Rlwy Regt, 1877, AF Inf, —.
Bombay Bn, 1877, AF Inf, —.
Bo Fen Regt, 1803, 17 Bo NI, —.
Bo Lt Hse, 1886, AF Cav, —.
Bo Lt Patrol 1933, AF Cav, —.
Brahmans, 1903, 1 Inf, 150; 3 Inf, 150.
Brownlow's Punjabis, 1903, 20 Inf, 151.
Bundelkund Legion, 1838, Be Irr Con, —; 34 Be NI, 64; Be Irr Hse, 54.
Burma Bns, 1890, Ma Inf, 4.
Burma Rlwy Vol Corps, AF Inf, —.
Cachar Mtd Vols, 1883, AF Cav, —.
Calcutta Lt Hse, 1872, AF Cav, —.
Calcutta Native Mil, 1795, 1 Be Lo Inf, 13.

Calcutta Presidency Bn, 1888, AF Inf, —.
Calcutta Scottish, 1911, AF Inf, —.
Calcutta Vol Rifles, 1863, AF Inf, —.
Candeish Bhil Corps, see Khandesh.
Carnatic Bns, 1769, Ma NI, 30
Carnatic Inf, 1903, 65 to 88 Inf, 152.
Cawnpore Levy, 1823, 62 Be NI, 28.
Cawnpore Lt Hse, 1886, AF Cav, —.
Cawnpore Rifles, 1877, AF Inf, —.
Central Bengal Lt Hse, 1884, AF Cav, —.
Chamar Regt, 1941, Inf, 179.
Chamba Inf, 1881, SF, —.
Champarau Lt Inf, 1815, 5 Be Loc Inf, 68.
Chicacole Lt Inf, 1811, 34 Ma NI, 32.
Chitral Scouts, 1919, Fro, —.
Chittagong Loc Corps, 1763, 7 Be NI, 24.
Chota Nagpur Regt 1891, AF Cav, —.
Christie's Hse, 1844, 9 Be Loc Hse, 54.
Circar Bns, 1769, Ma NI, 30.
Coast Sepoys, 1758, Ma NI, 30.
Coke's Rifles, 1903, 55 Inf, 152.
Cooch Behar Inf, SF, —.
Coorg and Mysore Rifles 1933, AF Inf, —.
Coorg Inf, 1902, 11 Ma Inf, 131.
Coorg Regt, 1941, Inf, 179.
Cortlandt's Levy, 1861, 31 Be Inf, 125.
Cureton's Multanis, 1857, 15 Be Cav, 95.
Cutch State Inf, 1929, SF, —.
Cuttack Legion, 1817, 10 Be Loc Inf, 81, 6 GR 155.
Darrang Mtd Rifles, 1887, AF Cav, —.
Datia Inf, 1923, SF, —.
Deccan Hse, 1903, 20 Hse, 145, 29 Lan, 145.
Dehra Dun Mtd Rifles, 1885, AF Cav, —.
Dhar Inf, 1924, SF, —.
Deoli Irr Force, 1903, 42 Inf, 151.
Dharangadra Makhwan Inf, 1909, SF, —.
Dinajpore Loc Inf, 1792, 4 Be Loc Inf, 81.
Dkolpur Narsingh Inf, 1920, SF, —.
Dogra Regt, 1887, 37 Be Inf, 125; 1890, 38 Be Inf, 125; 1900, 41 Be Inf, 125.
East Bengal Rlwy Bn, 1873, AF Inf, —.
East Bengal Vol Rifles 1900, AF Inf, —.
East India Rlwy Regt, 1869, AF Inf, —.
Ellichpur Bde 1788, 5 HCI, 81.
Ellichpur Inf, 1826, HCC, 60.
Erinpoorah Irr Force 1903, 43 Inf, 146.
Fane's Hse, 1857, 19 Be Cav, 95.
Faridkot Sappers & Miners 1900, SF, —.
Fatahgarh Levy 1817, 63 Be NI, 28; 9 GR, 126.
Fatehgarh Levy, 1857, 34 Be Inf, 97.
Ferozepore, Regt of, 1846, Be Loc Inf, 68; 14 Be Inf, 124.
Fitzgerald's Hse, 1824, 6 Be Loc Hse, 54.
Frontier Force Regt, 1922, 12 Inf, 178.
Frontier Force Rifles, 1922, 13 Inf, 178.
Gardner's Hse, 1809, 2 Be Loc Hse, 19.
Garhwali Regt, 1890, 39 Be Inf, 125.
Gauhati Rifles, 1885, AF Inf, —.
Ghaut Lt Inf Corps, 1847, Bo Loc Corps, 81.
Ghazipur Lt Hse, 1887, AF Cav, —.
Gilgit Scouts, Fro, —.

Goojramwallah Levy, 1859, Be Inf, 97.
Gorakhpur Lt Inf, 1818, 11 Be Loc Inf, 68.
Gordon's Hse, 1903, 30 Lan, 145.
Gough's Hse, 1823, 5 Be Loc Hse, 19.
Great Indian Peninsula Rlwy Bn, 1875, AF Inf, —.
Guides Cavalry, 1846, Pu Cav, 57.
Guides Inf, 1846, Pu Inf, 71.
Gujerat Irr Hse, 1839, Bo Irr Cav, 54.
Guzerat Pol Corps 1852, Bo Loc Corps, 81.
Guzerat Provincial Bn, 1845, Bo Loc Corps, 81.
Gwalior Contingent 1838, Be Irr Con, —.
Gwalior Inf, 1822, SF, —.
Gwalior Lan, 1833, SF, —.
Gwalior Regt, 1857, 41 Be Inf, 97.
Hariana Lan, 1903, 7 Cav, 144.
Harian Lt Inf, 1836, Be Loc Inf, 68.
Hawke's Hse, 1824, 7 Be Loc Hse, 54.
Hazara Gurkha Bn, 1857, 5 GR, 97.
Hazara Pio, 1904, 106 Inf, 153.
Hill Rangers, 1818, Ma NI, 34.
Hill Regt, 1846, 2 Sikh Inf, 72.
Hodson's Hse, 1857, 9 Be Cav, 93.
Holkar Inf, 1927, SF, —.
Holkar Lan, 1892, SF, —.
Hyderabad Inf (1–6), SF, —.
Hyderabad Lan (1–3), SF, —.
Hyderabad Regt, 1922, 19 Inf, 179.
Hyderabad Rifles, 1882, AF Inf, —.
Idar Cav, SF, —.
Idar Inf, SF, —.
Jacob's Hse, 1888, 6 Bo Cav, 120.
Jacob's Rifles, 1857, 30 Bo Inf, 99.
Jaipur Inf, 1923, SF, —.
Jammu and Kashmir Inf (1–9), SF, —.
Jat Hse, 1857, 14 Be Cav, 95.
Jat Lt Inf, 1903, 5 Inf, 150.
Jat Regt, 1922, 9 Inf, 178.
Jund Inf, 1837, SF, —.
Jodhpur Inf, 1918, 142 Inf, 155.
Jodhpur Inf (1–3), 1922, SF, —.
Jodhpur Lan, 1888, SF, —.
Junagarh Inf, 1924, SF, —.
Junagarh Lan, 1891, SF, —.
Jupur Legion, 1835, Be Irr Con, —.
Kamroop Regt, 1857, Be Inf, 97.
Kandahar Hse, 1778, 2 Be NCav, 17.
Kapurthala Inf (1–2), 1857, SF, —.
Kelat-i-Ghilzie Regt of, 1842, Be Loc, Inf, 68; 12 Be Inf, 124.
Kemaoon Levy, 1857, Be Inf, 97.
Khairpur Camel Corps, 1914, SF, —.
Khaki Risala, 1857, Be Irr Cav, 95.
Khandesh Bhil Corps, 1825, Bo Loc Corps, 81.
Khyber Rifles, 1878, Fro, —.
Kolapore Loc Inf, 1845, Bo Loc Corps 81.
Kolar Gold Fields Bn, 1903, AF Inf, —.
Kolhapur Inf, SF, —.
Kotah Contingent, 1843, Be Irr Con, —.
Kotah Inf, 1929, SF, —.
Kumaon Bn, 1815, 9 Be Loc Inf, 68; 3 GR, 126.
Kumaon Rifles, 1918, 50 Inf, 152.

Kurmool Hse, Ma Irr Cav, —.
Kurram Militia, 1900, FRO, —.
Lahore Lt Hse, 1857, Be Irr Cav, 95.
Lakhimpur Mtd Rifles, 1888, AF Cav, —.
Lal Paltan Bn, 1757, 1 Be NI, 24.
Lind's Pathans, 1857, Be Irr Cav, 95.
Lingayat Regt, 1941, Inf, 180.
Loyal Purbeah Levy, 1857, 17 Be Inf, 97.
Lucknow, Regt of, 1857, 16 Be Inf, 97.
Lucknow Rifles, 1903, AF Inf, —.
Lucknow Vol Cav, 1857, AF Cav, —.
Ludhiana, Regt of, 1846, Be Loc Inf, 68; 15 Be Inf, 124,
Lumsden's, 1903, Guides Cav, 145.
Macaulay's Hse, 1857, Be Irr Cav, 95.
Madras and Southern Mahratta Rlwy Rifles, 1910, AF Inf, —.
Madras Fencible Regt, 1804, Ma NI, 34.
Madras Native Militia, 1819, Ma NI, 34.
Madras Rifle Corps, 1814, Ma NI, 34.
Madras Sappers Militia, 1857, Ma Inf, 91.
Madras Vol Bn, 1801, 40 Ma NI, 34.
Madras Vol Gds, 1857, AF Inf, —.
Mahar Regt, 1941, Inf, 179.
Mahratta Hse, 1857, 18 Be Cav, 93.
Mahratta Lt Inf, 1903, 103 Inf, 153; 105 Inf, 153; 110 Inf, 154.
Mahrattas, 1903, 114 Inf, 154; 116 Inf, 154; 117 Inf, 154.
Mainpura Levy, 1823, 63 Be NI, 28.
Malabar Vol Rifles 1885, AF Inf, —.
Malaun Regt, 1903, 1 GR, 155.
Malay NI, 1798, 29 Ma NI, 76.
Marine Bn, 1777, 21 Bo NI, 36.
Masulipatam Bn, 1799, Ma NI, 32.
Mayne's Hse, 1858, 1 CIH, 96.
Meerut Hse, 1857, Be Irr Cav, 95.
Meerut Levy, 1857, 37 Be Inf, 97.
Meerut Vol Hse, 1857, AF Cav, —.
Mekran Levies, FRO, —.
Mewat Inf, 1880, SF, —.
Mewar Lan, 1908, SF, —.
Meywar Bhil Corps, Be Loc Inf, 68.
Mhair Regt, 1857, Be Inf, 97.
Mharwara Bn, 1822, 14 Be Loc Inf, 68; 44 Inf, 151.
Mooltan Regt, 1903, 119 Inf, 154.
Moradabad Levy, 1857, Be Inf, 97.
Moplah Rifles 1902, 17 Ma Inf, 132.
Moulmein Vol Rifles, 1877, AF Inf, —.
Multani Regt of Cav, 1857, 15 Be Cav, 95.
Mulwa Bhil Corps, 1840, Be Loc Inf, 68.
Mulwa Contingent, 1845, Be Irr Cob, —.
Mundlaiser Bn, 1825, 15 Be Loc Inf, 68.
Murray's Jat Hse, 1857, 14 Be Cav, 95.
Mussorie Bn, 1871, AF Inf, —.
Muttra Hse, 1857, 17 Be Cav, 95.
Mutra Levy, 1818, 64 Be NI, 28.
Mynpoorie Levy, 1857, 35 Be Inf, 97.
Mysore Inf (1–4), 1761, SF, —.
Mysore Lan, 1799, SF, —.
Nabha Akal Inf (1–2), 1889, SF, —.
Nagpore Irr Force 1854, Be Irr Con, —.
Nagpur Rifles, 1860, AF Inf, —.
Nain-i-Tal Rifles, 1871, AF Inf, —.
Napier's Rifles, 1903, 125 Inf, 154.

Narsingh Inf, 1918, 143 Inf, 155.
Nasiri Bn, 1815, 6 Be Loc Inf, 68; 1 GR, 126.
Nawanagar Lan, 1914, SF, —.
Nilgiri Vol Rifles, 1878, AF Inf, —.
Nimour Pol Corps, 1845, Be Irr Con, —.
Nizam's Cav, 1826, HCC, 60.
North Bengal Mtd Rifles, 1875, AF Cav, —.
North West Rlwy Bn, 1880, AF Inf, —.
Northern Scouts, 1900, FRO, —.
Nowgong Mtd Rifles, 1888, AF Cav, —.
Nundy Regt, 1800, 36 Ma NI, 76.
Nussaree Bn, New, 1830, Be Loc Inf, (GR), 68.
Oudh and Rohilkund Rlwy Vol Rifles, 1903, AF Inf, —.
Oudh Aux Cav, 1838, 9 Be Loc Hse, 54.
Oudh Cav, 1776, 1 Be NC, 17.
Oudh Irr Force, 1835, Be Loc Inf, 68.
Oudh Light Hse 1887, AF Cav, —.
Oudh Mil Police, 1856, Be Irr Con, —.
Oudh Vol Rifles, 1865, AF Inf, —.
Outram's Rifles, 1903, 123 Inf, 154.
Palamcottah Lt Inf, 1811, 3 Ma NI, 30.
Palanpur Iqbal Inf, 1922, SF, —.
Panna Inf, 1923, SF, —.
Pathans, 1892, 40 Be Inf, 125.
Patiala Regt, 1918, 140 Inf, 155.
Patiala Inf (1–4), 1889, SF, —.
Patiala Lan, (1–2), 1889, SF, —.
Pegu Lt Inf, 1853, Be Loc Inf, 68.
Pegu Pol Bn, 1857, Ma Inf, 92.
Pishin Scouts, FRO, —.
Poona Aux Hse 1817, Bo Irr Hse, 21.
Poona Vol Rifles, 1887, AF Inf, —.
Porbander Inf, 1923, SF, —.
Probyn's Hse, 1903, 11 Lan, 144.
Punjab Lt Hse, 1893, AF Cav, —.
Punjab Rifles, 1861, AF Inf, —.
Purbeah Levy, Loyal, 1857, 17 Be Inf, 97.
Rajpipla State Inf, SF, —.
Rampur Inf (1–2), 1910, SF, —.

Rampur Lan, 1840, SF, —.
Rangoon Vol Rifles, 1860, AF Inf, —.
Rajput Lt Inf, 1903, 2 Inf, 150.
Rajput Regt, 1922, 7 Inf, 177.
Rajputana Inf, 1903, 120 Inf, 154; 122 Inf, 154.
Rajputana Rifles, 1922, 6 Inf, 177.
Ramgarh Lt Inf, 1778, 31 Be NI, 26.
Ramgarh Loc Bn, 1795, 2 Be Loc, Inf, 68.
Ramghur Irr Cav, 1857, Be Irr Cav, 95.
Rampura Loc Bn 1818, 12 Be Loc Inf, 68.
Rangpur Lt Inf, 1817, 10 Be Loc Inf, 68, 6 GR, 155.
Ratlam Rifles, 1930, SF, —.
Rattray's Sikhs, 1864, 45 Be Inf, 125.
Revenue Bns, 1787, Ma NI, 32.
Rewa Inf, 1942, SF, —.
Robart's Hse, 1857, 17 Be Cav, 95.
Rohilkund Hse, 1857, 16 Be Cav, 95.
Rohilla Cav, 1815, 3 Be Loc Hse, 19.
Russell's Brigade, 1813, 1 HCI, 81.
Rutnagherry Rangers, 1852, Bo Loc Corps, 81.
Sam Browne's Cav, 1903, 22 Cav, 145.
Sawunt Warree Loc Corps, 1845, Bo Loc Corps, 81.
Scinde Camel Corps, 1843, 6 Pu Inf, 71.
Scinde Irr Hse, 1839, Bo Irr Cav, 61.
Scinde Rifles, 1903, 59 Inf, 152.
Sealkote Inf Levy, 1857, Be Inf, 97.
Semana Rifles, 1897, FRO, —.
Settara Loc Corps, 1857, Bo Loc Corps, 81.
Shajehanpur Levy, 1857, 40 Be Inf, 97.
Shekhawati Bn, 1835, Be Loc Inf, 68; 13 Be Inf, 124.
Sibsager Mtd Rifles, 1884, AF Cav, —.
Sikh Irr Cav, 1857, 11 Be Cav, 95.
Sikh Pio, 1903, 23 Inf, 151; 32 Inf, 151; 34 Inf, 151.
Simla Rifles, 1861, AF Inf, —.
Sind Rifles, 1879, AF Inf, —.

Sipni Con, 1861, 41 Be Inf, 125.
Sirmoor Bn, 1815, 8 Be Loc Inf, 68; 2 GR, 126.
Skinner's Hse, 1803, 1 Be Loc Hse, 19.
South Andaman Vol Rifles, 1884, AF Inf, —.
South Indian Rlwy Bn, 1884, AF Inf, —.
South Mahratta Hse, 1850, Bo Irr Cav, 61.
South Provinces Mtd Rifles, 1904, AF Cav, —.
Suket Inf, SF, —.
Surma Valley Lt Hse, 1886, AF Cav, —.
Sylhet Lt Inf, 1824, 16 Be Loc Inf, 68; 1/8 GR, 155.
Sylhet Vol Rifles, 1880, AF Inf, —.
Tennaserum Bn, 1917, AF Inf, —.
Tehri Garhwal Inf, SF, —.
Thal Scouts, FRO, —.
Tiwana Lan, 1903, 18 Lan, 145.
Tochi Scouts, FRO, —.
Travancore Inf (1–4), SF, —.
Trichinopoly Lt Inf, 1811, 31 Ma NI, 32.
Tripura Rifles, AF Inf, —.
United Provinces Hse, Northern, 1909, AF Cav, —.
United Provinces Hse, Southern, 1904, AF Cav, —.
United Provinces Regt, 1916, 131 Inf, 155.
Upper Burma Vol Rifles, 1856, AF Inf, —.
Vaughan's Rifles, 1903, 58 Inf, 152.
Wales' Hse, 1857, 11 Be Cav, 95.
Wallajahabad Lt Inf, 1794, 23 Ma NI, 32.
Watson's Hse, 1903, 13 Lan, 145.
Waziristan Militia, 1899, FRO, —.
Wellesley's Rifles, 1903, 104 Inf, 153.
Wilde's Rifles, 1903, 57 Inf, 152.
Yercaud Rifle Vols, 1886, AF Inf, —.
Zhob Militia, 1894, FRO, —.

Bibliography

Books

The Army in India and its Evolution, Government Printing Office, Calcutta, 1924.

Ackermann, R., *Costumes of the Indian Army*, Rudolph Ackermann, London, 1844–1849.

Atkinson, G. F., *The Campaign in India*, Day and Son, London, 1859.

Barthorp, M., *Indian Infantry Regiments 1860–1914*, Osprey, London, 1979.

Bowling, A. H., *Indian Cavalry Regiments 1880–1914*, Almark, London, 1971.

Bremner, F., *Types of the Indian Army*, F Bremner, Quetta, 1897.

Broome, A., *History of the Rise and Progress of the Bengal Army to 1767*, Thacker Spink, Calcutta, 1850.

Cadell, Sir P., *History of the Bombay Army*, Longmans Green, London, 1938.

Cardew, F. G., *A Sketch of the Services of the Bengal Native Infantry to the year 1895*, Government Printing Office, Calcutta, 1913.

Carman, W. Y., *Indian Army Uniforms, Cavalry*, Leonard Hill, London, 1961.

Carman, W. Y., *Indian Army Uniforms, Artillery, Engineers and Infantry*, Morgan Grampian, London, 1969.

Chappell, M., *British Infantry Equipment, 1808–1908*, Osprey, London, 1980.

Chappell, M., *British Infantry Equipment, 1908–1980*, Osprey, London, 1980.

Dupuy, R. E. and T. N., *The Encyclopedia of Military History*, MacDonald, London, 1970.

Elliott, Maj-Gen J. G., *A Roll of Honour, The Story of the Indian Army 1939–1945*, Cassell, London, 1965.

Harris, R. G., *Bengal Cavalry Regiments, 1857–1914*, Osprey, London, 1979.

Haswell Miller, A. E., and Dawnay, N. P., *Military Drawings and Paintings in the Collection of Her Majesty The Queen*, Phaidon Press, London, 1966.

Heathcote, T. A., *The Indian Army, The Garrison of British Imperial India 1822–1922*, David and Charles, Newton Abbott, 1974.

Hughes, Maj-Gen B. P., *The Bengal Horse Artillery*, 1800–1861, Arms and Armour Press, London, 1971.

Hunsley, W., *Costumes of the Madras Army*, Madras, 1840–1841.

Jackson, Major D., *India's Army*, Sampson Low, London, 1940.

Leslie, N. B., *Battle Honours of the British and Indian Armies*, Leo Cooper, London, 1970.

Lovett, A. C., and MacMunn, G. F., *The Armies of India*, Adam and Charles Black, London, 1911.

Mason, P, *A Matter of Honour, An Account of the Indian Army, its Officers and Men*, Jonathen Cape, London, 1974.

Mollo, A., *Army Uniforms of World War 2*, Blandford Press, Poole, 1973.

Mollo, A., *Army Uniforms of World War 1*, Blandford Press, Poole, 1977.

Mollo, J., *Military Fashion*, Barrie and Jenkins, London, 1972.

Rivett-Carnac, S, *The Presidential Armies of India*, W. H. Allen, London, 1890.

Wilson, W. J., *A History of the Madras Army from 1746 to 1826*, 4 vols, Government Press, Madras, 1888.

Articles

Abbott, P. E., *Dress Regulations of the Madras Horse Artillery*, JSAHR. 57.

Annand, A. McK., *Col Francis Brown, 1st Bengal European Fusiliers*, JSAHR. 50.

Appleby, C. B., *Captain George Jolland*, JSAHR. 39.

Bullock, H., *Major Abraham James, 67th Foot*, Military Author and Artist, JSAHR. 39.

Cadell, P., *The Uniforms of the Madras Army*, JSAHR. 27.

Cadell, P., *The Beginnings of Khaki*, JSAHR. 31.

Cadell, P., *The Raising of the Indian Army*, JSAHR. 34.

Cambridge, Marquess of, *Notes on the Armies of India*, JSAHR. 47, 48.

Carman, W. Y., *The Bengal Light Cavalry from beginnings to disbandment in the Mutiny*, JSAHR. 58.

Fosten, D. S. V., *Some Notes on Military Costume worn during the Indian Mutiny*, Tradition 29, 30.

MacMunn, G., *Dress in the Indian Army in the Days of John Company*, JSAHR. 7, 8.

Nicholson, J. B. R., *Special Indian Cavalry Issues Nos 1 and 2*, Tradition 50, 73.

Nicholson, J. B. R., *Madras Native Infantry 1845*, Tradition 42, 43.

Nicholson, J. B. R., *2nd Bengal Lancers 1901*, Tradition Nos 5 to 12.

Norman, C. A., *Further notes on Military Costume worn during the Indian Mutiny*, Tradition 62, 63.

Steele, R., *The 1st Bengal European Light Cavalry 1858–1861*, JSAHR. 20.

Steele, R., *5th Madras Cavalry, c1855–1859*, JSAHR. 18.

Steele, R., *Uniforms in the Indian Mutiny*, JSAHR. 26.

Wylly, H. C., *The British Cavalry of the Honourable East India Company*, Cavalry Journal 1930.

Regulations

Chapter 1 (to 1824).

Grace, H., *The Code of Military Standing Regulations of the Bengal Establishment*, Cooper and Upjohn, Calcutta, c 1791.

Grace, H., *The Continuation or Supplement of, the Code of Bengal Military Regulations*, John Johnson, Calcutta, 1799.

Carroll, *A Code of the Bengal Military Regulations*, Government Gazette Press, Calcutta, 1817.

Code of Regulations for Various Departments of the Military Establishment of Fort St George, Madras, 1806.

Aitchison, J. W., *A General Code of the Military Regulations in Force under the Presidency of Bombay*, Mission School Press, Calcutta, 1824.

Chapter 2 (1824–1857)

Standing Orders for the Bengal Native Infantry, Scott & Co, Calcutta, 1828.

Standing orders for the Regiment of Artillery, (Bengal), no imprint, 1845.

Artillery Regimental Standing Orders (Bengal), Smith & Co. Calcutta, 1828.

Regulations for the Dress of General, Staff and Regimental Officers of the Army of Fort St George, J. B. Pharaoh, Madras, 1838.

Ibid. Adjutant General's Office, Madras, 1851.

Standing Orders for the Light Cavalry of the Army of Fort St George, Adjutant General's Office, Madras, 1833.

Ibid. J Wright, Madras, 1848.

Plates of Officers' Dress of the Madras Infantry, Adjutant General's Office, Madras, 1847.

Standing Orders for the Native Infantry of the Madras Army, J Wright, Madras, 1848.

Bombay Code of Regulations, Bombay, 1832.

Regulations for the Dress of the General, Staff and

Regimental officers of the Bombay Army, 1850, Education Society's Press, Bombay.

Standing Orders of the Brigade of Horse Artillery (Bombay), American Mission Press, Bombay, 1829.

Chapter 4 (1861–1903)

Regulations and Orders of the Army of the Bengal Presidency, Government Printing Office, Calcutta, 1880.

Bengal Army Dress Regulations, no imprint, 1885.

Standing Orders for the Native Cavalry of the Bengal Army, Adjutant General's Press, Simla, 1866.

Standing Orders for the Bengal Cavalry 1875, Adjutant General's Press, Simla.

Standing Orders for the Bengal Infantry, Adjutant General's Press, Simla, 1874.

Dress Regulations for the Punjab Irregular Force, no imprint, 1865.

Madras Army Dress Regulations, no imprint, 1885.

Bombay Army Dress Regulations, no imprint, 1884.

Standing Orders for the Native Infantry of the Bombay Army, Education Society's Press, Bombay, 1868.

Army Regulations, India, Volume VII Dress, Government Printing Office, Calcutta, 1886.

Ibid. Government Printing Office, Calcutta, 1891.

Ibid. Government Printing Office, Calcutta, 1901.

Chapter 5 (1903–1922)

Army Regulations, India, Volume VII Dress, Government Printing Office, Calcutta, 1913.

Regimental Standing Orders 8th Cavalry, R. A. Press, Jhansi, c 1910.

Regimental-Standing Orders 2nd Queen's Own Rajput Light Infantry, Victor Press, Secunderabad, 1909.

Regimental Standing Orders, 35th Sikhs, Central Press, Delhi, 1908.

Regimental Standing Orders, 40th Pathans, Gouldsbury Press, Jhelum, 1908.

XLVII Sikhs, Regimental Standing Orders, City Press, Sialkot, 1903.

Standing Orders, 103rd Mahratta Light Infantry, Israelite Press, Poona, 1913.

Standing Orders, 127th Q. M. O. Baluch L. I. Poona, 1913.

Chapter 6 (1922–1947)

Government of India, Army Department, Dress Regulations (India), Government Printing Office, Calcutta, 1925.

Ibid. Government Printing Office, Calcutta, 1931.

Ibid. (reprint 1942) (incorporating amendments up to and

including Amendment No 90 of December 1941), Government Printing Office, Calcutta, 1942.

3rd Cavalry Standing Orders, Crown Press, Ferozepore, 1936.

Standing Orders of the 7th Light Cavalry, Pioneer Press, Allahabad, 1925.

Standing Orders of the 18th K E VII O Cavalry, privately printed, 1938.

Standing Orders 5/12th F. F. Regt. Q. V. O. Corps of Guides, Albion Press, Lahore, 1923.

Standing Orders of the 1st Battalion 17th Dogra Regiment (P. W. O.), no imprint, 1939.

Battle honours	Date of action	Date of award	Regiments granted award (1824 titles)
MANGALORE	1783	1841	1st
MYSORE	1789–1791	1889	1st, 3rd, 4th, 5th, 7th, 8th, 9th
SEEDASEER	1799	1823	3rd, 5th, 7th
SERINGAPATAM	1799	1823	3rd, 4th, 5th, 6th, 7th, 9th
EGYPT 1801	1801	1804	2nd, 13th
BOURBON	1810	1855	4th
KIRKEE	1817	1823	2nd, 12th, 13th, 23rd
CORYGAUM	1818	1818	2nd
PERSIAN GULF	1819	1854	Marine Bn
BENI BOO ALI	1821	1831	3rd, 4th, 5th, 7th, 13th, 18th, Marine Bn